STEPS ON THE PATH OF
transformation
Volume 1

channeled through Robert Shapiro

Other Books by Robert Shapiro

EXPLORER RACE SERIES

1. The Explorer Race
2. ETs and the Explorer Race
3. The Explorer Race: Origins and the Next 50 Years
4. The Explorer Race: Creators and Friends
5. The Explorer Race: Particle Personalities
6. The Explorer Race and Beyond
7. The Explorer Race: Council of Creators
8. The Explorer Race and Isis
9. The Explorer Race and Jesus
10. The Explorer Race: Earth History and Lost Civilizations
11. The Explorer Race: ET Visitors Speak Volume 1
12. The Explorer Race: Techniques for Generating Safety
13. The Explorer Race: Animal Souls Speak
14. The Explorer Race: Astrology: Planet Personalities and Signs Speak
15. The Explorer Race: ET Visitors Speak Volume 2
16. The Explorer Race: Plant Souls Speak
17. The Explorer Race: Time and the Transition to Natural Time
18. The Explorer Race: ETs on Earth Volume 1
19. The Explorer Race: Are You a Walk-In?
20. The Explorer Race: Totality and Beyond
21. The Explorer Race: ETs on Earth Volume 2
22. The Explorer Race: ETs on Earth Volume 3
23. Steps to the Path of Transformation Volume 1
24. Steps to the Path of Transformation Volume 2

SHAMANIC SECRETS SERIES

A. Shamanic Secrets for Material Mastery
B. Shamanic Secrets for Physical Mastery
C. Shamanic Secrets for Spiritual Mastery
D. Shamanic Secrets: Lost Wisdom Regained

SHINING THE LIGHT SERIES

Shining the Light I: The Battle Begins!
Shining the Light II: The Battle Continues
Shining the Light III: Humanity Gets a Second Chance
Shining the Light IV: Humanity's Greatest Challenge
Shining the Light V: Humanity Is Going to Make It!
Shining the Light VI: The End of What Was
Shining the Light VII: The First Alignment; World Peace

ULTIMATE UFO SERIES

Andromeda
The Zetas: History, Hybrids, and Human Contacts

SHIRT POCKET BOOKS SERIES

Benevolent Magic & Living Prayer
Touching Sedona
Feeling Sedona's ET Energies
Mini Book of Transformation

THE EXPLORER
RACE SERIES

STEPS ON
THE PATH OF
transformation

Volume I

channeled through Robert Shapiro

LIGHT
Technology
PUBLISHING

For information about special discounts for bulk purchases,
please contact Light Technology Publishing Special Sales at
1-800-450-0985 or publishing@LightTechnology.net.

ISBN-13: 978-1-62233-045-4

Cover image: *Geometry of the Soul, Series Two,* © agsandrew
www.ShutterStock.com

Light Technology Publishing, LLC
Phone: 1-800-450-0985
1-928-526-1345
Fax: 928-714-1132
PO Box 3540
Flagstaff, AZ 86003
LightTechnology.com

Dedicated to the
true nature in all beings,
which is unconditional love.
— Robert Shapiro

CONTENTS

CHAPTER THIRTEEN

The Polarity Reversal Affects Men **131**

Grandfather • May 26, 2011

CHAPTER FOURTEEN

How to Reconnect with Your Magical Powers.....................**137**

Isis and Grandfather • June 13, 2011

CHAPTER FIFTEEN

Earth and Humans Are More Electric Now...........................**146**

Element of Electricity • June 17, 2011

List of Benevolent Magic

List of Living Prayer

Introduction

Isis

January 12, 2017

As you read this material, this is what to keep in mind: Your path might be completely different from what this book — okay, it will say it in both books — is attempting to show you. So when you read this material or listen to it, don't think, "I can't possibly do that." Rather, think about what is familiar to you.

You will experience times when you have read a page or two and something feels as if it resonates within you. It might not be a sequence of words that you find in a paragraph. It could be words that came together from different paragraphs, creating in you a sense of familiarity. This tells you that these books are not just about thoughts or ideas. The books are about transformation.

Even if you have difficulty reading the books in the language they are in, go through them and put your hands on some of the pages, or touch the pages to your arms or other parts of your body to see whether the books — with all the words, letters, symbols, and numbers — can in some way trigger a dream, a vision, or a moment of inspiration in you that helps to bring about a better life for you and those around you.

Good luck, and good life in this pursuit.

CHAPTER ONE

You Traverse to Your Home Planet in Deep Sleep

Soul Portal

February 4, 2010

Greetings. I work as an intermediary between worlds. There are many of us in existence — millions, many millions. We are part of the living spirit world that must be close to you all, all the time, to keep your world stable and to allow for your comings and goings. All of you on the soul level are from other planets, and you are not at home on Earth. As a result, you must go to your other planets in your deep sleep state and recharge your existence. Beings like myself will connect to anywhere from thirty or forty individuals — and sometimes some groups of individuals up to a hundred, sometimes even more — to act as intermediaries to support moments of passage of your unconscious sleeping self to your home planets in this universe or beyond. This is why there are so many of us here.

We do not originate on this planet, but we have the capability to be present on your planet without any adaptation or training. We seem to be some of the few who can do this, and we are not here for anyone other than the human being. This allows you as individuals to traverse, then, perhaps three or four times in a twenty-four-hour period. This traversing often happens in between teachings with your guides, teachers, angels, and so on. At the deep sleep state, you might go temporarily to your home planet, but what you do there is not what you might think.

You may not know that this is necessary, but even though you are not physical there — you might even appear like a spot of light. Occasionally you might appear in the form of life associated with the planet that you identify with — what you do there more than anything else as a soul being, almost the first thing you do when you go to your home planet, is to breathe. By "breathe," I do not mean that you take in air as you do here on Earth, but rather you take in the energy of that place, just a deep reception that I would call breathing, but you do not exhale anything from Earth.

The reason this happens is that we are connected there, meaning we have the capacity to function as intermediaries, which is like a living portal, creating a truly conscious portal by which you can make such a journey instantaneously so that all other beings — including the planets — are insulated and protected from all that you are on Earth that may be uncomfortable to them. And anything on the home planet that may be incompatible with your soul does not affect you or cause any detrimental influence to affect your life on Earth.

I personally have been functioning in this capacity on your planet now for about 1,000 years. As we get more experienced and have been here longer, some of us grow larger. When we are newly arrived, some of us are smaller, but this is not a fixed situation. Sometimes [chuckles] some stay small no matter how experienced they are. But we are not assigned, you see, to souls, so we might have thousands of experiences with different souls, many experiences with some souls, or anything in between.

Generally speaking, the dots that seem to make up our being have to do with one or more traverses, so what you're really seeing is something that's a tube. If you were to see a tube in a cross section, it would look very much like a circle. So that's what you're really seeing. It isn't a plasma that makes us up. If you were to see us in our natural state, we usually would appear as a single color and there would be none of this "little circles" stuff [chuckles]. I'm getting used to your language here.

Your Souls Have the Same Shape We Do

I cannot tell you where I am from, because I have been told it's vitally important that this remain a secret from you. I can say that it's at the outer boundaries of this universe, but that's all I can say. This may be why we are able to help Earth souls traverse to a home planet beyond this universe, because we are used to being in our state at home. We are used to being at the border of things. Perhaps this is why we can function in an unusual capacity this way. Generally speaking, we do not stay in this capacity for more than a thousand years. I have lingered a bit, and I might linger for a couple more years, but soon I will return to my home place. We are not humanoids, as is obvious, but we do have lives. We also do not have a fixed amount of life but exist in an ongoing fashion.

We would call that immortal, right?

Yes, but this is what you are too when you are not in your adventurous mode exploring different life forms. You do not look exactly like we do, but on examination, you would be circular in form. This is perhaps why we were requested to come, because your souls have the same shape that we do. When you are at the deep sleep state, you are most at ease with beings who are circular like yourselves. In this way, there is a natural built-in compatibility.

What do we do when we get there? Just take in the energy?

You do the same thing, yes, with the energy. It's like when you take a deep breath of fresh air and feel that sense of exhilaration and refreshment. It's very much like that experience, which is part of the reason a person can have a nap for twenty or thirty minutes and wake up profoundly refreshed, whereas that same person might sleep for four or five hours and not really have that experience of refreshment.

So it means you went home during that time?

That's what it always means.

Our Different Colors Accommodate the Soul's Different Feelings

I saw the picture of you that was taken close to Bradshaw Ranch in Sedona, and you had many, many, many colors in these little tiny circles [see **Merging Dimensions** *by Tom Dongo and Linda Bradshaw, Light Technology Publishing, 1995]. Are you saying that each one of these represents a traverse for souls?*

Yes. The reason there are different colors is that it accommodates the soul's different moods. When the soul is coming from Earth, traversing wherever it needs to go, it will still have feelings. Even at the deep sleep level, there are strong feelings. The colors accommodate those feelings, both going to the home planet and returning, so that when you are, say, passing through Earth, you leave those feelings, and by the time you get to the home planet, you are in a state of being in which you can be totally

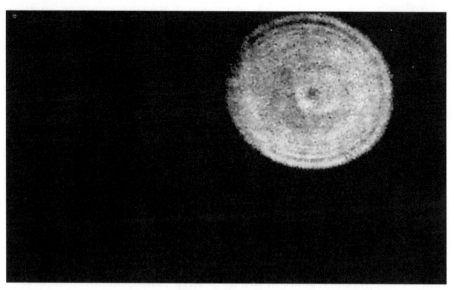

Figure 1.1. An enlarged photo of the being speaking through the channel.

receptive. But when you return, you must pick up at least a portion of those feelings so that you are reminded of who you are and can return at ease without resistance to your physical self. Otherwise, you would not want to go back to your physical self.

So the colors have to do with feelings. We do not feel these feelings, although they are within the tubes as you might see them within us. Thus we are insulated from feeling the feelings, but in some photographs I've seen that are taken here and there over the world, you can see the energy feeling. Different colors are not always associated with the same feelings. It depends largely on the individual or the individual's family of souls. Some groups of souls will radiate "this" or "that" color for the same feeling, and other groups of souls might have an identical feeling and radiate a different color. I have noted that there's much variety.

Do the humans in deep sleep go to you, or do you go to them? How do you connect with them?

It is not a problem of time or space. Wherever I am and wherever they are is not a difficulty. Once you are in the deep sleep state and your soul can traverse, there is no limit to where you could be. I could be inside a mountain — just as an example, though I don't do that — and you could easily come and make your passage.

Okay, but do we go to you? Do the same souls always go to the same beings like you?

Oh yes, you would come. You would have to come to make a safe transit.

So when you first came here 1,000 years ago — that would be AD 1000 — how much did you see of Earth?

Not very much. In order to perform such a function, I need to have a strong connection to my home planet so that I do not lose myself, my personality, with such passages. So I do not really observe your history, your culture, or anything like that. To the degree I know you, it is in my relationship with your souls. It is not based on your experience on Earth. My relationship, then, is that I feel you with your essential mood as you make your traverse through and then into your home zone, so to speak. When you come back, you are a bit more comfortable for me because you are completely clear, but then you traverse back, and I release some of that matter of your feelings, as I said before. So I do not observe your history and manners and mores and all that.

Stabilizing Your Energy

How did you happen to come here? Did someone go to your home planet and request that you do this for the humans on Earth?

That's how all of us have volunteered to do this. We were requested to come here to create a much better stabilized energy. When the first humans were on Earth — not really your people — it wasn't necessary, because Earth in those times was benevolent. But once the Explorer Race, as you are deemed, came and there was some discomfiture, there needed to be not only a means to stabilize your traversing to your home planets, as I've mentioned, but also a means to insulate the planet and the planet's other life forms from such jolts, you might say, to the veil system that protects your planet and protects other planets from what happens on this place, on Earth. So we were asked to come in as great a number as needed. That's why I say there are millions of us, but one can perform such services for many souls. Even though you might have billions of individuals, millions of us are enough.

What was your life like before you came here?

Oh, very calm: a benign and benevolent existence with communication of ideas and concepts, like that. I wouldn't say we were purely intellectual, but that was part of our pursuits.

Do you have a form there?

We look the same here. We look the same with the exception that you do not see all the little circles. We are of one color, but we would not be circular.

Ah! So before you come and then also after you go back home, all the circles are gone?

Yes, because the circles …

Are the portals.

That's right, the traversing mechanism. It is not part of our physical functionality. Some have said it is a kind of plasma that makes us up, and as well-intended an analysis as that is, that is not the case. In our natural state, we would just be circular and no "tubes." I'm using that as a simplified means by which you can imagine in your mind's eye what that might look like, because you are familiar with tubes.

You said you keep a strong connection to your home planet. So then are you able to connect with the rest of the beings there while you're doing this, or do you have to not do that because of the discomfort?

Usually I would do that — speaking for myself — when I am not having traversing going on. I cannot have traversing going on for a few time segments and then connect to my home planet to refresh myself. For you, such a refreshment would come in sleep. For me, it is more of being present there, during which time I do something not unlike what you do. I take the energy in. But I don't exhale in that sense.

You take in the energy of your home planet?

That's right, and this refreshes me.

And it gives you the strength to keep doing this?

Strength is not actually a factor. We have a natural endurance.

This is amazing. We knew we had to go somewhere during sleep to get recharged, but no one ever said before how the process worked.

This is my experience of it. I do not claim to have all knowledge, but I'm sharing what I know based on my experience.

You've given us incredible information that helps us understand how our lives are possible here.

I believe on your world, with you as souls in human form, that you are constantly surrounded in every waking and sleeping moment with a vast fabric of spirit and other physical forms that make it possible for you to continue the delicate balance of your lives on Earth. From what I have been guided before coming to this place, it is a very delicate balance indeed. Yet from the angelic messenger from Creator who came initially to explain why and what and so on about your service on Earth as souls, I believe that your intention is of the highest, and I wish you well along your pathway to accomplish such a worthy goal. Good night.

Thank you very much. Good life.

CHAPTER TWO

Solar Flares Bring More Creative and Astrological Capabilities and Talents

Zoosh

September 14, 2010

There are elements of the Sun's personality that are unknown on Earth. They affect the relationships of the planets in this solar system to each other as well as to the Sun. The Sun, obviously, is spherical, but the assumption is that the Sun has mass all throughout its interior. There is a different relationship that the Sun has to all other suns as well as to the center of spiral galaxies such as the one you find yourself in.

All suns are associated directly in this galaxy (I'm going to keep it to that) with the center of this galaxy. And there is a very powerful cord that you cannot see — and I don't think you ever will on Earth — that connects all suns, and of course your Sun, to the center of this galaxy, where suns are born. Let's just say that's a pretty good description of what happens. In the center of spiral galaxies is a concentrated energy that not only is of creation itself but also has a capacity to compact light and to create form and substance. Literally, what is going on here is the mechanics of creation, which has been mentioned before in *Explorer Race* books.

The issue that I'm bringing up now, however, is about how this element of the Sun's personality causes the changes the Sun goes through — as with, say, flares or what are also called sunspots. That's what causes

7

those to happen within an exact timed sequence. It's not just a matter of how an astronomer might say, "There! Oh, I wonder where that sunspot came from? How does that come about, and can we predict the next one?" It may not be possible to predict the next one until you have better views of the center of the galaxy, but some day that will be possible.

For now, just know that the center of this galaxy is about creation. When there is a surge in the level of creation, there will immediately be a large flare that comes from the Sun and radiates out, usually to impact all the planets in this solar system and beyond. If that creative energy has to do with you on Earth here as the Explorer Race, then what you have is a stimulation seemingly coming from the Sun but in fact coming from the center of the galaxy. When Creator is involved in a creation — and of course everything is created — of a gradual evolution of a group of beings such as your own here on Earth, things are meant to happen in a certain sequence.

Becoming Your Soul Selves as Your Day-to-Day Selves

Right now, this sequence is about remembering who you are so that you can literally become your soul selves — also known as your spirit selves — as your day-to-day selves. You'll still be physical, albeit in a little different form physically than you're in now. But you will be able to do many things, things that one might associate with spirit — benevolently, you understand — or soul, not necessarily things that you would associate with human physical and social life.

This doesn't mean your physical and social life will go away; it just means that you, as the Explorer Race, have completed what you came to Earth to do, and it's very gradually being implemented in other parts of the universe. So given that completion, you can then begin to experience the relationships now — not only astronomically, not only physically, but astrologically as well — between yourselves and the other planets in this solar system.

So I want you all, if you would, to get a basic book on astrology. You can get the advanced version [*Astrology: Planet Personalities and Signs Speak*, Light Technology Publishing, 2010] as well and get lots of information about the personalities of the planets, and so on. But get at least a basic book about astrology so that you can understand what the planets in this solar system represent. You can generally condense the basic things that they represent down to a few sentences. And if you don't want to get a book, then go see an astrologer and have them tell you; they can do that.

Here's the reason why: You've all been born on certain days at certain times, and that sets your astrology so your soul can pursue what it needs to pursue in this life and learn what it wishes to learn. That's all part of creation. But since you are now becoming your soul selves as your day-to-day selves, what will happen on the soul level is that you will not only have that specific delineation that you have in astrology.

Over the next forty to sixty years — some of you will be around for that entire time, and most of you will be around for some of that time — what is going to occur and then increase at a faster rate is that instead of having only your personal astrology, you're going to gradually begin to assimilate all of the characteristics of all of the planets in this solar system. And to a lesser degree, you will experience the characteristics of all of the star systems that are used to define the various signs in the zodiac, but that will take place a little further away.

A Wave of Astrological Balance from the Sun

Right now, I want you to focus on what the planets stand for in this solar system. You don't have to guess about planets beyond Pluto, for instance. Just focus on the basics, and those of you who want to do more can always do more. You will be assimilating those characteristics but not on an equal basis. It will come from the Sun outward. You'll be assimilating basic characteristics of Venus, Mercury, Earth, and so on, all the way out to Pluto and beyond.

Initially it comes out from the Sun as a wave, so you'll experience that wave, all of you, in the next three to five years. And you'll notice it because after the wave, some things about your personal astrology that have been very specific — your interests, for instance, that you're very interested in doing this and not so interested in doing that, as you find very often in astrological readings — will become much more across the board. You'll be very interested in lots of things, and you'll find that you're getting better or you'll find that lots of things are a lot easier than just the few things.

Now, because of your astrological setup, everybody is born with certain things that come easy. They may not be a snap, but they're easy for you compared to other people who are born with things that are easy for them, and so on. For instance, some people can very easily make lots of money — it seems like it comes easy to them — and other people can very easily work with things that are mechanical or scientific. That seems to come easy to them. Granted, it may not be as easy as it seems, but individuals have certain trends and capabilities that are associated with their astrology.

Now, you're going to find an evenness in your capabilities in the next three to five years, as there is going to be a wave, and you're all going to experience this wave. Once you experience that wave the first time, there will be many times when you feel that the focuses and relationships that other people may have with the planets in this solar system — based on their association with their special astrological birth date, time, and place — that you don't have because you don't have that birth date, for example, you're going to suddenly find that those relationships are going to be equalized for everybody. And as time goes on, this will become more so because in your soul and spirit self, you are not specific to a birth date or a birth time.

This does not mean that astrology is going to go away in terms of its interests or in its pursuits, but it does mean that the more you become like your soul or spirit self as a day-to-day personality, the more you're going to be able to access all of the things the planets are known for and not just the ones that your specific birth date is associated with. So if one person can make money easily, then you'll be able to make money easily. If one person can do mathematics easily, then you'll find that even though some of you have never been able to get a handle on mathematics, it will suddenly seem very obvious. I wanted to tell you about this, because this is part of the Sun's personality, and it directly relates to the center of this galaxy.

Energies from the Center of the Galaxy Come to You in Waves from the Sun

That's absolutely wonderful. Say more about the center of the Sun.

It has a core that is essentially summed up in one word: receptivity. It has to be focused in receptivity, and that tells you something really important, doesn't it? People tend to think of the Sun as a male figure and the Moon as a female figure, but that is not the case. The Sun is balanced; it can do both. The center of the core of the Sun is entirely feminine, and it has to be, because it is totally receptive to what comes from the center of the galaxy.

I think that's pretty interesting. It puts a different cast on things, and I want astrologers to take particular note of that because of the tendency (by some astrologers, not all) for the astrologer to represent the Sun as a more masculine thing to people who do not understand the subtleties of astrology. You really need, as astrologers, to explain to your clients and others that the Sun is a balanced energy that is sometimes *perceived* as a masculine energy because it radiates. Nevertheless, on the inside, it is entirely receptive. And I'm not talking about some pinpoint on the inside. Once you penetrate, say, about one-quarter of the way into the Sun, from that part forward straight into the center, that's all receptive. So the Sun is basically receptive, and the outer quarter, say, of the sphere is entirely projective.

So there's like a massive connection running through all creation, from the center of all suns to the center of each galaxy, and then there's some connection between the centers of all galaxies?

No, I'd say that the relationship is entirely like to like. Two apples may not be atomically exactly the same, but … like to like. It's like that. The relationship is familial in that sense. A sun is a sun. Large or small doesn't make a difference; a sun is a sun.

So we're getting energy from the center of creation all the time to the center of each galaxy and then out to each sun?

No, I said spiral galaxies.

Oh! Only spiral galaxies?

That's right. I'm trying to keep it to spiral galaxies so that it's relevant to the reader. If I say all galaxies, then you'd have to create a mathematical best guess as to what the center of the galaxy is, whereas in a spiral galaxy, you don't have to make that guess; it's obvious. So let's just keep it to spiral galaxies. Otherwise, you're challenging mathematicians to find the center of a galaxy that isn't spiral, and that just makes it controversial.

Okay. That's exciting, because even though we're isolated and insulated here on Earth, we're actually receiving energies from the rest of creation all the time?

Yes, you're receiving energy from the center of the galaxy. But as you said yourself, the Earth planet as it exists with you human beings on it is insulated so that you do not impact the rest of the planets, and so on, in the galaxy. Nevertheless, there is a route by which physical energy enters from a completely different place. And I'm saying physical energy; the Sun is physical, is it not? And physical energy comes from the center of this galaxy to the Sun and is broadcast physically. It's important to say that, because of course outside of the context of your physical bodies — and even when you're at the very deep sleep level — you are in fact connected to All That Is, and so on.

So I'm talking about the physical level. If you keep it strictly to the physical, then you're looking at an issue where you might be insulated — the more accurate thought is that everybody else is insulated and protected from Earth as it is now — but that doesn't mean you're cut off from creation. It just means that the route from creation has to be through a totally pure being. And all suns are totally pure.

Perfection Found Stumbling in the Dark

Okay. So the new abilities that we're going to absorb aren't something that we ask for or seek or strive for — it just happens with these waves of energy from the Sun?

That's right. It's not something you can try to make better or faster or something like that. It just happens. It's part of the process of waking up. You understand, a lot of this process of waking up is entirely unique to your planet. This whole thing of the Explorer Race is entirely new in terms of waking people up. Everybody else every place else *is* awake.

So here you have this unique group of people — humans on Earth who are not awake — and you have to function at the asleep level so that you can sort of stumble around in the dark. I'm not saying that's what was set up for you, but it feels like that to you. And in the process, you re-create many things that many people have assumed every place else are perfect.

Your job on Earth as the Explorer Race is to find the other perfect things that other civilizations and other peoples in the universe have not found yet. Your job is to discover these other perfect things that are useful and applicable in many societies all over the universe but simply have not been discovered because the conditions didn't exist whereby you could find them by stumbling around in the dark. And you know, if you were here right now, what would I say?

Never forget that!

That's right, and that is a very powerful point. That's why you're here. And that is really the only reason you're here, because why would any soul wish to experience — and you don't wish to experience suffering — but why would you come to a place where you can be pretty sure that at some point in your life, you're going to be unhappy or in pain? Why would you even want to do that, unless you were going to discover some portion of creation that is so absolutely perfect that it could be applied to many different civilizations? When you take in the varieties of how it could be applied, it can be applied to every civilization everywhere in this universe, but it hasn't been discovered yet. Only for something like that would your soul say, "For that, I'm willing to come." Otherwise you, as a soul, would never choose this. You, as a soul, are a purely benevolent being. Why would you want to suffer? You don't want to, but you'd be willing to take the risk to discover such a wonderful thing.

And that's why, as has been said numerous times in the Explorer Race books, if you're going to come to Earth and have a life on Earth with human beings here on Earth, you must have had at least one life where you've become a spiritual master so that you have the depth to fall back on when you come up against things here on Earth for which you have no preparation. That's going to happen at least one time in every single life. Sometimes it's just an embarrassing moment, and other times, it's much more extreme. But if you've been a spiritual master at least once on any subject, you have great depth to your soul, to your spirit, and ultimately, at various levels. Even though it may not be conscious and it may not be something that you emanate as a personality, it's there in each and every one of you. You might find it hard to believe that someone that you're around or have been exposed to could have such depth, but I assure you, no one is allowed to have a life on Earth without that prerequisite.

We need to look beyond the surface and start searching in each other for this depth.

Yes, or when you feel it yourself and you notice something about your personality you hadn't noticed before and you just feel thunderstruck by it, make a note and scribble a few words down, because it may not be obvious every single moment. In time it will become obvious every single moment, but if you can scribble a few words down or grab a recorder and say a few words, "I just had this most amazing experience," and so on, then later on, when you have forgotten that — and it will happen in the course of life, because you do other things — then you'll be able to read that note or listen back to that recording and write about it and so on and think about it, maybe even recall it at times when it might be useful. By "recall it," I don't mean think about it; I mean re-call the moment so that you can utilize that wonderful thing about you that you didn't know you had.

You Have Done It!

Can you give me an example of something that we have discovered that is, as you said, usable by others that we didn't know about — that no one knew existed?

No, I won't, because if that's discussed, it becomes an intellectual thing. I will allude to it (you know how I am). I will say this: Part of the capacity to be all things to all people in moments and to demonstrate that through different personality traits in ways that feel totally benevolent to you and to others is associated with one of those things. Now, don't get confused and say, "Oh, that's one of those things." It's *associated* with it. And that's all I'm going to say.

It's not your job to find out what those things are, because remember what I said: You have done what you came here to do. Those things have been completed, and they're being applied. Even now as I speak, they're being applied on other planets and to other cultures all over the universe, because it's not necessary for you to go there and say, "Hey, why don't you try this?" You don't have to think about it. You don't have to demonstrate it for it to have taken effect.

Because we radiate that energy out?

No, it's not you. You did it; you discovered it. You proved it could be done. It used to be that a lot of ships came here from other planets, but there are not that many coming anymore. And it's not entirely because your governments have the capacity to zero in on them and say, "Hey, what are you doing?" [chuckles] in one way or another — sometimes not so pleasant. It's this: When you do it, it just automatically becomes available to everyone everywhere. It's discovered.

You are a portion of creation even with the discomfort that you experience. The only reason your planet is insulated and the other planets are insulated against you is entirely about the level of discomfort on your planet — that's it. But happiness, joy — all kinds of other stuff that doesn't have anything to do with discomfort — isn't kept from the other planets. They're only protected from things on Earth that would harm them, but everything else is just a portion of the universe.

So when you're told that you are one with the universe, you are one with the universe! The only disconnect is the discomfort. So if you become aware of something or you achieve something or you discover something, do you think it's withheld from everybody else just because you have discomfort on your planet? No, they're applying it now, and they've been applying it for the past ten years of your Earth time. You did it, and now you can wake up because you don't have to do anything anymore. It's been done.

You discovered three major things, but I'm not going to tell you what they are right now. You have to understand that they're major because they involved complexities of life that you do not experience on Earth, all right? If I were to tell you right now, it would definitely disrupt your ability to become your soul selves as your day-to-day selves.

So when the ET ships that used to come to harvest the latest thing or see what we were doing ...

Well, the issue is — thank you; I hadn't finished my point — that all those ships were coming because they were checking you out to see what's happening. You know, "We know why you're there; you're there to discover these things we don't know about." And so they were checking up to see, you know, "How's it coming?" so to speak. And now they're not coming so much anymore. The vast reason that they're not coming so much anymore is because they say, "Oh! You accomplished it!" There's no reason to come to check up on you anymore, because you did it. So there's no reason to come. So now, if you see these ships from time to time, they just happen to be in the neighborhood, but they're not coming to check up on you.

ET Visitors Are Now Coming to Help Wake You

And they won't come to talk to us again until we're benevolent and can be social and trading partners, right?

Well, yes, that's in your future, naturally, as it is with all planets, but they'll also ... they might, from a few places, be allowed to appear momentarily in the sky if it will serve to help you to wake up and become your soul selves as your day-to-day selves, and only if that's the case, then they'll be allowed to be seen. If it won't serve that purpose, that won't happen. So there are times and places on Earth, and places where the ships are from, where they might be allowed to do that if it will help you to wake up.

Those places will largely have to do with the places where the genetic makeup of the human being on Earth is now, where that's from. And I think that's been discussed in other books, but as a quick reminder, some of the places are Orion, the Pleiades, Sirius, Andromeda, and a few more. So if you see a ship in the sky, it's probably going to be from one of those places or other places that have contributed to the genetics of the people on Earth. If they haven't contributed directly, they probably will not be in the sky. You won't see them.

Sometimes there's a contribution that you can't imagine because the beings don't look exactly like you, but generally speaking, they'll at least be humanoids, if not human. There are parts of you, you know, in your genetics that are not strictly of human beings, and that was necessary because if you were strictly made from the genetic makeup of other human beings around the galaxy — to say nothing of the universe — you'd probably be too vulnerable to deal with the discomfort level. So you have, oh, 3 or 4 percent of your genetics that is not human. So you might say that you're a hybrid. [Chuckles.]

Can you say anything about the beings whom that 3 or 4 percent came from?

You can ask that question at a later time.

Changes in Your Physical Bodies as You Become Your Soul Selves

Okay. We have physical bodies, and we reside in them as souls ... or as immortal personalities. We are gloved in this soul essence of the Creator, and all of that fits into the physical body, and then there is the soul of Earth that's in the physical matter of the body. Is that correct?

I see where you're going. You're trying to differentiate that the soul is one portion of the spirit. Is that where you're going? So let me put it this way: To become your spirit being as your day-to-day self, you have to become your soul first, and then it sort of expands into being your spirit being. But you can't be 100 percent your spirit being and be physical. You *can* be 100 percent your soul self and be physical *if* the Earth is totally benevolent. But if you're 100 percent your spirit being, you're going to be a multiple of lives, okay? You can't be physical then. But a single, unique soul is going to be associated with one being.

So what we're doing, then, is waking up to that piece of the spirit that is the soul?

Yes. And then you will expand further. But of course, every time you die or your physical body returns to the earth and you return, you go zing, straight through the few bits of time, so to speak, experiential time, as your soul and then on to your spirit.

I always thought that the soul body was completely separate from the physical and that when you become your soul, you are no longer physical, but from what you're saying, that's not correct.

No, it's not the same. On Earth, it's completely different, because you came here to do something that was totally unlike anything happening in the rest of the universe. So the set of rules that might apply everywhere else in the universe does not apply here; you've got your own rules.

Will our physical bodies be a little more refined? How will our physical bodies change as we become our soul selves on Earth?

That's a very good question. For one thing, you will probably find certain likes and dislikes changing. You'll have less interest in eating meat and more interest in eating things more along the lines of vegetarian, because your physical body will be more inclined to feel. Your feelings will become very prominent, and you'll need that so that you'll be able to tell when any member of the physical human community on the planet needs help or is in distress.

So as a result, you will have your senses heightened in that way, and you'll feel the same distress in any animals you might consume, and it will feel pretty much the same. You won't be able to experience distress like that and just shuck it off as if that's part of life — no shucking off anything. So you won't be eating animals. That's one of the big things.

Now, you're asking how the physical body will change. There will be subtle changes as a result, but you won't notice much change right away. The main thing you'll notice is likes and dislikes. You'll probably like everybody, you'll have special friends, and so on. You'll still have your basic social structures, but there won't be any judgments on people. There won't be any crime or anything like that. Everybody will have what they need.

Our identities, then, will shift from being bodies to being souls in a way that we're conscious of?

No, you'll feel like yourself; you'll feel like your personality. You'll have more of your personality present, and you won't have to sublimate any elements of your personality at all. Everybody will be very pleased to experience you as you are, not as you've had to become to disguise elements of your personality because some people around you didn't approve of them, for whatever reason.

There are no actual elements of people's personalities when they are born in normal times — meaning not when you're going through this wake-up process, say, go back three, four, five hundred years and then forward forty or fifty years — that are not appropriate on Earth. Most personality traits even now are appropriate. There are a few that are temporary because they have to do with waking up. I'm not going to go into all of that because it would take a year to explain.

All right, but that's excellent. It's more of who we are, but within a safe, slowly expanding experience of ourselves. We become our soul selves while in the physical body, have different traits, different personality traits coming up. Everybody would like each other. We don't have to hide anything.

Good enough.

The Unification of Personal Astrology
Brings Out New Talents in You

Now, here it is in a nutshell: You have had a relationship to your soul that can be at least partly intellectually defined through the study of your astrological horoscope. But the change that's taking place is a unification in which everyone's capacities and talents are going to be somewhat balanced. It doesn't mean that your specific talents that you've honed, perhaps, to your advantage are going to go away or that you're going to lose anything. It's rather that you will notice you've gained something.

That's how it's going to be for everyone. Everyone's going to gain more capabilities because the astrology is sort of unifying. I wanted to bring that to your attention because even a casual study of astrology these days will help you to see — especially as you understand what the planets stand for in the astrological zodiac — and then you'll get a pretty good idea of some of the talents that you can expect to come to the surface that you didn't know you had or that you identified with.

There are twelve different personality types in astrology. As astrology merges, do we have access within each of us to all of those personality types?

For starters, there are *thirteen* different types. The astrological calendar is based on a physical calendar that's not real. The real calendar is the moon calendar, so you really have thirteen months; you don't have twelve months. So you can do that as a follow-up at some point. But you know, we put it out as twelve months because most people follow that calendar. But it's really thirteen signs: thirteen months, thirteen signs.

Okay, fine. As they merge, do we then have access to all of them? Do we become all of them?

No, because that would suggest that there's only one soul personality and that everybody has the same personality. How do you think you'd find that on Earth? Kind of boring, eh? No, you have access to the planets, not all the signs. Look up the planets in this solar system somewhere — get a book or something. What do the planets stand for? And then when you do that, *that's* what you're going to have available to you. Some of the planets stand for "this"; some stand for "that." And let's just say that depending on where you reside in your personal horoscope, you have greater or lesser access to those planets.

Obviously, you have access to all the planets, but until now, you have had greater or lesser connections to those planets, and it gets kind of mathematical there. But now your horoscope won't change; you'll still have that. You'll still have your personality, but if there's something missing — maybe, for instance, you don't have a lot of Jupiter influence in your horoscope, and you'd like to have it, since it stands for some neat stuff — you'll find that it's going to be available.

You don't give up anything. You don't lose your personality. You just have access to things that other people have — not everybody. If you didn't have access to it, you would suddenly find you have access to it. Look up the planets, find out what they stand for astrologically, and then check your horoscope to see what the influence is from those planets in your horoscope. If there are things missing, planets missing — meaning you don't have much influence from that planet; there might be some, but not a lot, and you'd like a little more — you'll have it.

By asking for it or automatically?

Automatically. It's unasked for. Personality doesn't have anything to do with it.

We just add a little more of "this" and a little more of "that," like some spices or something.

There you go. It's capabilities. But remember, I used this as an example. Some people are just naturally good at some things. You've noticed this, eh? And other people are good at other things. That's where you pick up things — the things that somebody's really good at, and you wished you were good at that too. You'll find that you'll be better at that or other things associated with that planet's capabilities or characteristics.

Good night, and thank you incredibly much.

Good life.

CHAPTER THREE

Allowing Perception without Judgment Moves You to 3.56

Grandfather

October 14, 2010

It is time for you to hear that because of your change of motion from one path or timeline to another, you are experiencing a global shift of perception. Perception allows you to gravitate in this case to seeing more than you have seen before. For most of you, this involves a reacquisition of your spiritual abilities — and by spiritual, I mean your own capacities to see more, to do more, and to be more.

For those of you who are seeing, for example, unexpected lights — a typical thing these days — out of the corners of your eyes or even in front of you, a quick twinkle of something, this always has to do with spirit that is always present and almost always benevolent. So your sense of time now is bending, like the curve as generally interpreted in Einstein's famous theorem. Time is a curve. It is not a straight line, though it appears to be a straight line.

You have reached a point in your shift from a past-anchored dis-comforting timeline to a future-anchored benevolent timeline, and the point you are at is beyond the timeline you have been in with a strong connection to the future-oriented timeline. Specifically, you are con-nected more to the future-oriented timeline than you are to the past one. This is part of the reason many things are being seen that have always been there.

These days, you are also seeing more and more sky vehicles from other planets. They have always been there, but you did not have the perception available to you as much as you do now. Now not only are you seeing them more, but they are quantifiable, meaning that your instruments for perception are picking them up and even showing details that have not been seen before. These things have always been present. In the past— going back hundreds of years and certainly more so in the past, say, thirty or forty years — there have been people on your planet who could see these things and experience these things. But now many people, if not everybody or most, will see these things on a regular basis.

Don't let it frighten you. This is part of life. It is part of the welcoming of your planet into a universal community of planets all set up to support each other, to provide what is needed when requested, and to generally create a broader and more pleasant social community.

These signs that you are seeing — and the repetition of numbers is a sign — do acknowledge your change as spiritual beings from one dimension, as you have said before (you like that term), to another dimension. Those who are attached to those numbers or have an interest in them will be interested to know that you are now at 3.56, and while you may not maintain that and will waver back and forth a little bit, you will not waver more than one point either way. As a result, you are now more connected to the future timeline and releasing the past one. I thought you might be interested in that.

You Are Now Seeing More without Judgment

That's awesome! Zoosh said it would be two or three years before we reached past 3.50! What changed?

The change was that you are now seeing without judgment. That's the most important thing. People, for instance, all over China now are seeing many things in the sky. They are noticing things in the clouds, of course. With such an ancient culture as exists in China, even with its tumultuous government in recent years, still there is depth there. And people have noticed things in the clouds and used them as predictors as well as constants.

A great deal is being seen in the skies, and one of the more wonderful things going on is that people are not judging. Look at it and, of course, say, "What is it?" and discuss what it is, but don't quickly come to a conclusion that "It's up there; it must be bad." Judgment is what holds you back from friendships — friends, allies, and in the largest sense, the global community.

The Desire for Control Is Leaving Your Planet

Well, this is absolutely fantastic, because this is over the hump! Now we can't go back to the old negative, past-anchored timeline or be pushed back by those who want to control or be pushed back by those who want to control us now, right?

Right. Things can move forward rapidly — not always at that speed, but things can take a jump forward when perception becomes accepted and not rejected. In the past, for various reasons, some perceptions were rejected because of things that happened to individuals or because of their desire for control. But since a certain aspect of control is leaving your planet, then that kind of attempt to control will leave as a general influence in the lives of all human beings on the planet as well.

Control is a desire brought about largely by fear, but sometimes it is also brought about by greed. As these symptoms are analyzed and treated by those who can help and there is sympathy and understanding, then the global community can benefit. For example, MIBs, also known as Men in Black, are leaving your planet now and will never return. One of the primary things that these beings did — I'm not talking about the fictional ones in the movies, but the real beings — is that they were afraid of your culture and were afraid that it would somehow harm theirs, and therefore they came here to attempt to control you. In the process, though unintentionally on their part, they spread a great deal of energy and fear around control.

But they are leaving your planet now, and while all desire for control will not leave your planet, fully 10 percent of that energy affecting human beings will leave your planet. And within a year to a year and a half at most (maybe two years at the outside) they will be gone and will never return. And equally during that time, you will all notice less of a desire to control, less fear that prompts control. This is how you have made a jump forward, because they began leaving not too long ago.

I thought that they left years ago.

No, I'm just going to say that they came and went, but others were affected. Once upon a time, the impact of that energy of control was 40 percent, and now it's reduced to the numbers I suggested.

So do you mean 10 percent of that energy is left, or we only have 10 percent of that controlling energy on the planet now?

Ten percent of their energy left. You will have what you have, but it will no longer be stimulated or agitated by that energy.

But who have they been contacting?

Nobody. They have been quiet inside the earth, underground. They have been quiet, and now they are all leaving and taking all that they brought with them as well. They are taking automated equipment that was underground with them, so there will be nothing left from their being here. They no longer feel the need or the advantage to control you.

What was that automated equipment doing?

Controlling, period. Controlling in general.

Well, that's good that they are gone.

Move Beyond the Mental

Your expanded perception helps you to be the more that your self truly is. Now, as you move in that direction of creation and allowance and even in the expectancy that the impossible will be solved easily, you will discover that that which has apparently been impossible to resolve (and there are many things out there that are impossible to resolve mentally only) with the addition of attitudinal change — not pie in the sky, as you say, not pretend, but an attitudinal change, for example, that the impossible can be done — then it is possible to integrate greater depths of your personal spirituality as part of your day-to-day life otherwise known as perception without judgment. Discernment, yes — this goes "here" and that goes "there" — that's fine, but not judgment, which limits and can breed contempt.

When that is bred into a culture, sometimes you can go thousands of years on the wrong path. And then something — possibly spirit, angels, guides, or Creator — will have a way to bump you off that path and help you to recover who you truly are so that you can become who you are in the global community and then who you are in the universal community. Then you discover that even as a physical being, you are simultaneously a spiritual being. Good news, eh? Good night.

[Laughs.] All right. Thank you very much. This is fantastic. Unbelievable. Nobody can push us backward. We can't fall backward. This is blessed! Good night. Thank you. Good life.

Ongoing Support, Release of the Past, and the Eleventh Planet Help Move You to 3.56

Zoosh

October 25, 2010

All right. Zoosh.

What do you see as the reason we suddenly jumped to 3.56 in our movement to the next dimension?

You are assuming there was just one cause, but in reality, you are in a period of ongoing support that is pulling you forward into that more benevolent timeline by the desires of people on the world for better lives. You're also releasing the old timeline in some ways. That's the hard part — releasing the old timeline — because with releasing that, people must release their attachments to a great many things that they want to change. By attachments, I do not mean that people are attached to having better lives. In this case, they might want to get in one more punch before they move on, if you get my meaning — get back at someone, have revenge — and that kind of attachment is just something you're going to have to let go of.

You're going to have to accept that almost everybody you know who you're angry with is actually totally different and you're not seeing the true personality. I'm not trying to apologize for anybody here; I'm stating that the true personalities of most people are displayed maybe 3 to 5 percent of the time. I'm referring to most adults. Of course, really young children display their true personalities most of the time, but even when they get to be four or five years old, they already know some of the rules of the house or the culture, and their personalities start to recede a bit into the background.

But without going too much into that, I'll simply say that what Grandfather said is true, and I feel you're over the hump. As far as connecting to the future timeline, that's solid. The only thing right now is that there is still a lot of desire to pay back "this" or "that" group or person. It's going to be tough, but you're going to have to let that go.

Can you say a little bit about some of the processes that happened, like an overview of how it happened so quickly, just in a month or so?

This mostly has to do with a planet not mapped in your solar system yet — but referred to, I believe, in the *Astrology* book — that has begun to have a little more of a physical countenance and is now beginning to influence the outcome of your civilization: planet eleven. [See *Astrology: Planet Personalities and Signs Speak,* Light Technology Publishing, 2010.]

That's the only real difference, but you know all these things affect your day-to-day lives. As a simple aside here, it's kind of interesting that if the planet Saturn were only half the size it is now, the personality characteristics astrologically that go with Saturn would be reduced by about 10 percent in everyone. So if you have a planet that's becoming more physical — although I'm not saying Saturn should do that — then it's going to affect your personalities, and your personalities have everything to do with the timeline you're moving on. It's not just the physical matter in your body. It's not just the physical matter of Earth. Primarily, it's about your personalities and your awareness of them.

Okay. What does that mean for us now? How do we go forth, besides letting go of anger and judgment? What particularly do we need to do now to keep this momentum?

Just try to be yourselves, and find out more about your actual personality. It's not a bad idea to consult with an astrologer or an astrology book. Try to find out more about your true nature, and attempt to support those qualities. That's what I recommend, because astrology, numerology, and other practices like that can help you to become clearer about your actual personalities. It may not map your personality for you, but you'll recognize certain traits in there that you'll like and that you'll identify as yours. I'm not talking about some generalized astrology that's put in the newspaper to amuse people; I'm talking about very specific astrology. So see your astrologer and find out more about you, and try to be you. Good life.

Thank you. Good life.

CHAPTER FOUR

A Stable Pathway to the Next Dimension Was Created on 1/11/11

Il Pacht, a Pleiadian Teacher of Motions

January 12, 2011

My name is Il Pacht.

Greetings.

I am here to welcome you to a new era on your planet. This era will see you smoothly into your next spatial shift. There are, all around this planet now, focuses of benevolent energy — some of it radiated from vehicles from afar, but most of it synchronized with a timed event that has taken place and has created a pathway for you to move from your current place in sequence to the next one. From my point of view, other than people working on their spirituality and making an effort beyond that which they have been making to get along with others, the passageway is clear for that motion. You do not have to do much other than be kind and patient to your fellow humans and be as kind and patient as you can with the other beings on the planet. The pathway has been pre-chosen by those beings who look after your planet — Creator, I am assuming, and the various "assignees," is that the word?

I am on a vehicle from a distance, a very large ship, and we are radiating an energy that helps. It's not too much, really, compared to the rest of the energy that's coming from your Sun and four other suns that are roughly in a pattern that is — I think you'd call it a trapezoid. I'm not sure what you call those places, but these four suns and several of the outer planets in your solar system are now supporting the energy for Earth. There are also many peoples on other planets that have sent emissaries in the past and are even seen in your skies from time to time who, in their culture, are what you would call meditating every day about the same time. The meditation is to help Earth and all the beings upon her to make this transit. [See the chapter "All Life on Earth Is Being Transformed to Benevolence as Beings from Many Galaxies Focus Benevolence on Earth" in *Steps on the Path of Transformation,*Volume 2.]

So I wanted to come through and speak on this matter, since I feel it's important and it now relieves you of a considerable amount of responsibility for trying to do this on your own. Understandably, to move from one (let's say) dimension to another while one is embodied in a living form is really not typical for any place, much less Earth, where you are really examining minutiae in order to learn about elements of creation. We are all somewhat in admiration of you for doing that. But at the same time, if I were to ask around on the ship, I don't think I'd find a single volunteer who'd wish to come and do it with you. So we admire what you're attempting to do, but I must say, we keep our distance, eh?

There Are Many Focuses of Benevolent Energy Supporting Earth Now

We, in our vehicle, are from the star system you refer to as Pleiades, and there is a great deal of energy on your planet right now. Some of our beings are there in spirit form. I know the channel here — the person who is communicating my communication, if I can be redundant — has seen a lot of lightbeings. One of us managed to come just a few minutes before this session, and I am actually connecting with that being. It is a spirit being that is at home on the Pleiades, but it is visiting and is in the room with Robert right now, making it easier for me to communicate in this way, because this kind of communication is difficult for me.

I am a type of being who is a teacher on the Pleiades, but the way I teach is nonverbal. I teach with motion. Therefore it is very difficult for me to do what is going on right now, but having this other being there in the physical space where the channel is makes it possible. So what's actually happening is that I am on the ship making motions, moving, doing something you would say is an elaborate form of dance, and the being is interpreting, and the channel is speaking that interpretation.

Why were you chosen to talk to us if you don't usually communicate in words?

Because I have knowledge that I can pass on. Most of the other people on the vehicle are doing the tasks they always do when the vehicle goes from place to place, and they do not communicate in this fashion. But at an early age, I took a vow of silence. I can speak, but I have taken a vow of silence when I do my work. However, when I am in my private moments with family, then I speak quietly to them.

Well, I'm glad you're doing this. Can you say what four suns you mean? Would we have heard of the solar systems of these four suns that are helping us?

I don't think so. They are vastly far away, but they seem to have some direct relationship to your Sun. This leads me to believe that your Sun might be migratory, meaning perhaps it was in motion and came to the place it is now in.

Yes, he said so in the Astrology book. Yes.

As a result, the connection between the other suns might be so strong because perhaps your Sun was once closer to them.

Yes, the Sun said he came from somewhere else. And the planets? That would be which ones?

Pluto, then ... what's the next one in?

Ah, Neptune.

Yes. Then what's the next one off Pluto?

That would be what they're calling the Tenth Planet, I think. It doesn't have a name. It's not visible.

That one.

Then there are two more that are not visible.

But it is not them.

Okay, Neptune, Pluto, and the Tenth Planet.

Yes, and then the one that's closest to the Sun.

Mercury.

Yes.

The people of the Pleiades — you are really helping us. We've had another group who talked to us. They are putting energy into all the mountains on Earth to facilitate feelings of benevolence and unity among all humans on Earth, and they were asked to do it by your people.

Ah, very good!

They're putting this energy into all the mountains all over the world. They said they do favors for people, and the Pleiadians asked them to do this because they loved

us and wanted us to have all the assistance we could get. But they couldn't do this themselves because they are not able to handle the discomfort on Earth, and these other beings can.

This might be why the channel has been seeing so many of the "little blue lights," as he calls them. [Laughs.]

Ah, the little blue ones are Pleiadians?

Not all, but some are.

Communication in Motions That Inspire Action

So tell me about you. How do you know so much about us?

In the course of my education, I have studied with those who have lived on Earth who are able to express communication through motion. I have studied with so many people, mostly mystical people (I think you say shamans) — men and women and one child. One was even recently alive on your planet, and I studied with that person, who is now in spirit. Doing the dances with these spirit beings formerly living on Earth, I have come to know everything about them, and they have come to know everything about me. This makes it easier for us to communicate, and this is how I have, in that course of events, assimilated a certain amount of information about you. As I say, the recent one was on your planet, I think until last year — something like that.

Okay. How do you find each other? Do you put out the need to know more about speaking without words, and they respond?

Yes, and I put it out — as far as Earth people, in going along with your previous inquiry — so that they will come and communicate with me in spirit form. I don't try to visit people when they are, say, having a dream. When they're doing that, they're still in life on Earth, and it could just complicate their lives because such a communication would have to take place over many nights, and it would interfere with their guides and so on. So I usually have these interactions with them after life. Of course, after life, many beings just go on, but there are many opportunities for the spirits of beings who have lived on Earth to also participate in different projects. For some beings, especially ones who have some affection for people still on Earth, the idea of remaining fairly close by, even in spirit form, is appealing. So not everybody volunteers to work with me, but many do. And of course it's not permanent. We do this for a while, and then they do what they are going to do.

Who do you teach after you have learned all you can? Who are your students?

What I'm really learning, you understand, are different ways to communicate. You might say different languages. I teach only those who have an interest in these things because, as you may or may not know, it is possible to do certain motions, and those motions bring about actions. So I am happy to teach these things to anybody who wishes to study with me. As I say, it would look to you very much like dance motions, but in fact, they are motions that inspire activities or actions — not of others, but it might, say, inspire some portion of a planet to do something a little differently that might be desirable by the population that lives there. This is particularly helpful for planets that are strong and vital, such as Earth, which has powerful weather activities and earth motions and volcanoes and so on. If you have a living planet with that kind of personality and you're on that planet and you have that many people as well as other beings, sometimes people ask, "Would somebody help?" So I sometimes help — not directly, but I help those who wish to learn.

People who are, you say, mystical people — and there are sometimes others — need to have support to learn these things. So I might work with those people's guides, you see? Then when their guides teach them "this" thing or "that" thing at the deep sleep level, I might pass that on as well. And then somebody might make a motion or several sequences of motions that turn out to have some good effect. Maybe, for instance, the volcano stops flowing for a time — something like that. The person might not even be aware of what he or she did, but it's not necessary to be aware; it's only helpful to make those motions.

Sometimes certain events also trigger a person to make those motions. People work with their guides all the time, and sometimes a guide will suggest that you feel something if "this" happens or "that" happens. It's described as the breath of an angel. "When you feel that," the guide might say, "then you make those motions, and good things will happen." Guides speak in even simpler terms than that, but I'm being more elaborate so you understand the answer to your question.

Humans Interact with Earth
Emotionally and Physically, Not Mentally

What is this process or this dynamic? You make a motion with your hand, your foot, your body. How is that translated into action by the planet?

It is because the planet is a motion being, and the planet interacts with all beings on the surface of the planet — animals, humans, and plants, you understand. The planet interacts with you first on the physical plane. The planet does not interact with you at all on the mental plane. Your mind might think about things associated with it, but the planet does not interact with you that way. The planet — you say "she," eh? — interacts with you physically and, to a degree, through your feelings, because the planet also has strong feelings. She has strong feelings, and between feelings and physical actions, that's how this equality takes place: balance. So naturally, things would be triggered through physical motion rather than thought.

So humans make certain motions. They extend their arms, they turn — they do something — and Earth feels this? She sees it? She ... what?

She responds. It requires the breath of the angel, though. You would call that energy. It requires that energy plus the right motions in the right sequence in the right timing. But individuals get instructed on how to do that, and of course there are people on your planet now who are of the mystical nature, men and women and sometimes young people as well, and they are learning what they are learning in those activities as well. So if they suddenly get the feeling to make certain motions, it fits right in to the rest of their teaching and learning. And they might say, "Oh, I'm going to do this now." Then because they would be observant people — and certainly the teachers who work with them might also be observant — either the student learning or the teacher teaching would notice, because when you're doing that work, you have to notice what's going on around you. And if one of them notices something, then they'll probably say, "Wait, stop!" or something. Or they'll say, "This happened." They'll talk about it, and then they'll try to reproduce that again. If it happens again, then they'll just use that as a regular thing. They do it to communicate with Mother Earth by making a request with motion and energy.

How many different planets have you affected by communicating your knowledge to the guides who give it to the people on the planet?

I have worked with people on nine different planets this way. Is that what you were asking?

Yes. And can you tell me about some of them?

Only one, and that's in the Pleiades, which is a huge place, just like your own galaxy. The planet in particular that I happen to be from is a planet where people have integrated motion into their language. I think maybe, from looking at your planet a little bit, I have seen some cultures on your planet who speak — you have perhaps seen this as well — with a lot of gestures. Have you seen that, people talking and gesturing all the time? This is something that I feel directly relates to the planet that I'm from in the Pleiades because that is what we do but even more so.

When you are, for instance, walking with a friend, instead of just making a regular pace and walking, you might look as if you're dancing, all right? And the dance itself represents something. Have you ever been in a situation where you were attempting to explain something to somebody, and the person just didn't understand it? In this situation I'm describing, when you start making those motions that look like a dance while you're walking along, it's as if you've shown a file card to the person. They immediately know what you're communicating, and therefore they're not floundering around, trying to understand what you're talking about. It's like that.

See, I think that on your planet, you have a variation of that. Some of your people make gestures, and the gestures themselves communicate feelings. They help people to understand that something, perhaps, is a loving gesture, something else is an aggressive gesture, and so on. So it would be as if somebody's flashing that file card, saying, "It falls under this classification," so you can set everything else aside. That's an attempt to correlate it to your culture.

What was the situation on the planet that you were affecting?

You would call it kind of political. There were peoples visiting the planet who had a common language with those on the planet, but they kept misunderstanding each other. It turned out that the same words in their language meant different things. I think that you have this sometimes on your planet, and that's what happened. So there needed to be something else added to the language so that people could understand what it was about — that word meant "this" rather than "that," so to speak. I'm oversimplifying, but you understand.

Yes. But you weren't dealing with a volatile planet that is in motion like Earth, so it was more of a situation just with beings.

If you're asking if I have ever done anything like this with a planet like Earth, no. But tell me: Where is there another planet like Earth? I don't know of one.

Using Gestures Simplifies Communications in Some Cultures

How did you figure out what motions to transmit to the guides who would give it to the people? How did you communicate?

You understand, it's not mental; it's based on feeling. I either visited their guides or, more often, the guides visited me, and they would, through a form of what I call communion, help me to understand the feelings and the general nature of the people they are guiding — not their whole lives or anything, but their feelings, their general nature, their frustrations, their difficulties, and so on. Then I would demonstrate to the guide what gestures might work if they were included in the people's lives. I think you could find people in your own cultures on Earth who started using gestures — they knew not from where — and those gestures somehow made it easier to communicate with other people. The others just couldn't understand them, and then all of a sudden, they could. You'll find that, I think, and I'm not just talking about sign language. While some cultures do not do this, some do, and you'll find that in those cultures, communication is greatly simplified.

Probably the more feeling-oriented cultures rather than the mental ones would do this, right?

Probably, but some cultures are also cultures within cultures, meaning they might be people, for instance, who are more dramatic, or theatrical. As a result, the idea of suddenly breaking into a dance that expresses a feeling so that everybody understands that "this is what we're doing now" might make complete sense. And it doesn't require much thought. There are also some people on your planet who do not communicate with words very well — something I understand very well. As a result, without having physical gestures, motion, or just being able to perform the way they're feeling, they would not be able to communicate much at all.

One sees this very often in children. Young children, after all, do not have much of a vocabulary, but they might do something, and the parents will understand the physical gesture or the motion of what the child's trying to communicate. Frustration would be an obvious one when the children sort of jump up and down — partly because they're upset, but the upset is almost always caused by the fact that the people they're attempting to communicate with don't understand them. This happens to almost every human being on Earth, from what I can tell, and as a result, you sort of learn that kind of difficulty in communication as a feeling, and it happens throughout your whole life. I feel this is probably how friendships are formed — because people understand each other. When people understand each other, they gravitate toward each other as friends, don't they?

The Explorer Race's Attempt to Re-create the Universe

Yes. Now, what is it about these other eight planets that you can't talk about? They would be so far from our experience that we wouldn't understand — or you just can't talk about it?

Three of them I just can't talk about because they're planets that your people will visit in the future, and I don't want to predispose you to anything. The other ones I can't talk about because about four of them are just impossible for you to understand and for me to put into words, so I just can't.

Okay. You're on a ship right now, what I guess we would call a mothership, a really huge one, right?

Yes, very long. You know. It's not circular, it's just very, very long.

How many people are on it?

It comes and goes, but there are never fewer than 7,000.

Is it parked out here, or do you come and go? Do you come and go to the ship, or does the ship come and go?

It pretty much stays where it is.

We had a wonderful Pleiadian who was out by the space station and talked to us through Robert. He had what he called a jalopy, an old small spaceship, and he was going to visit a friend somewhere. He called these big motherships rest stations: He would go from one to the other in his jalopy on his way to his destination. [Laughs.]

Oh yes. Yes, I have some idea — not who that is, but there are some really old vehicles that some beings just like to fly in. I think that they are older members of the community, and they might have ...

Used it when they were young, yes.

Yes, exactly.

Yes, he was absolutely delightful. So I didn't let you finish the answer. Did you come to this ship in another ship or do you move? If this ship stayed, you came to it, right?

Yes, in another vehicle.

And you're here for a while?

I've been here for about twenty years of your time. I expect to stay for another ten or twelve years. My family is with me, so there's no urgency to get home. When we come, if we're going to come for a long mission, we're always invited to bring family members. One does not bring one's entire family, of course, but I have my wife and my children with me. Of course, there is more family, and they sometimes come to visit.

May I ask — different people feel that different things are too personal, so just tell me if you don't want to answer them — how long do your people live?

Well, our particular people from our planet live anywhere from 700 to 750 years — what you would call years.

Where are you in that cycle?

Right around 600, a little bit before that.

So you're very experienced. Do you spend a percentage of your time away from your planet? I mean, do you go out on these trips frequently?

Oh, I will go out every hundred years or so, and I might be on a trip for, say, thirty of those years. So you might say maybe 30 to 31 percent of the time. If my family wishes to come with me, they're always welcome, and on this occasion, they did so.

How did you first hear about Earth? When did you first learn about us?

Oh, when I was very young, I heard that there was some project going on in this galaxy that they didn't talk about with really young children because they apparently thought it might upset us. As I got older, I was educated to the degree that was possible about your attempts to really re-create the universe, from what we understand. And of course, when I first heard about that, I came up with the usual young person's question, which is "Why?" — you know, because things are so nice where we were. So it took quite a bit of education for me to understand and appreciate that you're not attempting to totally change things but to just sort of add a little a little spice.

When was your first chance to come here?

Well, I came here once about a hundred years ago, but I didn't really interact with too many people then — just a few guides who were getting a sense for what would work — and I didn't stay long, less than a year.

But during your whole time now this time, in these twenty years, that's basically what you do, then: work with guides. Is that true?

Yes, I work with guides or the spirits of beings who are on Earth, as I described before. But yes, that's what I do. That's what I do for you and Earth.

At the same time, you may be working in some other way too?

Maybe.

Maybe at a distance or something. And the people on the ship ... how long has that ship been there?

Oh, hundreds of years.

I know you can't say where it is, but is it there as a gas station, an R&R place, or is it there because Earth is here? Is it on a trade route or something, or what?

No, I think it's just there. It's been in this position for, well … I'll ask somebody. Just a moment. [Pauses.] About 1,300 of your years. So it's not on the way somewhere.

I see. Well, the Pleiadian guy with the jalopy said that once you create them, they last for millions of years.

Oh yes — there's not a problem with wear and tear. We may not be able to go much longer this time.

The Benevolent Energy Intersection

I'm trying to think of what the most important things are here that we can learn from you. Was the event that you just discussed — with all of the energy from the suns and planets and people on other planets — on 1/11/11? The event that created this pathway?

Yes, because the pathway required an intersection of a considerable amount of benevolent energy — I think that's the term, "benevolent," and that means not just a good energy, but it means an energy that *intends* to be benevolent. So there's an intention there as well as a circumstance. It's hard to say that that's two things, but it really is two things. Perhaps you could understand it in a way that a person might be benevolent in personality but also be intentionally benevolent, something like that. So that energy came into what you might call an intersection and is now readily available for usage. And really the only thing that you have to do on Earth as individual human beings is to work on your personal clarity, on your balance, and as I said before, on treating each other well and treating other beings on the planet well.

I would say that at some point in your future, you will no longer consume living beings in terms of flesh-and-blood type beings. I think that eventually, you will be vegetarians. In this way, the population of other beings on the planet will decline, because a lot of the beings you have on your planet on what you call farms (is that it?) would not normally exist in such numbers if they were not artificially encouraged to do so. Some of them will then also want to migrate, probably go to their home planets. I believe that there are some beings on your planet now who have decided to go to their home planets and …

Yes, the birds and the fishes are leaving in vast numbers right now.

Yes, and I know many people are alarmed about that. But sometimes they wish to go all at once, and if many of them wish to go, they will often come together and do it. In the long run, I think you will find that people will become vegetarians and find foods to eat that provide what they need and do not cause any suffering in other beings. I think a lot of the beings who are leaving are apparently having difficulty living on the planet with the human culture.

They are also suffering from the pollution — that's part of it too, right?

Yes, that has a lot to do with it.

This energy that I felt yesterday — I was able to do something I had not been able to do before, and it was just sort of like a dreamy day. The whole world was just wonderful yesterday.

Well then, that really sums it up. That's what happened, and it has created — I feel my word "pathway" really does describe it. It's as if someone opened a door, you see, and now you're really primarily responsible for what I mentioned, but you don't have to —

Struggle so much.

Exactly. You don't have to struggle so much. Very well said.

For this, then, we're grateful to our Sun and the four suns and those four planets. Did they somehow create that intersection?

I think that other beings were also involved, but the suns and planets were very much involved in helping that energy occur. This is apparently something that was planned a long time ago, and the repetitive nature of the numerals in your calendar really has less to do with it. It's not about so many ones or anything like that. It could have been any date, but it was at that time. I think there are other calendars on your planet, but it was at that time that this event took place on that calendar date. I may be making this more complicated than it needs to be.

No, I know. You're saying that the point in our time sequence was pre-chosen.

Yes, well said. I don't have too many of your words.

[Laughs.] You're doing great. I'm so grateful that you're explaining this.

Working with Guides

You don't teach individual humans? You don't actually interrelate with the humans themselves?

No, those of us who do this feel that would be interfering. If you had really, you know, long lives — 700 or 800 years or more — then we would be open to that, but your lives are so brief that it is better to work through your guides, because your guides know what and when and how and all of that, and they are the experts. So we work with them, and then they help to inspire the humans they are working with or interacting with. They know exactly when to do it. And that's why: It's because your lives are so short by comparison.

Now, that's interesting — you said there's a group of you. It's not just you; there's a group of you?

Yes, there are others. I am not the only one.

Ah! How many of you?

Oh, there's another one on the ship, there are five or six more in my general community, and there are quite a few more on the planet. Yes, that's the way. You can't just have one person doing this. It would be too much responsibility.

So it's almost like a profession.

It *is* a profession.

So you were an apprentice or something?

Oh yes. That's why I can talk about student-teacher relationships.

I see. And how long were you an apprentice? What period was that in your life?

Oh, it was maybe twenty-seven years of your time here.

Then you get to go out and do it. Do you have apprentices now?

I do not, but I'm rather hoping that my son will come into this work. He has some interest in it, but he's also interested in other things, and I'm not pressuring him. As he said so eloquently, if I may say: "I'm not ready to give up talking yet, Dad." He doesn't call me Dad, but I'm putting it in your terms.

Oh! That is a major commitment. I can feel the energy of that.

Yes, and so I honor that. It's a major commitment. But you know, we'll see. [Laughs.]

That is a wonderful thing that you are doing. You are helping so many, not just people but — do you realize? How can I say this? It's a feeling I'm trying to get across. By doing what you're doing, you're not just helping the people on Earth but the entirety of All That Is. Not only our creation but all creations everywhere will feel the energy of what we're trying to do.

Yes, that's why I volunteered for this task — because one likes to make a contribution, eh?

It is so far-reaching!

Well, everyone feels that you're all trying to do that too, so that kind of enthusiasm does tend to generate more. You are that. Now the channel is tired.

Bless you. Thank you so much for coming through. Many, many people will read this on paper and in books and electronically. Thank you.

You're welcome. I wish you all on your planet many happy lifetimes, wherever you go.

Good life.

CHAPTER FIVE

The Stabilized Passageway to the Eden Version of Earth Is Ready

Zoosh

January 26, 2011

All right. Zoosh.

Oh, welcome!

It's very important for everybody to focus not so much on the ending of the way of struggle and strife on this planet but rather to focus, meditate, envision — whatever you do; whatever works for you — on the benevolent version of Earth that is coming closer. That benevolent version of Earth will essentially provide you all with little hints of its existence over the next three to four months. Sometimes you will look up in the sky and say, "Oh, what's that?" It will seem almost like an overlaid image. At other times, you will see that kind of overlaid image there, just for a split second when you are looking at something else, and then it will be gone.

This will usually not happen when you're doing something important, such as driving a car or operating machinery or something like that, unless you are pulled over and parked or unless you're taking a coffee break from that machine — that kind of thing — because it's not meant to distract you from life's important ventures. But it is meant to remind you that the world on which you are now living, the time sequence you are living in, and the dimension that you occupy are shifting, and as a result, the time of struggle and strife is drawing to a close.

Now there have been so many things that are upsetting, such as the sudden death of animals and the poisoning of the oceans, even when it was meant to help the oil disseminate, as it was with the release of the chemical by the oil company in the Gulf of Mexico. But that caused a poisoning in the ocean. I know they didn't mean to do that, but this poisoning is affecting the oceans globally. And while it may not be obvious that the oceans can globally affect lakes and rivers and the water in general, it is so.

Human beings, of course, can drink filtered water — water taken from its natural state or its polluted state, filtered by your water companies, and delivered in your home taps in a way that is safe for you. Or you can purchase filters and so on. I urge you, if you're not sure about the water that comes out of your tap, to get a filter — even though if you're in a big city or even a small town, chances are it's perfectly safe. But if you're not sure, get a filter, and drink filtered water.

The issue here is that the animals, of course, do not have filters on their water, for the most part, unless they are pets or even farm animals. But the issue of pollution is overwhelming now, not only because of so many people on the planet and so much crowding and so on, but also to gently prod you, you might say, to sort of release your grip on this old struggle-and-strife world. This is not being done by beings who are trying to harm you. Rather, it is being brought to your attention more.

So I'm not saying that the cause of the pollution or any of the struggle and strife between people is caused by spirit beings. Rather, your means of knowing of these things, the news of such events, the technology, even phone calls, is what's going on for you now. You can know almost instantaneously when something happens on the other side of the world through many good, quality news services, to say nothing of eyewitness reports.

Practice Letting Go

All of these things cause you to feel a great deal of dismay, and I sympathize with that. However, it is important for you to let go, so practice letting go a bit, okay? If you're not sure how to do it, this is the simplest way: Just grab on to the arms of the chair you're sitting in sometime (turn the ringer off on your phone, and try and do it at a time when there's the least amount of distractions). If your hands do not work too well, tuck your legs under the chair and pull. In short, grab something, even move your legs together and push, and then gradually let go. And as you're letting go, exhale, and while you're exhaling, simply say, "I give up," like that. All right?

Now, I know that it's not in your nature to say that you give up, but you have all had to do that at one time or another, perhaps because you were at the end of your endurance for some physical activity or something. There is no shame attached to this, all right? You need to be able to give up, and sometimes the thought of letting go can be a bit vague. So that's what I recommend. It will help immensely if you do that, because the more people who do that letting-go exercise — say, once a week or even twice a week, if you like — the easier it will make the transition from the polluted struggle-and-strife planet to the benevolent ease planet: It's the same planet, just at different dimensions.

Here's the big change going on for you: It's not about moving gradually through some decimal point — "You're at this decimal point: 3.47, 3.52," or all the other kind of comments that have been made before. It is possible to make the switch quickly. I'm not saying that it will happen instantaneously, but it is possible, and it is important to make it as possible as you can.

So here is also a living prayer you can say: First ask for all the most benevolent energies available to you to be all around you — and with these things, always say the words out loud, all right? If you're in a crowded situation, or if there are other people present, you can whisper; that's fine. Again, try to have as little distraction as possible, then say:

Living Prayer

"I am asking that my shift and the shift of all others to the benevolent planet of ease, also known as Mother Earth, now take place in the most benevolent way for all."

Or if you prefer, you can say this version:

Benevolent Magic

"I am asking that I now be able to easily and comfortably be on the benevolent ease version of Mother Earth in the most benevolent way for me."

Try to use one or the other of those living prayers. If you wish, when you're asking "for me," you can also add, "and my family and my friends," or something like that. You can do that, but really the reason I don't recommend you do that is because it won't work for the others. Everyone has to do it for him- or herself and any language is perfectly acceptable. You each have to do it for yourselves, because no one can bring you along. You have to *want* to be at such a place.

Now know this: There will be no struggle or strife in the benevolent ease version of Mother Earth. There will be no disease there. There will be an easy lifestyle there, and everyone will be comfortable. I know it sounds like heaven as it has been described in various books, and it's not unlike that. I must tell you something else that might surprise you: It depends on how you look at it, but looking at it on the experiential time level, which is where I am at the moment, that version of Earth is about, oh [chuckles] seventy times bigger than the version of Earth you're on now.

That's why everybody can go, and when you get there, there will already be a lot of support in place. There are people living there now who are ready to welcome you. Some of those people are your future selves, but you're not going to have to give up your current self. They will welcome you, help you get settled, and show you the ropes, so to speak — how to live there and how to be there without any struggle, without any strife. Competition will not be necessary, nor is it encouraged. And you will have a good life.

There is room for everybody, and you will be able to continue your current birth expansion to the point at which the population of Earth, that Earth, will reach about 8 to 9 billion. Then it'll just stop, meaning that there will be an understanding that children will need to come less frequently because of the balance that is needed. The death rate will also balance equally with the birth rate. However, life on that planet — especially for people born there, but even for people who migrate there — will be extended so that you're living comfortably until you're about 147 years old. For people who are born there, though, life will be about 250 years or something like that. I need to give you these glimpses so that you will understand, roughly, that we're not talking about some vague thing that might happen. It is happening, and you need to give it some attention in the way I'm suggesting.

Earth Exercises Her Capabilities to Purify Herself

I will simply say that you need to try to let go of the struggle-and- strife-polluted Earth, because what's going to happen on this level of Earth will not make it a friendly place for any beings. When you leave (and actually, it's beginning now, as you might have noticed), Earth will exercise her own capabilities — her personality, you might say. She uses volcanoes, earthquakes, and all of these things, (especially rains and winds) to clean herself. She might even experience another ice age, but I don't expect that. I would expect her surface temperature to rise and for there to be more volcanic eruptions, because ultimately it is what comes out of volcanoes that does the purifying.

So this will go on with heat and steam and so on, and you really won't be able to live here. But it's not meant to eradicate you from Earth; it's meant to just remind you that Mother Earth is on her own clock, her own schedule, and you need to let go. I know you were born and raised here, and this is the home you know, but you need to let go, because the newer version of Earth is waiting, and life will be so much better there.

In my lifetime?

One hopes. The whole point is to make it as possible — as quick, you understand — and as immediate as can be, so that's why I gave the recommendations for the exercises. Other people are also giving exercises, and those are perfectly fine, but I wanted to add my voice, because I feel it's really important now to understand what is going on. I do appreciate that the entire ascension movement is about moving to a higher dimension of Earth, and almost all of those exercises are perfectly valid to use in this situation. But remember, if you're practicing ascension, understand that everyone must go at once. So nobody is to be left behind, okay?

What is the impetus for this sudden urgency? Is it the state of the planet?

The state of the planet. The issue of the pollution of the oceans is really catastrophic, but it won't affect you in your home that much because of water-processing plants and the care that goes into the modern city. Whether big city or small town, there is great care that goes into protecting and supporting the local citizenry through clean waters, good sewers, and so on. This is wonderful, but of course the animals do not live in that world unless they are pets or, in many cases, farm animals. So you are seeing in the animals what would happen to human beings if you didn't have this infrastructure, these people working in these places to make your water clear and pure, to take care of the sewers, and to bring you electricity — in short, people in various public-service jobs. If they weren't doing their jobs, what is happening to the animals would be happening to you and to all human beings.

You Can Make the Leap

An ET said that on 1/11/2011, the Creator, our Sun and four other suns, four planets in this solar system, plus people meditating all over creation created a pathway at an intersection to this new place. Do you concur with that ?

I do.

Can you say a little more about it?

There's not that much more to say about it. The fact that you can make the leap has everything to do with it. You can make the leap now, but you will all have to try to do this together. And I recognize that you cannot do these things simultaneously. For some of you, quite obviously, the leap will happen during your sleep state. For others, it will happen when you are awake. For still others, you might find yourselves driving down the road in the car, and suddenly you will be in some completely different space. It will feel warm and loving, and many of you will feel wonderful. At first, you'll wonder if something happened and you died and are in heaven. But no, after a few moments you'll certainly be in this other place, and it will be wonderful.

Explain a little more about the process. We're in a car, and suddenly we're in a new place. Do we still have the house and the car and the clothes and the family and everything that was here, or is everything different?

Many things will be different. You will still have your beloved friends and family. I am not prepared to say that you will have every single product that you currently own. On the other hand, you'll be happy, you'll be completely safe, you will enjoy all the people you meet, and they will enjoy you. You have to decide whether products are more important than safety, happiness, and fulfillment.

Okay. Is it a completely different kind of life from what we know here?

It is a completely different kind of life from what you know here. If you're asking, "Is everybody going to have everything that they've got now?" and are hanging on to that for dear life — no, you won't. But you won't miss it one bit. You won't need to make a living. You will be able to do the work or the things you like to do in the most benevolent way, and you won't have to work for money. You will have everything you need to live well — everyone will. It's going to be a lot like heaven, only it will be a real, physical life. It won't be in spirit; it'll be a real life.

You will know yourself as you are, but your world and your environment will change. You'll have other things you can do. You won't have to make a living. You won't have to struggle. Remember, it's not about struggle and strife. Most of you really don't realize how much struggle and strife happens in your daily lives, because you've adjusted. You've been conditioned, yes, but you've also adjusted to the pain and discomfort level. There won't be any pain there; discomfort will be unknown and almost immediately forgotten to have ever existed.

Well, there are so many questions one could ask, but I don't think you want to answer them all right now.

Well, I don't want to give you all the details, Melody, because if I give you the details, people will not make the effort. This is entirely about believing in the value of benevolence and ease for all beings. If you do not want benevolence and ease for all beings, you might find it difficult to make this leap. You have to let go of your prejudices and your anger. So when you're doing the letting-go thing, don't say, "I'm letting go of my prejudices; I'm letting go of my anger." Just let go: "I give up." Do you understand? Just do that, and it will happen; things will fall away.

If you do that regularly, over time you will notice your prejudices and your anger decrease. They won't decrease so much that you will be unsafe in various situations; you don't have to give up your knowledge or your instinct, okay? But you do have to let go of the old chains that tie you to the past. It is that past — even though in the past there has been some good learning — that is holding you there, weighing you down, and contributing to your pain and your struggle. Just because you're used to it doesn't mean it isn't there.

So the Explorer Race will go out, not from this planet, then, but from that version of Mother Earth?

We'll see. Most likely, but we'll see. The reason I am making an issue about this, the reason I'm suggesting that it's important to practice your letting go, is that it may be possible to make the leap before "years and years down the road." I realize that it will take a while for word of this to get around and for other people talking about it to get around and for folks to accept that it might be possible, that it could be possible, and so on. But even so, get started now, because the benefits of letting go and doing a letting-go exercise serve much more than making the move to this other version of Mother Earth. It also serves and will serve your life in the most benevolent way. Good night.

Wait — let me ask you something else. Are there pyramids, constructed pyramids, in a country called Bosnia? I've never seen so much "yes and no" and "this and that" and "it's a hoax" and "it's real" as when I looked it up. Are there real pyramids there, 600-foot-tall pyramids made of manufactured cement or something?

You're talking about pyramids being underground, actual pyramids that happen to be covered with soil; is that it?

Yes. Actual real, created pyramids — five of them, one of them taller than the Great Pyramid in Egypt.

I will say this (I'm going to be a little vague): At least one of them is a real pyramid. And I want to also bring your attention to — though you may already know this — the fact that the whole area has been a source of struggle and strife and wars for years and years and generations and generations going way back. Partly, for the people who live there, it's because they're on the way to every place, and when you're on the way to every place, people see things they like, so that's problematic. But yes, at least one of those is a pyramid.

Vertical Time

When was the pyramid built?

No, Melody. We can't do markers anymore. You're not in that calendar anymore. The calendar you're using now with the years and all that business is a complete joke. You're not in that anymore. It's practical for "Monday, Tuesday, Wednesday, Thursday, Friday, Saturday, Sunday," but it's completely … you can struggle with a line back about 200 years and say that calendar's really still legitimate, but from there, forget it. And it's really becoming less so every day, so it sort of becomes a dotted line before it gets to that 200 years. It becomes a dotted line about 3 years ago.

So when you say that, it's just impossible to give you an answer like that. You really must let go of those questions, even though they are completely logical. The trouble with logic, you see, is that the logic that you use nowadays is completely linear, but you, as a human being, and all other human beings on the planet, are not linear anymore. Did you know that? You have already connected to vertical time.

Okay. I've never heard of vertical time. I've heard of vertical wisdom. What is vertical time?

Vertical time is what allows beings to traverse from one time sequence to another, which is what everybody does when they fly in their ships. You see their lightships in the sky and so on. Do you think they came by ticking off the miles? No, of course not. They came by moving through different dimensions, you might say — different time sequences (which is a so much better term, but okay; everybody accepts the word "dimensions"). By coming through these different sequences, they are able to traverse vertical time, and vertical time allows you, through various portals that are stable, to move from your sequence — meaning where you are, how you live, your people, your version of the universe, if you would — into other sequences for certain amounts of time, certain amounts of experience, okay?

When the ships come here, they can stay here only so long; they don't hang around forever. They stay until they start getting the feeling of being uncomfortable. The beings cannot tolerate that, but the ship itself will start to get that feeling, all right? And when the ship gets that feeling, it will signal that it's time to go. Or if the beings are distracted and the ship just goes *bing* — it will no longer be there, and they'll suddenly notice that they're back in their own time sequence. They will laugh and say, "Oh, well that's all there is to that! Maybe another time, but … the end." They'll make a joke about it and go on with their lives. That's really how it works. You are now connected to this vertical time, as all human beings are, which is another reason you're all starting to have some really wild and crazy dreams.

Some of you are dreaming about things or even experiencing things in those moments of waking up and remembering things. Sometimes they're not so good; sometimes they're crazy. Sometimes they seem violent, and when you wake up, it's "What was that all about?" You might wake up with your heart thumping.

I'm going to tell you what that's about. It's not that those things are coming; it's like you're setting an ordination, in a way. You're setting something up to try to change the past of the level of sequence that you're on now. You're trying to change it, to leave it a better place for whoever follows in your wake. You're not attached to who it's going to be, you just … it's like you want to rush to sweep up the porch because company's coming.

So many of you are involved in projects. These are the kind of projects that you usually do after life, but since you're moving or are going to be able to move from one sequence to another — or one dimension to another, in other words — you are trying to sweep up the porch, so to speak, before you go. You're not all doing that, but some of you are, and that's why your dreams are totally nuts sometimes.

I know some of you think that these dreams are prophetic. Generally speaking, they aren't prophetic. The way you will be absolutely certain that they aren't prophetic is that if you remember that something you're dreaming about (whether it happens at the deep level of dreaming or when you're waking up, kind of going through the stages you go through when you're waking up) is a news event — it's something that actually happened, or you can look it up, say, on the Internet and say, "Hey, this actually happened!" — then you can be darn sure that you are involved in a project with many others to try to recreate the events of that time so that it will be more benevolent for those who follow in your wake on this dimension of Earth, even though it might be millions of years in the future because the level of Earth you're on now will have to go through this whole cleansing process.

Nevertheless, that will take place in time, and so hopefully Earth will not only be cleaned up but the psychic condition, you might say, meaning the energy of Earth will also be cleaned up to welcome the souls of the beings who will incarnate on that version of Earth in that time, when it comes — even though you'll be long gone, living on another planet.

That's great. So can we say that the 1/11/2011 connection that you talked about, the connection to the next dimension, the pathway, was that the connection to vertical time?

Yes. Now, that's not widely known, but it's very important to put it out, and it just so happens that in this experiential moment, it's all right to say that. Now, there's another side to that dimension of the wild and crazy dreams. Some of you are having incredibly benevolent dreams that you wake up from, and you say, "Oh, I want to be there!" And that place that you want to be —

Is where we're going.

As long as it's really benevolent and everybody looks really happy and you feel wonderful there, that's where you're going.

All right. That's wonderful. So we are connected to vertical time!

That's right.

Is there any purpose in talking to those other four suns who helped make the connection? Are they from the area in space where our Sun was before it migrated here?

I don't think so, no, but it's very typical for suns, as true lightbeings, to be allied with other suns. All over the universe, suns are completely allied. They're like a single family. And in other places, it might interest you to know that ... you know, you experience the Sun as something physical, but of course at other levels it is something completely different. Do you know that if you go up a few levels, so to speak, in various planets or sequences, that the Sun does not give off heat? Do you know why?

No physical matter?

You don't need it. But the Sun does give off light, all right, and the Sun ... this is just for fun, but since we're yacking, here's the example: At a different dimension, the Sun is completely cool. It is cool heat, and it gives off bright light. You know, because you're a scholar, perhaps, that the Sun in other dimensions gives off this heat and so on — it's overwhelming, and you couldn't get anywhere near it. But you can literally walk through this version of the Sun. If it's a big sun, it might take a while. If it's a small sun, it doesn't take so long; maybe it just takes what you would now consider to be a day.

So you can walk from one end to the other, for instance, if you are a scholar and you decide you want something and need something. Generally speaking, though, your need wouldn't be urgent the way needs are here on Earth as you now experience them; it might be something simple you'd want, and you'd say, "I'd like to have the experience of walking through this sun that will allow me to become receptive to and magnetic toward _____." You know, you'd say whatever it is you want. So by the time the journey ends, you're either much more likely to come into contact with whatever it is you're seeking or desiring to be around than when you started, just to give you an idea.

Is that the sun that will be at the version of Earth we're going to?

No, it'll still be warm. You'll need that because you'll be physical.

That's right. What about the setup of that event? Did the Creator plan it long, long, long ago, or did something just go into sync and allow it to happen?

No, you can be certain that monumental events, when they happen, are always planned by Creator. So you can be certain that this was planned by Creator. Do you want me to check with him?

Yes.

Okay. [Slight pause.] Yes.

Did you know it was going to happen?

It's possible.

So despite what we did, not because of what we did? Let's see, if the date was set up long in advance, then it was like the alarm went off or something?

It's just the timing, yes, but the formula has to do with the number of beings, the need, and the opportunity. It's as simple as that. That's the formula. Granted, there are millions of other factors that go into it, but that's the core of the formula. You have to remember that generally speaking in the rest of the universe where there's no struggle and strife, the simple statement of "all needs will be met" is true. Needless to say, nobody there needs anything horrible to happen to themselves or anybody else, so all needs will be met. Need a chocolate ice-cream sundae? It's right there. However, the cows don't have to give the milk. It's just there. So no, natural time —

Is experiential time.

Simply, yes. Experiential time. Vertical time is a passageway. Just think of it as that. It's a passageway. That's how you use it. You don't always have it; you have it when you need it. When the ships come, you understand, if they're meant to be here for some reason — you know, to be seen in the sky and have people talk about them; "What was it? What was it?" and that whole business — they need vertical time to come here. And when the time comes that they need to go, they need vertical time to get back to where they came from.

Can we equate that to the wormhole in Stargate*?*

No, because that's fiction. The reason I don't want to connect to fiction is because different people view fiction in different ways. The one thing you can be absolutely certain of in current fiction is that it has to do with danger and excitement and resolution. So of course it does not relate to that. People find that exciting now, but you won't find that exciting at that next level. As a matter of fact, excitement as you know it will cease to exist. It will only be benevolent excitement: "Oh! What's that flower?" or "Oh! Who are those people? I can't wait to meet them." So you might be excited, but there won't be any danger, and the resolution will not be required in the way you have it now. Resolution will be fulfillment.

Okay, so they made a connection to vertical time, which is a passageway, or as the being said, a pathway. So we have to use it when it's there, right? Or is it that they made a connection so that when we need it, it will be there?

Closer to the latter. They made the connection in a stabilized way — stabilized so that it can't be messed with, okay? And it can't be accidentally triggered. It's not going to be that you're walking down the street someday, you trip, and suddenly you find yourself on this other planet. [Laughs.] You're going to have to want to go, okay? So there's that. That's the main thing. It's stable, and it will be there when you want it, when you need it.

I am so grateful. This is such a wonderful thing to be able to share with our readers and all people.

Okay, good night.

Good night.

CHAPTER SIX

Old Ways of Life Fall Away, and Eden Is Ahead

Visitor

February 9, 2011

It has begun. Science looks at it as a pole shift — and others do as well — but that is the intellectual way, to try to bind one to the past. It is not that. Others have said it is the feminine energy rising, and it is closer to that. But to be specific, it is the natural course of the human being coming to its completion.

In your natural states, you are souls, you are spirits, and you are family. And as with all family, there is a time when you love each other and a time when you have spats and a time when there are distances between members. But now the familiarity of each other in ways that can be felt will be noticed by all. It will become more and more difficult to keep your distance. It will be much more difficult to strike out in anger, even if ordered to do so. It will be increasingly easy to do things together.

This time is when Mother Earth rebirths herself. In the beginning, before you — as a people with a destiny — arrived here, this planet was (as is described in many books) like Eden. In Eden, the people serve each other's needs in the most benevolent, kind, and considerate way. You will find that such moments will be upon you now, and it will seem as natural and normal as anything you have ever known.

This will take many forms. One of the forms is that your tendency to withdraw into a shell will suddenly be gone. You will want to be around people. You will be happy to be with your pets, as you have always been, but you'll want to include people. You'll want people to be at your home, or you'll want to be at their homes. You'll want to go places together and have fun. And "fun" will be expanded. Fun might be helping neighbors build their home or make an addition to their home. Fun might be helping people to have what they need: food, shelter, and other things.

Weapons will become a decreasing factor in life. This is not to say that there will not be capabilities to help make the planet safe, but it will be as a planet, not as countries, not as races and nationalities. The family of Earth humans is coming together now. Some of you have noted that you feel much more friendly toward people you never thought you would. Some of you are so happy about it, you have to sing about it. Others accept it calmly, with gratitude and simple grace.

There will be those who will be confused for a time. They have perhaps found safety and predictability in the old ways that create levels, hierarchies, and circumstances that can be predictable, even though it is predictability with pain, regardless of your stratosphere in life, meaning your position in the hierarchy. So now is a time when the option for pain, as long as it comes with predictability and hierarchy, will seem less desirable. It is hard to imagine that pain itself would be desirable, but it is an aspect of predictability. And people have sometimes thought in the past of pain as something even like a friend because it was predictable and therefore can be planned for in some way.

All of these things and more will simply fall away. The struggle within an individual to maintain some outer image or persona will fall away as well. Your true personalities will be able to emerge, and people you've known for years — some perhaps well, some perhaps not so well — will be startled and pleasantly surprised to see the real you, and you will have fun displaying it. So much pain has been caused by holding personality characteristics within and struggling to fit into circumstances that are not natural for the human being — Earth or otherwise.

Embrace the Feminine Energy

There will be other phenomena: On Eden-like planets, cold weather is almost unknown. Oh, there are places one can find a little bit of snow for the sake of beauty at the top of mountains, and sometimes if one lives near a mountain pass, there might be cool breezes at night so that you can enjoy wrapping up with a shawl or other garment or simply gathering around a fire in a group, singing and perhaps telling stories, to keep warm. But there will be no vast ice fields. There will be no places where one can go to be cold, bitterly or otherwise, and the coldness in one's heart will also fall away.

For many, this will be difficult, confusing, and actually cause some temporary changes in your body chemistry. Some people will think, "Oh, they have flu-like symptoms; they have to go to the bathroom a lot!" But in fact, this may, for some people, be part of the letting-go process, and it will not be — nor does it have to be — something that is truly detrimental. Such things will rarely be accompanied with fever or other symptoms but just be a part of releasing, and they will be gone quickly.

People will not walk away from their jobs; there will still be work and much new work to do. There will be a lot of need to help people to move, for some places will no longer be safe to live. The water level will rise a bit because of the melting ice. This will not be catastrophic but will happen in such a way — as it is happening now in places — that there will be a general sense of notification. You can see it's happening; it's obvious. So the move to higher ground will be possible.

Some places that have been reserved for parks will be allowed to have neighborhoods, but there will be a desire by people not to have a house with a big yard and a means to keep people away with big fences. Rather, there will be a great desire to live in large groups. People will often find that living in a single building or a compound of buildings is most desirable, and no one will be without friends.

This is the true nature of the feminine energy. The feminine energy is, by its very nature, inclusive. It is not exclusive, and as such, it is associated with inclusiveness, with love, kindness, nurturing, and assistance. It will not matter if you are a woman or a man; this energy is upon you. And even though some of you won't know what to do with it and will be confused at first, that confusion will fall away, especially as you see others embracing it and enjoying it.

Know that some of you will be frightened of it, and many of those who are frightened will gather together, and that is completely all right. But give yourselves time, and be patient with others around you who are embracing this energy. It may, in the beginning, seem offensive in ways, but it will not be harmful. It will just be that life is changing, and it is changing in ways that seem unusual. But if it seems too unusual, just picture it as a family. In many families, especially big families, there are always individuals who go their own ways and who are frequently the subject of family stories — and often, the stories are humorous, and one can laugh with love about this.

If you picture that which is around you that you don't understand in that context, it will be much easier, and you will be able to laugh things off that, in the past, might have frightened or upset you. What you will see is the many aspects of love, and it will not be so terrible. Be courageous; choose to embrace this energy, and your life will get better.

Generally speaking, in the Northern Hemisphere, this change, this great and wonderful feminine energy, will be felt most powerfully. It will not be felt as strongly in the Southern Hemisphere where that energy has already been prevalent. But in the Northern Hemisphere, where there has been much more cold, even the seasons will experience vast changes. There will be much rain, yes, but in time, it will not seem like it's trying to make up for something, and the rain will settle down and perhaps be light showers that occur every other day.

Don't fight it. Don't feel you must build huge dams and try to stop it. It will find its own way in time. Try to live on higher ground, and don't make casual structures — meaning build something temporary, even a tent — in a place that looks as if it could flood at any moment or might be an area where a flood could take place. I am not expecting a major flood of as destructive proportions as in the past, but there will be some flooding, as you have noticed. Help each other, and note that especially in the Northern Hemisphere, this will be the situation. Some Southern Hemisphere places are experiencing that now, but it will pass soon.

The Northern Hemisphere will be particularly influenced by this energy because it will affect people deep within their own personalities, and the release of one's true personality might be dramatic. Perhaps you considered yourself to be austere, but gradually you'll embrace the fact that that is a characteristic you had to use to feel safe among your peers or even to receive approval and be acknowledged or even appreciated. Soon you will discover that you are not the least bit austere and in fact love music, motion, and the sea or the lakes or the rivers.

The reason there is more water coming now is that you will need the waters for travel, for people to consume, and for animals to replenish themselves and feel welcome (those who choose to stay). In other places, you will also find that as water is temporarily converted (not for too long) to fuel, the excess of water will be temporary because that flirtation with the transformation of water into fuel will still consume the excess water that you are finding yourself with now. And then once again the planet will have waters that you're used to on the surface in places where you expect to find them.

As this process continues, you will find that your brothers and sisters from other planets will welcome you into planetary societies and will help you — not immediately, but as you begin to move into your natural, native personalities, which are all goodness and not in any way destructive or self-destructive. This is a process that will not take as long as you expect, but during the process, you will have a shift in what you call dimensions. Therefore, the process is not measurable in years, but it will be measured in felt energy.

As you go through the shift, there will be a definite sense of recollection of how things once were, but that recollection will fade as you get more and more connected to the way things are as compared to the way things were. What was and the memory of pain immersed in what was — meaning what you're going through now and what you're letting go of now in truth — will cease to be something desirable.

Pain in general will be looked upon as "Why? We don't need that." But then quickly it will become "Why? We can let go of that." And then even more quickly it will fade from memory. Fully 90 percent of disease will also fade quickly, because much of disease is a signal from your body that it cannot bear the pain, the suffering, the restriction, and the other things that you know about in societies where you've been struggling to be happy and to be free to be yourselves.

Celebrate and Be Compassionate toward Others

This time, while predicted for 2012, is in fact happening now. After all, the prediction of 2012 was only the best estimation. In fact, by

2012 all those who have been struggling with trying to keep the feminine energy from them will have let go of the struggle and embraced it. And that is why the symbol on that calendar that everybody wonders about will be completely understood as being the feminine symbol. That's why those who made the calendar made such an effort to show it the way it is — not so it would be confused with vehicles or other suggested possibilities.

This is a time to celebrate, when you have those good feelings, and it's also a time to be compassionate toward others who are struggling. Don't fight off these things; they are inevitable. It is your true nature to be happy, to be good and kind, to be considerate. Some of you have had lives that are so difficult that you will have to learn how to be happy, to be kind, to be good, and to be considerate.

For people like that, others who can do these things must be patient. Don't be demanding or commanding that they be some way. To say "Be good" is not going to help. Show them what you mean by being good. Do this yourselves, but also take time and be patient and say, "This is what I do because it is a good thing for me. You do not have to do what I do," you might say, "but consider it. That's all I ask." Be patient. They will have to be led slowly, because after having lived lives of restriction or suffering (or worse), patience will be needed, and they must go slowly. You will not be judged if you do not act patiently toward them, but you might feel a sense of unsettled energy in you.

If you feel unsettled or nervous at times, it simply means that others are crying out for help. If you cannot find them in your midst, then say prayers to help them in whatever way that prayer works for you. Or let people know that you are feeling unsettled and that this must mean someone around them needs help. Be sure to communicate that you are feeling unsettled or nervous. This always means that someone needs help, whether you know that person or not. So if you tell others about it, it will be helpful, and help might reach those who need it sooner rather than later. And then the feeling within you of nervousness and unsettledness will simply fade away.

I know you have questions.

Who is talking?

I am a visitor. That's all I'll say for now.

Okay. What was the catalyst for this energy, for all these new changes?

It has been happening. It is important to identify it, to state it as it is, so that people do not become frightened and believe that, as with other transformations of the planet in the past, there would be catastrophes and other such tragedies. If one holds to that theorem, one could accidentally — if there are enough other people holding to that idea — bring that about. But that thought is unnecessary, and Earth will actually struggle against it, as Earth herself is attempting to re-create an Eden-like planet for you all to live on.

Mother Earth Must Be Herself

There's been a lot of talk among scientists about a pole shift, a magnetic shift, that doesn't seem to be balanced; it's more in one direction than the other. It doesn't seem that the planet is moving with the same number of degrees in the Northern Hemisphere as in the Southern. Can you talk about that?

Not too much. These things will be observable. They will be noted, and I do not wish to dispute or create arguments and polarities among people. By all means, scientists, take note of these things, but do not assume that it means catastrophe. I can understand why you would think so, looking at the past, but the past is not always a predictor of the present; it simply suggests possibilities. And as you know, science's job, when it is in the area of research, is to predict possibilities and to suggest potential directions that could be more useful, beneficial, or yes, benevolent. So by all means, make your observations, but do not be attached to the possibility of drama.

Many years ago, Zoosh told us that those with power who were in opposition to us at that time had gone back into the past and created a fold of time under the Middle East that was partially causing all the dissention and violence there. Have we moved far enough now in dimensional time, space, or whatever to get beyond that?

No, nor is it necessary. It is much more empowering for individuals to unfold it. It can be unfolded, so to speak, not unlike you would unfold a napkin to have a meal. And it is being unfolded even now. Even though there are people there fighting each other, there are strong desires to be friends, even among those who are fighting. And this is happening on all sides. Even within groups, it is a struggle to stay mad at other individuals.

This might seem to make no sense at times. So those of you in this struggle, do not expect it to make sense, but if you feel like having moments of friendliness with someone you think is your enemy, just let it be, and apologize for the fight in the past (or in the present and the immediate future) and promise in your heart to one another, or to others and to yourselves, that it will not be interminable, that it will pass.

So is what we're seeing with these revolutionary uprisings — you know, these peaceful uprisings now in which people are saying, "I have the right to be happy. I have the right to be free" — a manifestation of what you are discussing?

It is partly that, but the drama and violence with it are not just elements of resistance to it. It is also like the rubber band stretched out as far as it can go, and then *snap!* — it comes back. And with that snap, there is a sense of at least temporary violence. If allowed to progress, it will become peaceful in time. So it is important to make promises that are lived up to and that are genuine to be inclusive, to make societies over in ways that include people and that do not create hierarchies and even caste systems. So while it is a manifestation of drama in a way, it is in that point of the snap-back of the rubber band. So that is why there is the drama for those desiring that freedom and those resenting and restricting it. The change for them is too fast, but it will resolve itself.

For those of you who are in positions of power or influence in those places, don't assume, should you move elsewhere, that others will rule in an iron-fisted way and hunt you down to harm you. It does not have to be like this. Take a chance, and compromise a little. Promise and live up to your promises. Move on and allow.

Now, you said that Mother Earth is rebirthing herself. Can you say more about that specifically?

I have. She is changing. She is bringing about something that has long been planned for, and that is being herself. The reason you all must be yourselves now is not that I say so. It is that Mother Earth is going to be herself as an Eden-like planet. That is her true self. But as someone who is engaged in fighting to be herself with her volcanoes and storms and other dramas, this is not her nature. It just seems to be her nature because in the past, she has had to do that to fight to be herself. Now you do not have to be volcanic. You do not have to strike out. You can be yourselves, and as such, you can be one with Mother Earth and be your own Eden.

What dimension will this Eden be on — the one we're going to, or the one we are on?

It is just a becoming. It happens, and you don't think of it as a motion forward. Linear time as you know it will change, and you will not be needed anymore in linear time. Linear time was a way to understand how things happen, but when you move past a need to know that, then you come into time that is perhaps called experiential, meaning you experience moments, but you do not have to count time. You do not have to trace your experience or the experience of others from the past. You do not have to do this because of any anxiety about the future. All that will fall away, and therefore time will be experienced, but it will not in any way be an attachment. So it will not matter.

Zoosh said that on January 11 of this year, 2011, the Creator and five suns and four planets and a lot of ETs opened a pathway to the next dimension. Will we go through that slowly? I know you're saying there's no time, but I mean is that a "we're here and then we're there," or is that a process?

It's a process, and it's happening right now.

That's what's happening now?

Yes. But it's also other people's predictions — most notably, since so many people are interested, in that famous calendar. It was kind of the people to make that calendar. One assumes that they made it for themselves, but they always knew that they were making it for others that they would meet someday on the soul plane. It was always a gift.

The Mayas are from the Pleiades?

They are from everywhere, as are you. Fixation on individual places is understandable at this time, but in reality, it is all family.

Right, but they actually came here from the Pleiades at that time?

If you like.

Okay. Is there a reason you can't say more about yourself, or is it that you don't want to?

I do not wish to. It is better to think of yourself as having this knowledge. It is my job to remind you of that which you know absolutely at the deeper levels of yourself where you dream, where you are with your guides and angels. Everything I am saying to you now you know about absolutely there, but it's good in your now time to have it in print or otherwise be able to listen to it. Print is good, but I recommend that when you are able, put it out as a voice message. Print cannot accentuate the way the voice can. Don't you agree?

I agree. Can you give me details about how the place, Eden, might look?

The reason I did not talk about that is that this subject is similar to the way it is in families. When people have wishes, hopes, and dreams, they do not always correlate directly. Some things correlate broadly — that's why I have painted with a broad brush — but if I say, "Oh, it will look like 'this'; it will look like 'that,'" some people might say, "Oh, I'd prefer it to be something else." The new version of Earth will be what you desire it to be, and most importantly, it will be for you all a place where you feel welcome and happy and enjoy being alive and simply being. You will feel that way because you will love the place. It will feel like a friend. It's like, "Oh, come along!" or "Come along when you're ready." You see, feelings are everything, my friend. Feelings create; thoughts describe. You must make your choice.

What a dramatic change! I know we're in a completely different place even from a few years ago. It's all moved so quickly.

It's important to know that it's happening now. It also helps people to release anticipation or even anxiety about what's going to happen in 2012. It makes it much easier to say, "Oh! It's happening now!" [Laughs.] And one can laugh about it and say, "Oh, why wait?" So you can embrace it. By 2012, though, the difference is that everyone, even those who wanted to dig in and say, "No, no!" will have begun to embrace it.

Oh, that's great. Everyone — that's a powerful statement.

When something happens that is, like they say, an irresistible thing, in the beginning you might resist it a bit, but then you see everybody enjoying themselves, so many people having a good time. Perhaps you never felt that you could be a part of that, but you suddenly discover that people do not have the thoughts or feelings about you that you thought they did or that you were afraid they did, and they welcome you without exception. You don't have to conform; you can be yourself.

And you're saying that some of our planetary leaders and dictators in various countries, those who have kept such tight control, are going to change that fast?

You seem to misunderstand something.

They're changing now.

And? It is your job to what, punish them? No.

It's our job to welcome them.

It's all about welcoming, and it's all about inclusiveness. Write down what I said about the feminine energy as I defined it before. Write it down and keep it handy, because you will discover your life becoming more and more like that, and what you thought you were supposed to be — what you were told you were supposed to be and what you guessed you were supposed to be — will just fall away, and it won't be so hard. Remember, what you must do now is be patient with yourself and others. I will have more to say about this in time. Good life and good night.

Thank you. From my heart, I thank you.

CHAPTER SEVEN

Earth Changes and How to Help

Zoosh

March 15, 2011

I'll put on my end-time historian hat today, all right? So you're wondering what's going on and why it is happening all of a sudden. You know, you have to keep in mind something that's been said and discovered and noted for the past few years: How many people are talking about how time has sped up, yes?

Now, when time speeds up, that doesn't mean things that were going to happen don't happen. It means they happen, but they tend to happen all of a sudden, and they tend to overlap each other. If time hadn't sped up, all that you're experiencing now in the world — pirates, rebellions, the way governments seem topsy-turvy, catastrophic changes, Earth changes — all of that would have happened very gradually over time, and everybody could have handled it in a more benevolent way. But when time speeds up because of the many reasons that have been stated before, things have a tendency to sort of happen at once, like a twenty-one-car pileup, as they say, on the freeway. You don't like it to happen, but then it's over, and that's that.

So this does not mean your world is coming to an end. It means all the stuff that was going to happen in third-dimensional Earth is happening all of a sudden. So that's the main explanation. Now you're going to have to ask the questions, and keep them specific, one at a time, okay?

Earth Changes Create a Unifying Force

Why Japan?[1] After the Second World War, why do they have to face radiation again?

Well, I'd have to say that the worst part of [the event] is the tsunami. The earthquake, of course, was very extreme, very damaging, but the water — that was the issue. You could say symbolically, of course, that water is feminine, and they tend to have a more masculine form of government, but never mind; that's rather not the issue.

You're asking about why they're experiencing radiation again. It doesn't have any connection to World War II, all right? It has to do entirely with the fact that everywhere on Earth you need to let go of using atomic energy, even though most nuclear reactors around the world are run very safely and emit practically no radiation accidents. The industry has sort of banded together over time and said, "Let's not tell 'em anything we don't have to." And that's unfortunate, because of course it's not as if they don't leave traces.

But what you have with this speed-up in time are circumstances that do not really allow for any kind of human error that's catastrophic, because you're going to have all these Earth changes going on, and they're going to happen no matter what. So what I have been saying, what Isis has been saying, and what lots of other beings have been saying through Robby for these past five or six years is to tell people to move back from the beaches. And this is why. The tsunami went in about five or six miles. The predictions were all to move back and move inland, move in by five or six miles, and then people would be pretty safe.

Earth changes must take place because they create a unifying force. Look at all the outpouring of compassion for the people in Japan. It's not as if there weren't arguments and so on before this, but you understand that human beings have a very fine quality, and that's in emergencies and crises, there's a tendency to totally unite and care for each other, regardless of who they are. Even if you've been fighting with your next-door neighbor for years, you're going to help each other. That's a fine quality, and if there are only Earth changes, those fine qualities will come out, and everybody will discover that what you have that you're

---

1.   On Friday, March 11, 2011, a 9.0 earthquake occurred off the coast of Japan, resulting in a devastating tsunami. See http://www.livescience.com/39110-japan-2011-earthquake-tsunami-facts.html.

disagreeing about is not so important compared to what you have that you can work together on and agree about.

You Can No Longer Afford the Risks of Atomic Energy

So you cannot afford to be making serious errors that would add to that, and atomic energy is the most serious error. I don't want to sound as if I'm just picking on power plants, especially ones that operate safely. I'm also talking about atomic energy used for weapons programs. Anything to do with atomic energy always leaves residue that you can't put anywhere. You can't just put it in a barrel and throw it in the ocean and hope everything will be all right. Even if you wrap concrete around it, it will be all right for a while if you're lucky, but it's going to leak out at some point. All the people who have dumped stuff like that know that very well. You can't do that. You're going to have Earth changes, and that's ongoing, so if you know that, then you know you can't be fooling around anymore with other stuff.

So that's what it's about in terms of the radiation. You might say the souls in Japan said, "Okay." They didn't say this consciously, I assure you, but they said, "We'll volunteer to show people that atomic energy is only as strong as its weakest link." Now, you know human beings are often fallible, yes? So there's a tendency to say, "Well, how many safety mechanisms do we need?" and "Maybe we don't really need that many." In other words, there's a tendency to cut back and say, "Oh well, it'll be all right." So when you have an atomic power plant where there's been a lot of that, to say nothing of having a major earthquake followed by a tsunami (pretty serious business), then it's like the sky is falling, eh?

So that's what's going on. It's a demonstration that is putting out the evidence that atomic energy is just too risky. And the irony, as you brought up yourself, is that these people suffered through radiation already. A whole generation was affected, and oh no, it's happening to them again. The thing about it, of course, is that it's not just happening to them. Korea is very close; China is very close. The Philippines isn't that far away. Japan is surrounded by other countries, and of course there's the jet stream; that can't be forgotten. So it's a global phenomenon.

Now, this happened before in Chernobyl, and even though people aren't talking about it too much, a whole swath of land there was totally radiated. As they say, it doesn't go away. But even though that was a catastrophic meltdown, at the time people just said, "Well, really, let's just not build atomic power plants like that anymore." Okay? But these are atomic power plants built exactly the same way they're built all over the U.S. and every place else. And even though they're a lot safer than the one in Chernobyl, they're not absolutely safe.

So you'll have to really say, "Okay, this far and no farther" with atomic power plants and then phase them out. You can't just phase them out and say, "Okay, we're phasing them out." You have to say, "Okay, we're now building wind machines," or "We're going big-time on solar." You don't shut down an atomic power plant until you've replaced the energy-production capacity with something that's clean. Then you shut them down one by one. That's how that's done. Or you shut them down and say, "Okay, we're going to burn oil and have generators and so on."

Remind Uranium of Its Identity

Now these things are things that you know, but I'm answering your question the best way I can. I know you want a spiritual answer, but the answer is much more practical than it is spiritual. Do you understand? All right. Now, if you want homework, then this is what I recommend: For everybody on the planet, you understand that even though it's vastly been changed, the fuel in nuclear power plants was originally a portion of Mother Earth in a natural form — uranium. And what you can do is to essentially remind that fuel (at a distance, obviously) who it is.

Now, you can't, nor do I recommend that you do, put your hand on pitchblende. [**Editor's Note:** a form of the mineral uraninite that contains a small amount of a radioactive decay product of uranium.] But what you can do, those of you who are good at this kind of thing, is to imagine or even, for those of you who wish to and can do this, sort of project yourselves into some area where there is uranium or even residue. Or if you want to, you can project yourselves to where old uranium mines are, all right?

First ask the Sun — or if you choose, white light or gold light — to be between you and that uranium, okay? Then send that uranium or the energy of that uranium as best you can to nuclear power plants all over the world to remind those elements that have been transformed of who and what they originally were. That's a good start.

When materials that have been vastly changed remember who and what they are, they then tend to identify with Earth once more, and they begin to function in the way they functioned when they were in the earth. And uranium has to do with Mother Earth's memory, so if you remove enough uranium from the earth, Mother Earth tends to get a bit forgetful. She tends to forget about the people and the animals and the plants on the planet and how she was serving them. And she tends to start living her life as if the people are not here anymore, you see?

So the thing you need to do is to try to remind all of this transformed uranium who it is. Even though it's in these atomic power plants and will still be running there, if it remembers who it is, it might be able to help Mother Earth and her memory. That's something you can work on. Now, a lot of you out there are very spiritual folks, so just adapt this to your practice.

Remind Mother Earth of Who You Are

That's really what happened? She sent that tsunami out?

Oh, no, no. She didn't send it out, but she is functioning the way she normally functions, as if people weren't here. She didn't say, "Oh, I'm going to kill a bunch of folks in this country." It wasn't anything like that. She's functioning, though, in a slightly forgetful way. Long ago, you understand, there weren't that many people, if any. If you go back far enough, there weren't human beings on Earth at all. When she gets forgetful, she tends to go back to those times. And when she goes back to those times, the idea of moving her waters around with a certain amount of ferocity makes her feel good because she's cleaning herself.

Rain and tornadic storms — cyclones, you understand; you call them hurricanes — all this has to do with Earth washing her surface. Mother Earth is primarily a water being, and as a water being, she tends to identify with keeping everything as moist as possible. Do you know that if you take the long look and you look back at Earth as a planet, way back before human beings were here, deserts were almost entirely unknown? There were a few, but generally speaking, Mother Earth liked to keep everything as wet as possible.

That's why she was so welcoming of the trees, because in those days, they were rainforests. And even after it stops raining, the trees tend to keep dripping. That's the whole reason to call it a rainforest. So between rainstorms, the trees and the land tend to maintain high humidity.

Mother Earth thinks of herself — you could say it that way — as a water being. And therefore, when she becomes forgetful, she just resumes in that water-like fashion. So you see, you have everything to gain by helping Mother Earth's memory functions revitalize, okay?

Now, for those of you who want to connect to uranium that has been transformed and is in some kind of weapons' programs or even is in some pile of nuclear waste some place (in small portions, of course), you can do the same thing. It won't interfere with its function in power plants, and for that matter, it won't interfere with its function in weapon systems, but if it remembers who it is, that's important. Then it can help Mother Earth's memory. Mother Earth will say, "Oh, wait a minute; there are people there. There are plants. There are animals," and she'll calm down a bit. That's pretty important to know.

Extremely important. Do you see other instances of earthquakes and tsunamis coming of this magnitude?

There's a good chance of that. So when you read this, even if you're not feeling at home with the kind of spirituality that this publisher is known for, then put it into your prayers. I'll give you a living prayer. You can adapt it to your religion, if you like. That's perfectly all right. You might say:

Living Prayer

"I am asking that all of Mother Earth's memory materials be reunited with her, no matter where they are or what they are doing, and help her to remember all that she needs to remember now."

That will be helpful because the more that she is able to remember, the less she will keep on resuming her natural personality. You see, she's sort of set aside her natural personality to be a host to human beings and animals and even many species of plants. Orchids, for instance — just picking one at random — are not native to Earth, and they're very fragile for the most part. A lot of flowers are. But Mother Earth likes the plants, and she likes the people. She likes the animals. But right now, so much of her memory material has been removed and transformed that she's a little forgetful, and you can't really let that be.

Remember that as you gradually wake up everybody on Earth, you'll gradually remember that magic, as Grandfather calls it — true magic and all of this kind of stuff — is not something mysterious or scary or frightening, even though you have storybooks that talk about it that way. It's what you normally do in your soul and spirit state when you are on other planets or in your natural state. You don't call it magic; you just say, "Oh, this is how we create." So as you begin to wake up here, that will be comfortable. You'll be able to do that, but you can't wait, see? Because time is speeding up and everybody is waking up, you still need to do what you can to support Mother Earth as she is now. So that's what you do. Do it in the best way you can.

If You Help Her Remember, Earth Can Slow Down Her Changes

Are there other elements or substances that have to do with her memory that we've mined or removed from Earth?

Well, not her memory, but more what I would call her brain and nervous system, and those are crystals. So please don't take any more of that out of the planet, all right? Crystal has the ability, if it's not changed too much, to still function in its original manner, even though not as well. It functions much better if it's not broken apart and so on. So I recommend not messing with that, either. That's the main one, but right now the most urgent is uranium.

You don't like these "how long" questions, but is there any sense of the span of time that these Earth changes are going to go on?

You'll be shifting, you know, into another dimension, and they'll continue to go on in the third dimension. Right now, you're sort of in that midpoint between dimensions, you see, and as a result, you're more sensitive to things as a people than you used to be. Oh yes, you like to think you're not sensitive, many of you, but in fact, you're much more sensitive than you ever were. Everybody is. So the more sensitive you become, the quicker you're able to react. That's right. So try not to suppress that. The issue is that most of you are not engaged with the fourth-dimensional Earth, so the Earth changes will go on.

The more you can do to help Mother Earth remember, the more the changes will slow. You see, time can still speed up, but Earth changes that are that radical can slow down because Mother Earth will remember. So you can sort of have a superimposition in which time speeds up for you as people and even for many of the animals. That's why the animals are leaving. They can tell you're remembering who you are and that you don't need them to remind you. So that can happen — where time will speed up for you, but Earth can slow down her changes until you're gone.

When you all leave and the animals are gone — most of them, not all — then she'll resume what she's been doing, only much more powerfully. And then there will be a period when there will be no people as you understand people to be, meaning humanoids. There won't be any people on the planet. There will just be a few animal species who can get along under harsher conditions. That will go on for several thousand years.

Then the beings who will live in third-dimensional Earth will show up with needs that must be fulfilled. By that time, Earth will be calm enough to serve their needs. They won't be comfortable in an oxygen-rich atmosphere, and it will be a little bit too rich for them, but they'll adapt and be all right. When you first came here as the human race, you too were not that comfortable in such an oxygen-rich atmosphere. When you first got here as the human race, the planet was much denser with oxygen. Over time, you adapted to it. Then of course, because of the use of tools and forgetting how to create in ways that are gentle and benevolent — sort of a combination of those two — you started unintentionally eliminating the oxygen creators. The oxygen creators are the plant world and, to a degree, certain species in the sea, but there are not that many of them left.

Move Away from the Sea

So the most important things we can do, then, are to remind the uranium who it is and move back from the edge of the sea.

Try to move inland five or six miles. That was always the suggestion, you know. We've been saying that for a long time, and we didn't say it because we wanted to poke a finger in some person's face who's suffering. We just want to underscore the fact that we like to give you a significant amount of time for warning. See, we're not trying to say, "We're going to do this." We just want to be the messenger and say, "This is coming; this is going to happen. Move back."

As you know — and we know it's frustrating for you — we can't say it's going to happen on such-and-such a date, because it depends on too many variables mostly having to do with human beings. What we can do, though, is to warn you about things at the earliest possible moment we can say anything. This channel, Robby, has been channeling these suggestions and warnings for a long time, and now you see why — because it's very possible that you'll get that kind of situation again.

If you're not living on that sort of flat ground near the sea, you'll be okay. Some people have asked, "What if we're near the sea but at a high elevation?" If you have a higher elevation, then you'll be all right as long as you're not on the edge of a cliff or something. You'll be all right. So let's say, just to be on the safe side, that if you're eighty feet up, you should be fine, even if you're pretty close to the sea. But if you've built on a mountainside or a mesa or something that could fall away in an earthquake, well, that's not too safe. If the ground naturally slopes up and you're eighty feet above sea level, you should be fine.

That's the worst-case scenario. You're not likely to have too many 40-foot tsunamis, but I think in places in Japan, that water was about that high at times. So if you know that can happen and a 40-foot tsunami is possible, then give yourself that extra margin, because a certain amount of splashing will happen, of course, coming in at a pretty strong velocity and so on. So I'd say 80 to 100 feet. That should be fine, and then you can be relatively close to the ocean. But if you're not, then move five to six miles inland, at least.

Start Demonstrating the Qualities of Mother Earth

Okay. Is there anything we can say directly to Mother Earth to have her temper the ferocity of some of these movements of her waters?

No, you can't argue with her. You have to help her, all right? She's not like a crazy person running around the street with guns and knives. She's just a little forgetful. So you have to help her. When somebody is forgetful, you don't hit him with a baseball bat. You help. That's what you do. You can't argue with her, okay? So that's why I'm recommending it. You have to learn how to do things gently, because doing them harshly ... well, the history books are full of people doing things harshly. I know you don't want to do that. Also, you have to keep in mind that Mother Earth is ultimately your host. Doing things harshly is not a good idea.

No [chuckles], I meant like a living prayer or something.

Of course, I understand. The repartee between us is meant to be kind of amusing.

Okay. Is that why she's not doing the book she said she wanted to do on the history of Earth?

That's why, because everything changed. You're in a cycle right now in which the past is changing. So doing the history of Earth is kind of like writing about something that's gradually becoming untrue. If you're still doing this work in a couple of years, maybe you can do that, but it'll have to be the history of the future. If you try to write the history of the past, it'll be sort of like … as you're turning the bag inside out, you're desperately trying to have the bag the other way. It's not going to work. You'd be writing the history of things that people don't even remember or care about. Oh no, it has to be the history of the future.

Should have gotten it while I had the chance …

If you had, people wouldn't care about it.

Yeah. But the history of the future, now that's not bad.

All right, then I'll make some witty or pithy closing.

[Chuckles.] Okay, please.

In the past, living on Mother Earth has been the experience of living as well as possible. But now, as I've said, you have to help Mother Earth, which means you have to demonstrate some of the qualities of Mother Earth's personality. You are not without these qualities. Mother Earth is a material master, and you are learning that. Mother Earth is a spiritual master, and you've all been that in other lives or you wouldn't be allowed to be here. And Mother Earth also has the capacity to transform things, which is what quantum mastery is about. While that may seem to be impossible to you at this time, what Grandfather calls true magic is entirely about transforming things in the gentlest and most benevolent way.

I want you to read up about that. It's mostly on Robert's blogs, so you can read there. Transformation can be done very benevolently; materials can totally change. I'm not talking about a tree becoming a rock. [Chuckles.] That takes a while. What I am talking about is within an organism. An organism that might have been harmful to human beings, or animals for that matter, can literally transform into something more benign. There are ways to communicate and to interact energetically to encourage organisms to transform so that they are still vital and have lives of their own but are no longer harmful to human beings or animals.

This has been discussed at length on the blogs, so I'm not going to bring that up all over again. I am simply going to say that now is a time when you have to start demonstrating qualities that Mother Earth has. So read up on your true magic, and see what you can do. And remember that if something's going on in some part of the world — like radioactivity some place you'd rather it not be — then simply do this little extra homework, as our questioner would have us do here.

You begin by asking for all the most benevolent energies that are available for you to be all around you and all about you, and wait for a moment. Some of you will feel energy come up. If you don't, just wait a few seconds — twenty seconds or maybe thirty seconds. Then say,

Living Prayer
"I am asking that radioactivity transform and become something that is safe for all beings."

Good life and good night.

Thank you very much.

CHAPTER EIGHT

Shift Your Energy Production

Isis

March 18, 2011

For the past many years, predictions have come through this channel from various beings, and there have been urgings and encouragements from these beings to move inland. This channeling has been going on for fifteen years or more through this being to move inland five or six miles or at least to be on very stable ground eighty to 100 feet above the sea. I'm not saying, "Oh, you should have paid attention." I'm saying that this is an ongoing issue and it won't only be an issue for places that are earthquake prone.

It will certainly be an issue for other peoples in other places for a considerable length of time, because you've got the polar icecaps essentially melting, not instantaneously, but that kind of melting is going to affect the sea level, and it's going to be difficult on low-lying islands, and it's going to be more problematic when you consider the tides and potential tsunami and so on. So there might be a lot of people needing to move around.

To what extent do you see the water rising? Six inches? Six feet? What's going to happen to the shorelines of the world?

Six inches was stated in the past, while not even seeing it going up any more than eighteen inches, and I have to agree. I don't see it going up more than eighteen inches, but it is possible that it could go up to perhaps twenty inches. But in many low-lying areas, this is very serious. Now, I know people are predicting five to six feet. I don't expect that. But I do think that you ought to plan ahead for the sea level to go up and stay up for a while. And given that, it's something to seriously consider.

You've noted the world over that glaciers are melting, and places that used to be famous for glaciers are really becoming places that were named for glaciers but not necessarily ones where glaciers are as obvious anymore. This is all adding to the rise in various lakes, rivers, seas, and oceans. Of course, one can look at it another way and say that this is vastly adding to your potential fresh water, which is something you're going to need with the increased population you have at this time.

Understand that we're talking about Earth changes here in some ways. And we're also talking about a gradual recognition that atomic energy, as valuable a contribution as it has been, still has not worked out some of its serious problems, one of which — and it's a major issue that is not really that obvious outside of the industry — is what to do with the radioactive materials. And we're not just talking about spent nuclear fuel. There is a great deal of other material that is problematic that way.

It's not that far into the future before you'll have a different form of producing power with atomic energy, and such power plants can be very small and produce quite a bit of power and have absolutely no nuclear waste. But it's far enough into the future where you really have to seriously consider phasing out the type of nuclear power you have now with the type of reactors you have now until you can get that new system. All right? Essentially, what we're talking about doesn't sound mysterious; it's fusion. And fusion is possible. People are working on it. There's been considerable progress, but it's not here yet as something that can be disseminated widely and easily adapted in various areas.

Until that comes, I think it's better to shift over to some form of energy production that is well established, such as the use of oil as something to tide you over — though I don't recommend drilling in the sea anymore. And in terms of other types of energy, such as wind and solar, you can produce a tremendous amount of energy with wind. You essentially have to utilize the technology you now have; it's not like you have to invent anything.

I know that this doesn't exactly give you the power-generating capacity you need for factories, but oil will do that until you have some other means, and another means is coming. It's just not obvious for you yet. It will bridge a gap to provide the kind of energy you need for factories and so on until you have a really viable fusion reactor system that can be placed anywhere completely safely.

That other method — and I'm not going to say what it is — will be with you in about twenty to twenty-two years. But it will take from this point another thirty-five, forty, and possibly as many as forty-five years for fusion to really get going safely, acceptably, and in such a way that there will be no danger or almost no danger. This means that it will be — I'm not speaking for the atomic energy community here; I am speaking as a fact — about 99.5 percent safe, and the only hazard might be the very occasional vapor leak. This will be very occasional and will be monitored in great seriousness by an international body of scientists in no way associated with the atomic energy industry.

That's wonderful, but no clue as to what it is?

Why would I give a clue? I don't want to step on toes. There are people working on things, and I'm sure not going to betray what they are working on. It's in its infancy now, but it will become more well known in time.

Mother Earth Needs Full Shoreline Access to Renew the Oceans

There are still people all over this planet on the seashores living where they can just open their doors and walk out to the water.

As attractive as that might be, and romantic in many cases, I do not recommend it.

I know. But I'm talking about the ones who are already there; they're not going to willingly [move].

Well, I don't think there should be an invasion force that comes along and drags them out of their homes. If, however, there are unfortunate disasters, realize that they are part of Mother Earth's revitalization process. You don't want Mother Earth to die as a planet, I can assure you. If Mother Earth died as a planet and you were trying to live on her — well, imagine living on Mars as it is now or on the Moon.

No, you don't want Mother Earth to die. You have to allow her to revitalize, and one of the things she's going to need to do is to have full access not only to her shoreline but also to five or six miles in from her shoreline, because she's going to try to make her oceans more habitable places for the beings who live in the waters even though there has been serious overfishing. By serious overfishing, I mean dragging nets along the bottom of the water just to pick up certain types of fish — and killing all the others. That absolutely, positively has to stop. If it doesn't (and don't blame the messenger here, all right?), Mother Earth will continue to produce earthquakes at sea that produce violent tsunamis with the express purpose of destroying fishing boats. You must know this: Mother Earth will do this not because she doesn't like human beings or fishermen, for she is actually very fond of fishermen, but because of the abuses of a few.

I'm going to say even more about the dragnets: Generally speaking, using nets to capture fish must stop, because — and you know this, people in the fishing industry — a great many fish are killed that don't need to be. Very often you wind up with more than you can possibly carry on your vessel, but because they've been in this net and been in these circumstances that do not support life, they all die. We cannot have that. So find another way. You are creative; find another way.

Now, I'm not trying to scare you, but that's necessary. And I also want to make this request: Please, no more so-called sport fishing, all right? It's not okay. Mother Earth loves the beings of the sea, just as well as she loves the beings of the land: the animals and the humans. She loves everybody equally. If the beings of the sea were suddenly attacking the beings on the shore, she would do something about it to save the beings on the shore. Do you understand?

So she is doing something about the sea and her remaining beings. Please allow fish, as you call them — or the people of the sea, as I call them: turtles, whales, and so on. Just put something in effect where nobody fishes for them hardly at all, and try to live off of other types of fish that you normally consume. Please don't get attached to shark finning. This is a monstrous thing, and it was really a last straw, from Mother Earth's point of view. I'm not blaming the fishermen only from Japan. This is happening all over, and it's strictly because some people think that this is a delicacy and it vitalizes them in some way, but it's monstrous. All right?

So I must tell you these things. It is better for you to know. You must remember — I know it's difficult to remember in this age of technology and the wonders of technology — but Mother Earth will have the last word. There is no way you can stop volcanic activity, all right?

There is no way you can stop earthquakes from happening. There is no way you can stop tsunamis from happening, though you can get serious about building walls in an attempt to deflect them. But you will have to build those walls very high: forty, fifty, sixty, or seventy feet high, in some cases. Or you will have to move to higher land.

I'm not trying to spread gloom and doom. I think it's better for you to know. I'm putting this out one more time. Through this channel, this message has come out for the past fifteen years or so, and even earlier than that. This being has been channeling these things for years and years, and other people are saying it now too. Please, I know you might miss your beach property, and I think it's okay to get some kind of compensation from the government if you want to, but just know that to live near the beach — well, I'll put it like this: I recommend insurance companies put your money some place else. It's not going to all happen at once, but it is a hazard, and by today's standards, it is an uninsurable hazard, to put it in the business community's context.

Fishermen are to be honored. They feed the world. But please, find other ways to fish. Start fish farms. I know there are problems there, but work on it; you're creative. Your people can do things. Start fish farms, and substitute the fish from fish farms for the fish that you acquire from the sea and even from big lakes, in some cases.

You Are Here to Observe and Learn the Messages of Nature
Remember that you are here to create. You are the Explorer Race. You are here to learn, to notice what the animals are doing, notice what the plants are doing — in short, to be observant, and then to create on the basis of those observations, all right? People have done that for years. That's how people got started. That's how human beings managed to thrive, by noticing what nature was doing around them and then living as well as possible. But the more you got into the machine age and then technology, the easier it became to ignore. You removed yourselves from that further and further and further.

So now people grow up in cities around technology and machinery, and there's no observation of nature whatsoever. This is not new, what we're talking about. It's very old. But it was well understood in days gone by and by old cultures. Some of the oldest cultures of the world have chosen to live in high places, eh? They know what they're doing.

Figure 8.1. Stinging jellyfish floating in the depths of the Pacific
Ocean. © Itsmejust | Dreamstime.com

There aren't many animals around the seashore for people to observe.

There are; you just don't know about them, and they need access to
the beach. By access, I mean with no people around, nobody to interfere
with them. In time, their numbers will increase, but they need access.
An obvious example is sea turtles. Since people consume them, there has
not been much opportunity for them to increase their numbers. That's
just one example of many.

Sometimes the sea will get upset, so to speak, and produce many beings
who are dangerous for human beings to be around, such as stinging jellyfish.
The point isn't to harm people. The point isn't, from Creator's or Mother
Earth's points of view, to harm people. It's to say, "Look here: Stay away.
There is a reason. Stay away. Give the beaches back to the sea peoples, and
be safe, and live well." But because people grow up in the age of machinery

and technology, they don't observe nature, and they don't understand. It just becomes something to try to deal with rather than to understand it as a message. That's what it is.

I know this has been kind of dramatic, and we've wandered around and covered various topics, but I just want to say that you are really in the time of unification. It's not going to be "this" country and "that" country, "this" group within "that" country, or "that" group within "this" country. It's gradually homogenizing, and the age of the Internet has been very helpful in doing that. Many of you have friends in other countries who you will probably never meet but you feel close to.

There is a kinship, and this is going to increase. Europe has gone out of its way to create an international currency and to make borders more open. Soon other parts of the world will do that, and it's not that far off when you'll have the global Earth community. So learn to care for each other, learn to respect nature in a new way, and learn to understand so that you can grow, change, and adapt. Learn and relearn to understand the example and the message of nature. Good night.

CHAPTER NINE

Adapt Now to Survive
Patience and Discernment Are Your Tools

Isis

April 14, 2011

All right, this is Isis. You are now at another intersection. I'm not going to call it a crossroads, because it's not quite that, but it is another intersection that allows you to change, for that is entirely what these times are about: change and, to a slightly lesser degree, adaptation. What you're dealing with is the need to recognize that you cannot continue to do things the way you have done them, even in the fairly recent past, with as many people as you have on the Earth now. Even if the population were significantly smaller, the Earth has been largely polluted by the effects of so many people, even with industries that are attempting to keep things as clean as possible, because worldwide pollution is a reality. There is only so much you can do, and beyond that, there are accidents, and the planet gets polluted. There are rainstorms, and then your waste systems overflow and so on. This happens all over the place in the best of conditions, and the best of conditions do not happen everywhere. In many places, the conditions are not that good.

So even if you say, "Well, it goes downriver from here" or "It goes out to sea from here" or "It percolates into the ground from here," the planet is not that big when taken into account how interconnected everything is. You know, even if it percolates underground, whatever the waste material is, there are beings under there that might be affected. At the very least, your water is affected. And of course in time, people dig around in that ground to create foundations for buildings or to look for things underground — mining and so forth. So even if you don't remember or don't know that something was dumped there by accident or otherwise, it does come up, and you have to deal with it at some point.

Even natural conditions that have been survived by the population that exists are problematic. In the past, there were waves of disease because "this" or "that" organism that hadn't been on the Earth's surface for a time was revealed, either by earthquake (followed by the natural process of water moving through the earth and eventually affecting the water you drink or the food you eat), or by people digging in the earth. You can dig in the earth for the most important and worthwhile causes, and if you dig deep enough or just happen to dig some place where something had either settled or been buried or came to be for any reason — and how can you know about it if it happened thousands of years ago? — then up it comes.

Mother Earth Is Taking Care of Herself

Here is the situation: If Earth existed even in its natural condition today as it once did and the people lived lightly upon it without digging into it (let's say that was possible), even then, there would be some challenges because of the nature of living on a planet that is so vital and involved in life. Mother Earth has earthquakes, as they are called, but actually, she is just moving her body not unlike you do when you are uncomfortable. Most of the time, these motions happen deep within her, but sometimes they affect the surface.

So you have chosen, as the human race, to live on a planet that is at least as alive as you are. As a planet, she is always in motion; she is spinning. Of course, you don't necessarily think about that because you are on her as she spins, and you don't really have to know that. The effect can be seen, of course; the Sun seems to come up and go down when in fact the planet is spinning. You know this.

The issue is that what's going on in the world today are not only the events of human beings — the dramas and traumas as well as the happiness and joys — but also to a degree (human beings are inclined to find solutions to their problems, yes?), the naturally occurring application of many human beings finding solutions to their problems. Sometimes very good solutions are found. Other times, they're not so good. What you have is the planet, a living being who must take care of herself, as you do.

When human beings get to the point where they must take care of themselves, they do what they need to do. You eat, you sleep, you go some place. In short, you act. You do something. And Mother Earth is just like you. In the larger sense, you might say you are just like her, since even though Creator sparks your personality with your soul, everything else that assembles into a human being is through the process of building with the available matter, which is Mother Earth's body.

So given that, you must realize now more than ever that what's going on in the world is a direct result of needing to operate as if Mother Earth were a beloved human being you must take care of. Now you know these things, but knowing it and being able to do something about it with the technology you have presently, that's the challenge, because the technology you have presently tends to pollute. Even if it didn't, simply what human beings eat — what goes into you must come out at some point — also tends to pollute. If it's one or two people or even several thousand (or even quite a few million scattered around), this is not a great problem, but in time, it becomes one. However, now you have billions of human beings, so you need to do things differently.

Adjust Your Technologies and Populations

The big challenge for today, really — even though it seems to be "this" or "that" situation, political or otherwise, meaning in history — is surviving and thriving, using new technologies and transformation of waste products into something that is at least safe. So you also have to take a hard look at using technologies that are gradually destroying your world. You cannot really live on a world as you have in the past where you have sort of focused on things locally so that you could have various other things far away. There is nothing like that anymore, because people are living pretty much everywhere. So there isn't any "far away" anymore; it just seems like there is.

So here's the issue: It is a time now when you must embrace technologies that you understand can be used that do not pollute at all, such as solar and wind. I know that you know this, but you must do that, period. I know that there is a very distinct and understandable desire to use oil — you know it works and you know it helps. Oil provides not only jobs but also survival — no question about it — at least in places at times that are not likely to be survived. It provides survival for really large populations of people, say, in bitter cold or even in places that are way too hot for lots of people. But the reality is that even though the planet is changing, it's not going to change so fast that it will be able to support billions of people.

So it's very simple; this is not tough stuff. You're going to have to resign yourself, couples, to having no more than one child. This is going to need to be supported. Now, I know a lot of couples would probably choose to have children anyway, but there needs to be a simple way to reduce the population that does not cause harm to anybody. The ways you have been using unconsciously to reduce the population is to have battles, but this ultimately causes much harm. It is seriously problematic. And given the level of weapons, to say nothing of the sort of capricious effect of weapons, you might be trying to do something specific and wind up doing something general, and it's the general that often makes great and long-lasting problems.

So there's that, and there's more. I had to touch on that, though, because everything else takes place within that bowl I just laid out for you. Now you know that. These things are not secrets, but there are other things: There have been cycles of civilizations that have come and gone on the surface of this planet. You are now in (depending on how you count) the third or fifth cycle. And the reason I say that is that it has to do with time, and that's so complex that I'm not going to get into it here, because the whole purpose of this is to help you to understand your life, not to complicate your life.

To put it simply, you are now making your third attempt to get through the challenges and problems in the most benevolent way for all beings — and this includes animals and plants as well as human beings. Those are the challenges you've chosen to be here for and to deal with, to get through all that I just mentioned in that bowl in which you are living. And while you're living within those challenges, you're attempting to get through problems that have stopped your civilizations in the past. Some things take place that are just hard. One of the great problems is patience and to know the timing for when to wait and when to act. So in that sense, patience and discernment — I'm not going to use the word "judgment," because judgment can also be used to condemn something that is simply not understood — are the big struggles you have within the whole drama of what I laid out at the beginning of this talk.

In the past, there have been many attempts to bring some kind of technology to bear on a situation so that things would become better for all people. Sometimes this has been very helpful, and more benevolent medical science has made a huge difference, but there are ultimately other choices that you must make. Still, since you have had hostility toward interacting with peoples from other planets in a way that is benevolent — meaning benevolent in all ways, not just in ways that you feel are benevolent according to your culture or to the culture of those peoples that interact with those from afar — this is slowing you down.

Stability Does Not Necessarily Mean Benevolence

It was really intended for your civilization to have contact with helpful beings from other planets about sixty-five years ago. If you had had that contact openly and welcomed it — and by that I mean your governments have systems in place and you have philosophies and, yes, religions welcoming such contact — you wouldn't have any of these problems I've mentioned because all the means to transform that is readily available. People live on other planets in complete peace and happiness even though if they lived on Earth like you, they would quickly become like you are, so it is not a judgment on Earth people — and I'm using the word "judgment" specifically here. So I'm not judging you; I'm simply saying that conditions on Earth exist without you having certain means to adapt, so you are stuck, essentially.

When people are stuck and their numbers grow and grow and conditions — especially the ones I mentioned in the beginning — get worse and worse, there's a tendency to act out, strike out, and so on. That's why you're seeing things happening in places that appear to be stable for people from afar. Of course, underneath stability, if there isn't benevolence for all beings, there is struggle and suffering.

So in many places, there *appeared* to have been stability. In the Middle East, for example, there was a lot of struggle and suffering; it just wasn't readily apparent to the outside world. This is not to suggest that the Middle East is a problematic place because of the peoples; it is simply because it is, in your now world, laid bare. It is difficult to hide when not only tools such as the Internet exist but people also travel and see things and naturally, being curious, as you all are, talk about them. And there is a great deal more about technology and its impacts, just to mention one thing.

So the issue has been this in the past: What has stopped your civilizations from growing and thriving and has caused you to have to fall back and essentially start over again is the trouble you have with developing patience and discernment. Now, you might say, "Well, isn't it 'this' strife?" or "Isn't it 'that' strife?" But ultimately, you can trace the strife you are dealing with to the fact that patience and discernment are not being applied in the best way for all beings. I'm using "best" so that those of you who don't exactly understand "benevolent" know what I'm talking about. Benevolent is the best way that includes kindness, gentleness, and patience with all life.

You are all on this planet as human beings really like astronauts in space. You are trying to resolve things in a situation that does not obviously present resolution. Yet if you want to see how things are resolved in a way that is fairly balanced, even in your time, you need only look to nonhuman populations. There you will always find adaptation. It is really important in this Earth school now to study adaptation by the animal world and the plant world so you can create a workable, benevolent society. You need to study how plants and animals live and then apply what you learn universally to the planet for human populations. You can't just talk about it anymore — you must act.

You Must Change and Adapt Right Now

This is really going to take a unification of peoples. There's a lot of understandable fear of a global government, because people are afraid they're going to have to give up being who they are and things that are near and dear to them. To a degree, you will have to give up some things that are near and dear to you, but you have to decide whether everyone can survive benevolently if you keep those things. Some of the things you may have to give up are attitudes, opinions, and judgments that harm other peoples.

See, it is not complicated, but its application — and that's the key here to survival — might cause *temporary* discomfort. But it doesn't have to be the end of Earth. It doesn't have to be the end of the world. In short, it doesn't have to be so awful. Think about it on an individual basis: Sometimes, you might have some disease or discomfort that develops for "this" or "that" reason. Then you have to adapt. You are literally forced to adapt, just like children are forced to adapt to survive in the culture they find themselves. You have to adapt. As you get older and you're no longer young and vital, you have to start doing things that take your slightly more frail — at the very best, and often more frail in general — physical condition into account. In short, you have to pay attention to your body and its dictates, otherwise known as your needs.

So it's not as if adaptation is something foreign to you. You are here to discover how change can effect betterment. That's really it in a nutshell. That's why you're here as the human race. That's why you find yourself on a planet that is constantly changing, with other species of beings that are constantly changing and adapting, because if you're going to learn how to change and adapt so things get better, you're going to have to be surrounded by teachers.

It's not complicated, but it's not always easy to give up things that you love. Even if you've been raised in a society that is generally self-destructive and at the very least destructive toward others, you're going to have to give up those things. You're going to have to give up what's destructive to others; you're going to have to give up what's self-destructive. In other words, you're going to have to change now. And it's not going to be foreign; it's just going to be different.

You won't like some of the things you have to give up, but other things can be done. You might not like that you have to talk to the plants and encourage them to grow. These things have been done on other planets; they are being done now. How do you think people survive with planets that have large populations in other parts of space? They talk and sing to the plants and welcome them to grow, okay? They pray to their deity, whatever that is, but they interact with other life forms that provide food. Perhaps it is a fruit tree and it is old. Then you encourage that tree to give forth the means to grow a new generation of trees. You have that now. If everybody were suddenly to migrate from the planet, the trees would continue on, and they would increase their natural cycle of reproduction. And pretty soon, you'd have a planet covered with trees, including fruit trees. Of course, you're not going to migrate like that instantaneously — though you do migrate a bit around the planet, and you'll continue to do that.

What I'm saying is that you must change and adapt right now, and you're going to have to give up being destructive to others as well as being self-destructive. Now, it's all right to eat the fruit from the trees and the grains from the ground. And for a time, you'll have to continue to eat some beings, meaning the fishes and so on. But you're going to have to change. You can't just overfish the seas. Mother Earth has spoken — recently loudly — with the intention of you fishing much less than you have been. This is not because she doesn't love fishermen as people; it's that you cannot eliminate species who live in the wild just because you don't know them and you don't understand how they keep you in balance.

The world's populations balance each other out simply by their existence. Imagine that this is a chorus — you know, people singing. If some people sing only certain levels and tones, the song doesn't sound quite right. It's the same thing in an orchestra: Not everybody in the orchestra plays the melody. Some of them play different parts of the tune. If you eliminated whole pieces of that, the tune doesn't sound the same, and you notice the absence. Just because you don't understand what some other form of life is doing to balance your life and make your life better doesn't mean they're not doing it, and overfishing is a perfect example of that. You will have to quit doing that and allow the seas and oceans to repopulate. Even though it's not your favorite thing, even though there are problems, you will have to. If you're going to eat fish — and you're going to need to do that a lot more as a substitute for eating other animals — they're going to have to be entirely from fish farms. I know I've spoken about this before, but I'm underscoring it now.

Everything Exists in Balance

Understand that the challenges that people have to face are overwhelming right now, and the reason they're overwhelming is not only because you can find out about it through global communication — meaning that there is a terrible disaster in a country named Japan, and there are atomic reactors that are spewing out harmful bits and pieces that are going to cause a great deal more harm as time goes on. It's not just that; that's a lot. It's that patience and discernment come into play here, all right?

It's not that there are some people from foreign governments trying to overthrow "this" government or "that" government in whatever part of the world — even though it may seem that way and, to a very small degree, might be that way. People the world over know that they must live in a better way, and very often one finds students striving for this because they are, after all, in school learning how things could be "if only." So I'm not saying stop them from going to school. I'm saying listen to "if only," because "if only" might be your best choice for survival.

Learn how to live together and embrace each other, meaning love each other. You don't necessarily have to love everything about your friends. Think about it. You have friends now, most of you. And even though you might like quite a bit about what your friends say and do, there is always something, isn't there — sometimes quite a bit — that your friends say and do that you don't like one bit, but because they're your friends, you tolerate it. It's the same for them with you. So that's a microcosm; it's like that all over the world. You're going to need to grow, change, and adapt into the situation that exists, so don't get any "bright ideas," like some people have in the past, of how you can eliminate "this" or "that" group of troublesome folks and solve all of your problems. In fact, that's not the solution.

Remember that everything exists in balance. If there are some people who are shy and retiring, there are also some people who are more outgoing. You've seen that in groups of people, and you might not understand why the outgoing people have to be *that* outgoing and boisterous, as you might say. And the outgoing people who are happy and like to express themselves may not understand why some people have to be so shy and quiet and rigid. You see, that's what they see, even though you might not be rigid at all, but to them, you are. You must learn how to understand that different beings acting different ways in different places are all part of the universal chorus. You must understand that even though the world seems to be in crisis about "this" or "that" situation, ultimately it can all be resolved with patience and discernment.

Discernment applies very well to a lot of technological problems. Yes, atomic energy works just fine, but it is delicate, isn't it? A lot of the systems are profoundly delicate, and they don't react well when Mother Earth expresses herself in ways that she suddenly has to do. She's not doing it because she doesn't like you; she's doing it in the same way you would if you were in a position that was very uncomfortable and you had the opportunity to move. She's doing it because she has to.

So you have to develop and use forms of that which creates energy to run your systems and technology and hopefully improve the lives of people. You have to run them in ways that even if Mother Earth expresses herself that way, you can all pick yourselves up afterward and say, "Wow, that was rough," and "How can we help each other and go on with life?" and not spend the next fifty years trying to deal with the impact of technology that wasn't quite ready because it was too delicate to withstand being broken open and spilling out onto the land and the people. Atomic energy works, but it's not yet ready to be applied on Earth because of its delicacy. So there's that.

Everyone Needs the Basics, but Treat Earth with Discernment

Don't get mad at people in "this" or "that" situation who simply want to express and be themselves in "this" or "that" part of the world. And don't get mad at people who don't have what they perceive other people have. Everybody needs to have the basics at the very least. You cannot believe that there will always be hungry people and that there will always be poor people, that there will always be people suffering. While I know there are some people who believe this, you cannot believe this anymore; you're going to have to give up this belief. If you continue to believe that, it's very easy to rationalize — in time if not immediately — that it is all right as long as you're not one of those people.

Everyone needs the basics: comfort, food, water, shelter. And then when everybody has that — and I mean everybody, including nonhumans — then you're going to be able to move forward. But of course, like it is with the orchestra, different instruments get used at different times. So move forward in the best way you can, doing the best you can in these times and in the times to come. I can assure you that in the times to come, you will need to have neighborhoods that help each other. You will need to have people, even if you don't know each other, from other neighborhoods who automatically help each other, because Earth must make changes — must use her wind and water, must move her body — to survive.

You can't dig around in her — you can't bring up stuff from inside her that she uses because she's a living being — indefinitely. In time, it's going to cause problems for her, and she's going to have to move more. It's just like if somebody were poking you, as sometimes happens when people play around or when they get agitated. At some point, you poke back and say, "Hey! I'm alive here!" And the other person says, "Oh, I'm sorry. I didn't realize that." It's like that. You've been poking Mother Earth for a while, and she's just saying, "Hey! I'm alive here, and I'm going to have to take care of myself. I can't just let you do what you want to do." So Mother Earth is taking care of herself now, and you will have to look after each other more and not just count on Mother Earth to be quiet and docile and gentle with you. She's going to have to be a bit more boisterous, you might say, right now. So you will have to look after each other.

Thus people will have to move around. At the very least, people who live close to bodies of water will have to move back. This is obvious. So that means room will have to be made for them to move back, okay? There are a lot of other situations, but I'm touching on some things you all know and understand so that you will realize how very much adaptation you need to make. It will be harder for those who grew up in a different system, meaning the systems you have now, but as new generations come along and adapt to the new systems you must have in which people can get along with each other and everybody else and help each other, then it will be, in time, as if it were always that way. As it has been in the past at times, so it can be now.

And you can't wait. You have to get along with each other, grow together, and thrive together. Enjoy each other and tolerate each other. If you don't always like what this person or that person is doing, you'll have to do that now. Do that while exercising patience and discernment.

All Humans Adapt, Even When Oppressed

Is the ability to adapt innate equally in all humans?

It is from birth, but when a human being is exposed to a culture that restricts you more and more from your natural abilities and even says simply, "You can't walk like that; you have to walk like this," (putting a dramatic edge on it) or demands, "You can't talk to 'that' person; you can only talk to 'this' person" — in short, essentially restricting your natural way of being — then just like with everything else, even if you restrict one thing, other things will change in concordance with that. As parents the world over know, when you try to control your children, they become at times uncontrollable.

The answer is not complicated. Keep in mind that as I've said, everything is in balance, whether you know it or not, so if something is restricted and the person is recoiling from that, whatever it is (it might be something completely reasonable), then they will … by coming into balance, other aspects of their behavior will be affected, or they might be affected in their health. Quite obviously, parents have to exercise certain things with their children: "Don't stick your finger in the fire, honey, or you might get burned," things like that.

But there are other things, other cultures — and generally speaking, all cultures — that restrict their people in ways that have simply become tradition. And tradition, while it might be the source of a great deal of humor, is also really engrained in a lot of you these days. Even though you have the awareness of traditions and you can compare your tradition with somebody else's tradition now, thanks to improved communications globally, you have to understand that what your tradition is can stifle adaptation.

Even when adaptation is stifled, you still adapt. For example, if you are stopped from being free to express something that is not going to lead to something terrible even though it might run against tradition, you might become bitter. And you might be able to control that bitterness, but at some point, that anger is going to burst through, and it might very well burst through for an individual in a completely inappropriate way — as parents the world over know and as societies know. And somebody who's embittered very often suddenly explodes in a situation that doesn't seem to make any sense.

You know, you have to take a good look at what's the best way to raise children and to understand that growth, change, adaptation, patience, and discernment are just a few of the many qualities it takes to become a benevolent citizen. So if adaptation is stifled, balance will still occur; it just won't be a balance you can live with.

Since most parents parent children in the way they were parented, what is the mechanism that is going to allow the change in the new children? How are they going to escape the conditioning?

Unfortunately, what you've always done in the past is that systems have broken down either because of the actions of human beings, as in battles and wars, or because Mother Earth is doing something she either has to do for herself — meaning wind, rain, lightning, earthquakes, and so on. That's how she moves herself about; that's how she helps herself. In short, things sometimes change from external reasons, and things sometimes change because of circumstances from other people. So it's either Mother Earth doing something — Earth conditions, Earth changes — or it is other people doing something.

Things are changing even now because people are discovering more about themselves and each other through improving world communications. But ultimately you are, as a species of beings, gregarious. You are, in your nature, friendly. Anyone can tell you that: Get a bunch of little kids together — babies, toddlers, okay? — and they will be, for the most part, very friendly to each other. They may be impatient — because you are born with a little bit of that, since in other existences every place else, you have what you need when you need it at all times — and feisty and so on, but they manage to work things out, and use a little gentle adult supervision in showing how things are done in order to share and share alike, then it makes it easier.

There Are Repercussions to Oppression and Imbalance

It's not going to be easy for you to change and adapt using patience and discernment. It might be easy in concept, but it won't be easy in application to change. But change you must, so one thing that would be helpful for parents to teach children and to learn themselves is that "change is going to happen, and it doesn't matter whether we resist that change, because it's going to happen. So let's make change be something that we all help each other with, not something we have to do because of trauma." Understand that sometimes there will be traumas, because you live on a living planet, and you cannot, intentionally or otherwise, try to stop Mother Earth from living. If by any chance she did stop living, you would stop too. You have chosen to be born of Creator with a soul, and you have chosen to be born out of the matter of a living planet. If the planet stopped living, the matter in you would stop living also.

I had heard that the new children being born were more resistant to being conditioned, that they wouldn't accept it as readily as earlier generations. Is that true?

It might be true, but there's a level at which resistance breaks down if authority is all-powerful. And that will happen in some cases; after a point, anybody will tend to break down and say, "Okay, okay," because there's a limit to how much absolute authority you can tolerate. So the children might be like that, but what comes with that also at times is an adaptation cycle you're not going to like, and that's that sometimes when people are born like that, they are forced or demanded to become like everybody else: "Why aren't you like other people?"

Then there's a tendency to disconnect from society and become less feeling. If you're not allowed your feelings, then there's a tendency to not only be impatient with your own feelings but to separate your feelings. Oh, they're there all right, but you don't respond to them, and you don't respond to the feelings of others. As a result, society might unintentionally create an entire generation of unfeeling people, and before you know it, you have a generation that can easily harm themselves and others and not really think about it.

It's like this: There's a complication with the new generation coming along that you referred to, and that's that in the course of making societies the world over safer for all human beings, there's a tendency to eliminate as much as possible anything that is predatory on human beings. So you eliminate dangerous animals, and to the best of your ability, you eliminate dangerous conditions for human beings — better homes, stronger structures, and better medical therapies — in short, creating as much safety as possible.

But as always, since you are living in a whole system, once you make a change like that, you very often do not take into account the lives of others: plants, animals, and so on. And very often there are repercussions. If you eliminate all predators — you cannot, by the way, because Mother Earth has lots of organisms — and do not allow, say, lions to have their own space where they can be themselves without human beings living among them, then imbalance is created. And you will do this because you don't understand how their energy contributes to your well-being in some way. As long as you're not trying to live among the lions, it's completely safe for them to exist, as an example. So I'm trying to condense all this, which amounts to an encyclopedic amount of information, down to the basics here.

Then you ultimately have conditions that prevail that can create a predatory class of people. You've noticed now — and not among children — that there are adult human beings expressing behaviors, killing other human beings, because they have become predators. It's as if they're filling in for other predators that were nonhuman. I know it seems complicated. What can you do? You have to begin with the children and raise them in ways that are completely benevolent the world over and try to protect them so that they can create a better Earth.

That's really what's going on. You're going to have to learn how to do things differently. You're going to have to find societies — there are a few; they might be small, but they do exist — that raise their children in a more benevolent way so that children, the kids, come out being really good citizens. They do exist. I'm not going to tell you who they are and where they are because it's actually known, okay? [Chuckles.] You can find them; they exist. It might even be a family in your neighborhood whose children are just fine and they don't harm themselves or others. Look for these things. Ask the parents, "How do you do this?" If they happen to have a religion that's not yours, then adapt it to your religion. If your religion doesn't adapt to it, then create a branch of your religion that does. In short, you know how to adapt and change, because you must. It is forced on you as the human race. So adapt and change.

ET Contact Was Avoided Out of Fear of Change

In 1945 to 1946, did we not interact with ETs because the planet as a whole was suffering after the war? Did we have a closed belief system? Or were we kept from it by various governmental figures?

Various governmental figures felt — and I'm not entirely disputing their decision — that people would not be able to "handle it," as they would say. They wouldn't be able to maintain who they were in that moment if they knew that some vastly more advanced civilization existed. In short, the governments were made up of human people, and the people who were encountering those beings from other planets or reading about other people's opinions from those who did encounter them were intimidated by it, and yes, to put it clearly, they were frightened. And they felt that if *they* were frightened — and there was just a very small group of people involved in the encounter with the ETs — if they were human beings and they were frightened almost to the point of being terrified of having such vastly superior-knowledged ET beings approaching them, then they were afraid that the world population would panic and essentially experience a much greater version of their own fear.

I'm not going to say that they had to control the situation because they were bad. It's nothing like that. They assumed that everybody else was like them. And to a degree, that may have been so, but it would have been possible to consult the philosophers of the time — just people saying, "People can do 'this' or people can do 'that'" — and say, "We could break it gently to them over time." And really, that's what the ETs who were making contact recommended. They said, "Well, let us just interact slowly over time. We know how to do this in a way that is completely safe and benevolent for all people."

They knew that because they had been contacting some people on Earth for a long time, even thousands of years, and they knew that they could get along just fine. Even though some of these ETs who were contacting representatives of "this" and "that" government around the world did not look human, they made it clear that the ones who would interact with human beings initially would look exactly like those human beings — different skin colors, different appearances, but they look exactly like you because, after all, there are different skin colors and different races of people all over the universe. [**Publisher's note:** Many of the ETs we have talked to through Robert Shapiro (the sessions are published in previous issues of the *Sedona Journal* and in books such as *ET Visitors 1, ET Visitors 2, Zetas, Hybrids, and Human Contacts*, and *ETs on Earth*) have said that they have had many discussions in their councils about that first contact with Earth humans—that if the Pleiadians on board the ship who landed had been the ones meeting with the humans instead of the Zetas and others, the outcome of that meeting might have been different, because the Pleiadians look just like Earth humans.]

That's how it would take place. They didn't say, "Okay, we're all going to come along to your planet looking whichever way we do, showing up looking overwhelming and scaring your people." It wasn't like that. But even taking that into account, the Earth people at the meeting then took the extra step to say, "No, can't you just wait?" And thus, you had situations where some peoples from other planets, having what you would consider to be extremely minor problems but what they considered to be serious problems, said, "Well, then we do need to interact with your peoples at times and in places just to see whether we can cure situations for ourselves." And your governments grudgingly said okay, but they still were trying to devise ways to protect your planet.

Do you know what they were really trying to protect your planet from? In the larger picture, they were trying to protect your planet from growing and changing — ultimately, from changing. It's very easy, when you are raised [to think] change is terrifying and undesirable (even if it threatens tradition), to grow up like that and become an adult human being so that when somebody comes along who says, "We can help you. We can help you cure all your diseases. We can help you with food and shelter so that you will always have enough and nobody will suffer. But we also need to interact with you at times," it would be very easy to be terrified because it represented change — change you weren't used to, change that was different and represented the unknown.

You have had times when you've been up against the unknown — everyone has had that experience — and sometimes it didn't go well, but other times, it was just wonderful. So quite understandably, not having all their own capabilities for them freely to use because they'd been raised in "this" or "that" tradition, as a result — as you might say, "this" or "that" culture or "this" or "that" nationality — as a result, they were afraid of change. So yes, it was intended for you to have that interaction in or around 1945.

Welcome ETs on an Individual Basis

It's still intended; it's kind of like a rubber band that's been stretching ever since. So when you allow the ETs, they're going to essentially be at that point. You're not all going to have to go back and relive the year 1946 and beyond, but essentially what they would have done in 1945, '46, and '47 is going to be what they will do. They're not going to rush you, but they will be able to help you to eliminate things that are causing harm from the technological basis, to learn how to put Earth to rights — meaning to help your planet to live and thrive so she can host your forms of life, all forms, and to help you not only have all that you need to thrive as human populations but also to learn how to live well with each other. And they're still available to do that. It's still possible.

How do we facilitate this process of interacting with ETs when most Earth governments are so against it?

You might have to welcome them on an individual basis. There's been a lot of instruction on the blog and on the videos of how to welcome them, and it's very simple. You know how to welcome somebody. When someone you haven't met before comes over to your house (maybe somebody else brought that person), you know how to welcome him or her. It's not something foreign to you. So you might simply look at the sky and say, "I welcome people from other planets who come here to help us in benevolent ways." But you can't just say it.

You have to feel it?

You have to feel the welcome. So work on the feeling of welcome — and you've been welcomed before, most of you, and you've welcomed others before, most of you. So get into that feeling through remembering, if you can, and then say that and practice it. Don't just say it once; practice it by welcoming other human beings. Get used to practicing it. I grant that you cannot welcome all human beings into your life at all times, but try to learn how to welcome other human beings into your life, even if it's just something simple, all right?

Learn how to welcome each other. Learn how to support each other, and don't always expect something in return. You may not get it directly from that person in return. It might come to you out of the blue, so to speak, as a favor from somebody else — because remember, all systems (and there are all systems) must be in balance. If the balance is based on an imbalance, then you will have imbalanced balance. So try to create as much benevolent balance as possible. Begin by learning how to welcome each other. Then, as you have asked, just look into the sky and welcome people from other planets to come, be themselves, and share their cultures, and ask them to help people the world over.

We are, at this time, much closer to them in consciousness and technology than we were sixty-five years ago, so it should be easier, right?

No, you're not any closer, because you are who you were then. The people you were then as human beings are exactly the same. Your technology has changed, but a lot of it is destructive or self-destructive or harmful to the planet, which is ultimately harmful to you. So no, you're exactly the same people, so it won't be any easier from that point of your question. On the other hand, you are also curious. Children are born curious, and children are also friendly when they're not told not to be and when they're not restricted in other ways. It is in the nature of young children to be friendly. I grant that when they learn and adapt to "this" family and "that" tradition and "this" culture and "that" culture, they might become less friendly and less welcoming, but they're born friendly. So understand that you are as a people exactly the same as you were then.

This Is Something You Need to Do Yourselves

I'm confused. I thought we had expanded in consciousness, awakened, or begun to awaken.

You have begun, okay. And some of you are past the point of beginning, but that is a small population compared to the vast population of

Earth. No, I'm not going to give you numbers, because the entire human race … you could come from another planet, and your job is to report on the situation of the human race. "How are they coming along?" someone says to you. "Go down to the planet and find out what they're like now." If you happened to meet somebody who is awakened, as you say, then you might go back and report, "Well they're coming along. I think we can interact with them just fine now." Or if you happen to meet someone who's angry, upset, and violent — self-destructive — you would go back and say, "Oh, no chance. We'd better wait another thousand years."

So it's not about those who are awakened; it's about those who aren't awakened. Yes, you are waking up as all people, but not everybody is sufficiently that way to automatically welcome that which is completely different — meaning, for instance, an ET who doesn't look like a human being. That would still scare a lot of people. So you're not any different when taken as an entire group of beings, though there are ones among you who would welcome ETs who do look entirely different. See, even though there are more people who are awakened, you cannot say, "Well, everybody's awakened now." You know for a fact they're not.

So how do you see it, then? When will we interact?

It's not my job to say that. It's my job to encourage you to grow and change and to let you know that the ETs are not in existence to save you. It's not about being saved externally; it's entirely about doing it yourself. Do you know why? Because you came here to learn about change and adaptation, and if ETs came to save you, after a couple of weeks of being saved and everything's fine and you feel good, you're going to say, "But I came here to grow and change." [Laughs.]

Really, think about that. This is really something that is an element of human nature. Yes, you want to be rescued, and of course you want to feel better and to be able to survive and thrive. But even after surviving and thriving — just as you do after your life, and you're surviving and thriving as mind and spirit — how many of you really get restless and want to do something more exciting, more adventurous? Really, all of you in the Explorer Race felt exactly that. You were living before you came here in absolutely ideal conditions — meaning before you were born on Earth — conditions every one of you would love to live under right now. But after a few weeks or a few months or a few years (at the very most), you and your personalities would say, "What do we do now?"

Now, it looks like that. It's up to you how to believe. And when the ETs come, they're going to know that they're not allowed to change you. They can rescue a bit, just like if you're having an accident: The emergency people come, and they help you. Maybe you were doing something that you probably could have done better; you were up on a rickety ladder to fix something, and you fell off the ladder and you got hurt. The emergency people came and helped you, and eventually you got better. How many of you might just use that rickety ladder one more time? It's up to you. They'll help you, but they won't save you.

You Came Here to Change

So are we like the little kids who push away somebody trying to feed them? I mean, are we subconsciously pushing them away or something?

You're not subconsciously pushing them away. Really, you came here with an absolute motivation to explore change and adaptation. And it's at the core of your being, because what's at the core of your being? Your soul. Your soul is your personality, your spirit. And a spirit, a soul, has certain things it wants to do, but at the core of that is to explore. You are the Explorer Race. You want to be exposed to change so you can explore and grow — otherwise known as adapt. So there is a degree to which you will accept help, but after a while, you want to do it yourself. Okay?

So even though you might come as a soul with things that you want to explore, there is also going to come a point when it's not good enough to be fed. You want to have a spoon *you* can use. And even though you're not very good at it and food tends to fly all over the place and you look a mess when you're done, you will feed yourself if it's the last thing you ever do! [Chuckles.] When you see children trying to feed themselves, it's really kind of a spectacular mess. Usually they do it with their hands, and that's not surprising. Eventually they learn how to do it with a spoon. So you will do it yourselves, but much more help is available, and that's what was attempted in '45, '46, and '47. They'll help you, but they'll know when to back off and let you help yourselves. Anything else?

No, I think you've covered it magnificently.

Well, thank you very much. For you to live, first do this (this homework's been given numerous times by numerous people, and I'll add my voice to that chorus): Next time you glance in a mirror, don't look to see what's wrong; look to see what's right. Good night.

Good night. Thank you for responding to my need to know what's going on.

CHAPTER TEN

True Change
Will Require Patience

Zoosh

April 18, 2011

Greetings. Zoosh.

Isis gave a magnificent overview of the present state of the challenges that humans face on Earth on Friday, but she said one thing that I would like more information about — that there has been no change in human consciousness since 1945 except that some individual humans have awakened. I would like another perspective on that.

Let me explain what was meant by that. From the way the question was phrased and the way the question was answered, it was meant that the thinking process, the way one thinks, has not changed, whereas in the thinking process in the Earth human, say, from a few thousand years ago, there has been a big change. What has changed underneath the thinking is the coming to the surface of the spirit.

So the answer that was given related more to thought. "Consciousness," after all, if you look up the term in the dictionary, does not really mean anything beyond thought or sentience. So if you say "depth," if you just add that one word — the depth of consciousness or awareness or what have you, spirit — then there's been a significant change. And you could get that response out of Isis as well.

But in terms of the thinking *process*, there hasn't been that much change in the last, say, eighty years. What's going on, however, is that the human thinking process is like a river with tributaries. The tributaries are flowing strongly into the river, but the river — as happens with

101

physical rivers — is simply absorbing what's coming in and is influenced by it but is not cognizant, meaning consciously aware, of what it means. So putting that in more practical terminology, it is not unusual to find people who are having experiences of spirit, but in their mental bodies, in their minds, they don't know what it means, and they're searching (as you well know) hither and yon to find out what it means.

The General Public Does Not Always Get All the Details

Of course, one of the first places the general public goes for answers to spiritual questions is religion. That's why there's been such zeal and zest for religion with the unfortunate side effect that when one is desperate for awareness and an explanation of what this all means, it's very easy to be attracted to something that represents a view of God and creation as being "the Word." And people understand that the Word in religion is to be taken literally. People who are more in the business world or in, say, the Western consciousness recognize that that goes hand in hand with the flow of life, but other people who live in more incubated conditions are more inclined — and this includes many people in the Western world — to embrace the fundamental acceptance of the Word as being rigid.

Looking for answers and finding the rigidity of the Word is very appealing to people in that situation. It does create a source of explanation for these unknown physical and instinctual experiences, experiences that are actually well-known and well understood in the spirit world — meaning your world beyond the physical form — but do not fit very comfortably into a world that embraces only words either written by well-intended human beings years ago or interpreted today based on what was written by well-intended human beings years ago.

As you know, the Christian version of the Bible, the New Testament, is highly edited. There is a great deal of material that was originally included that has not been published and accepted today as it was written originally. It would be very useful if all that material were included, but for the most part, it has not received wide distribution. Still, scholars and people of the priesthood have often read this material and understand that it is their job (from their point of view, understandably) to interact between an understanding of that material and creation and the general public so that the general public does not have to take all that in and can still live their lives.

This is actually intended to be a kindness, but in these times when spirit and an expansion of soul is taking place, [chuckles] what is occurring is that the intermediary priest class is highly stimulated and can understand things in a broader context, but still, if they're utilizing only the version of the accepted text for the general public, the general public is not able to take that in. So to put this a little simpler, it is difficult for the general public, who are all waking up, to be aware of, on a conscious, mental level, what it all means and thus be able to embrace it and recognize that it is like waking up from a long and deep sleep.

People in general have accepted that other beings on other planets are real, but not people in many — not all, but many — fundamentalist religions. And that's a big chunk of the general public, at least in the Western world at the moment. It's just the attitude toward it that is a problem at the moment. Attitudes are formed either through life experience or by other people's opinions. But that may not always mean that's how you demonstrate yourself. No, there's a considerable amount of fear of the new — not with everyone, but if you examine people's general attitudes, you'll usually find only select groups are really open to anything new.

Humans Naturally Welcome the New, but Organizations Fear Change

You understand that some things that are new are not good for you, and you have to accept that as a reality. After all, there are new illicit drugs that come out, and some people will say, "Oh, it's new; it's wonderful! It's not habit-forming. It doesn't cost much," and so on — the usual sales pitch. And you have one jolt of that, and you're hooked. It ruins your life, you understand, because the sales pitch is not about what it really is. So just because it's new doesn't mean it's necessarily wonderful.

It is in the nature of the human being to welcome the new, however. And you can see that with babies as they interact with each other. There is a welcoming of the new, and many of the babies born today are also more likely to carry their full range of spirit and soul through a few years — three to four years old — unless they've been very carefully nurtured to not believe it or even unintentionally nurtured in the most loving way, as often happens, to not believe it. And thus one is discouraged from believing at the very depth of one's own reality.

So religion right now is in a phase, especially among the hierarchies of religion, of being aware that things are changing. You know, the way some people might preach doesn't always mean that's what they believe individually, and many ministers, priests, and individuals of such classes of beings are very disturbed by their awareness and their general knowledge as well as their experience of the difference in spirit and soul now. But as is typical in any large organization, you might say — putting it in a business model for a moment — major change is slow to come about, and that's what's really going on in many organized religions now. Major change is slow to come about, but there is definitely a consensus — not one that anybody's voted on, but a general consensus — that a new model of reality must be presented to parishioners, because it's real, and the old model is not sufficient.

Since I'm using Christianity for the moment, it would be easy, actually, to pull up certain books of the old writings that really were taken out to form the more easily understood version of the New Testament as well as to simply make it shorter so it's not an overwhelming read. It wouldn't be that difficult to put those back in or to create something that says, "Okay, this is also real and needs to be considered." But it's still a challenge to do that.

I'm bringing up religion because I feel it is an important element, and we cannot overlook it. After all, a great many people in the general public would agree that society would have been more chaotic without religion. A great many people in society are able to live better because of religion, so we must accept that. Really, what you are teaching, Melody, with the publications, the journal and the books and so on is really another aspect of spirituality. As you know, spirituality is not only what [this is] but also comes up under the heading of religion, so we have to accept that. Not all religions try to convince people that what they are saying is true and to help them to understand it from their points of view, but this is a general thing, because their worldview of religion, while being different from your worldview, still relates back, if you take it back far enough, to the same source — creation.

Be Inclusive but Not Persuasive

It is to everybody's advantage now to continue being inclusive but not persuasive. There's a difference between including people and persuading people. So be inclusive, meaning make your material — or, in this case, your religion (bring everybody under the same umbrella here for the moment) available, but don't be attached to whether people accept it. If you are attached, you see, you become more and more persuasive. And I cannot tell you how many wars or even battles have taken place because of people trying to persuade.

I think there's a general understanding that this happens in political beliefs, and I think there is a general understanding that this happens in religious beliefs. That's why in some societies it's not polite to talk about religion. It's fine to have it, but you don't necessarily argue about it because it can create a breakdown in friendships. So I'm not saying "do this; do that." I'm saying be inclusive, but try to let go of being persuasive, regardless of your belief in whatever spirituality comforts you.

How is religion going to fall under the corporate model of the First Alignment — where we are going to have one transportation company, one communication company, one manufacturing company? What's going to happen to religion?

It's not a problem. Religion is at some point going to realize, and the priest and priestess class, as I'm calling them (even though in different religions one finds other names, of course), is simply going to recognize that they are all speaking about the same thing. If you look at religions, you generally find that there is more about them that is similar at the root of what they are talking about and in what they believe than is different.

So it will be recognized that Creator and creation are real (things like that) and that God is real, though there might be different words for God — "Creator," for example. And that will come about. It will be a synthesis of what everybody believes, but this will take time, as you might expect, since one's individual religion is often dear to one's heart. It's not going to go away overnight, and it doesn't have to go away. All it really needs to do is to let go of being persuasive. If it lets go of being persuasive, that's a big step in the direction of being openhearted and inclusive without being attached in any way to changing what people think.

Religion has to be thanked for bringing about a great deal more peace and stability in people's lives and very often helping people to get along. It's just that once it becomes persuasive, then there are arguments, and it can get worse from that point. It's the persuasive aspect that one has to guard against — even if one is a New Ager. So don't get too persuasive. Just say, "Here's what we believe. We hope you like it. If you don't, it's perfectly all right. Welcome anyway."

When you talk about being persuasive, you mean people trying to convert people, but it's the identity of the different religions as the only way that is the problem. So how do you see that coming into some kind of unity? Everyone thinks that their religion is the only way to whatever is the goal of the religion, and then they fight other people who believe that their own religion is the only way.

Religion doesn't have exclusivity on this. There are people who think that if you are "this" nationality or "that" nationality, you are somehow right, and if you are "this" race or "that" race, you are somehow right, and so on. Religion does not have exclusivity on that one. So it all evolves toward something more benevolent as people realize how very much alike they are, regardless of religion. And this is a wave that cannot be stopped. Generally speaking, young people the world over — younger people, and by that I'm talking about, say, teenagers and so on — are pretty much aware of that. So that's working. They don't all feel that way, but a considerable number of them do. So my one word answer to you is *patience.*

That's one of the hardest lessons there is.

Well, that's why it's for everyone. It's hard because it's not in your nature. Your nature in spirit form is that if anything is needed, it is there, either instantaneously or it is brought by someone who is a friend or becomes one. But in this slower world where one goes to school and learns how things come about — including attitudes, happenstances, and everything around that and beyond — patience is a challenge. Yet if you are going to create something that is wonderful, as parents the world over know, it does require patience.

CHAPTER ELEVEN

You Are Losing the Mask You Created To Survive

Isis

May 18, 2011

Hello, this is Isis. There is an issue coming up now. The reason certain religions — usually branches of other religions — are very popular now is that people need to be reassured. Many people are so overwhelmed by life that the idea of something very structured and organized is appealing. This is not about any one religion but about religions around the world and, I might add, some philosophies that go beyond religion. I don't mean the philosophies are better, but they are in a different category.

When people are overwhelmed by their lives, when they are in transition, whether they know it or not, they often find it very appealing to have some place where they can put their lives, so to speak. They put their lives into a dish with the lives of other people — not literally, you understand, but figuratively — in order to achieve a certain level of comfort and reassurance based on a community belief.

The Mask Isn't There Anymore

In recent years, the whole idea of community became very popular, and it really preceded this time you find yourselves in now. This is the time when your true selves come to the surface, and this is actually, on a practical level, very challenging for many people. You've spent almost your whole lives (most of you, though perhaps not the very, very young) trying to conform to your perception of what others wanted from you. This happens often in families and later on with friends, peers, and so on.

As a result, your true natural personality, the one you were born with — I am not talking about spirit or soul beyond Earth; I am talking about what you were born with — becomes completely submerged. The skills and even the skill sets that you were born with, while they remain with you throughout your life, do not always come to the surface as being something you offer if they do not fit in with the mask that you have donned. This is so not only because of your perception but also because of what people in general seem to feel safe with you being.

The reason the transition to being your true natural selves — which is literally what is happening and why so many people are nervous — is more difficult now is that it is almost like an unmasking. If you have ever had the experience or seen another having the experience of being revealed in public, so to speak, and that person just hit it on the button for you or for another, it could be shocking. By being revealed in public, I mean in print or the press or in a large group or, worse yet, among friends. Someone might say, "Well, I know this person, and this is what he or she is really like." Sometimes it makes you chuckle when it happens to somebody else and you believe that the person really is like that or when you are perceptive and *know* they are like that. Other times, due to the circumstances, it is horrifying, frightening, shocking.

What's making the press quite often these days are various well-known individuals, sometimes even celebrities, whose exploits — not their true personalities but their exploits — have been well hidden, sometimes even professionally so. They've been so well hidden that if you've seen them or interviews of them, they may have even been confronted with things they might have done as an exploit and they very expertly managed to disguise it.

I'm not saying this is good, bad, or anything; it is not my job to criticize. What I am saying is that what's occurring now is an exacerbation of the difficulty you are having in transforming to the true, natural selves you were born as, because here are these famous people being exposed, so to speak, being embarrassed, or being found out in other cases.

Whoever these famous people are in the world, in your country, or even in your community, for that matter (not necessarily world-famous), all of the judgments being hurled at them have made it even more difficult. In some cases, perhaps its deservedly so, but in other cases, it's just galling, painful.

Babies have personalities. There is a school of thought that personality develops, but you are born with personality. Granted, it develops and expands over time in its purest state, where you were born and welcomed into the world. But I'm here to tell you that the being you were born as — the personality you had, your true personality — is present, so the challenge exists in that what you have been trying to cover all these years at various times with a mask, well, the mask is not available now.

This is very nerve-racking to a lot of people. They don't know how to act. It is particularly difficult in families or in couple situations, where the other person expects you to be who you've been, and suddenly you're not that person anymore. You can't grab that mask; it's not there anymore. This is going to make for a lot of nervousness, and sometimes there will be arguments.

Move through Personality Changes as a Couple

Here is some homework. Couples, even if you've become a couple only recently — "recently" meaning in the past week or two — get used to touching each other. Even if you're not too romantic anymore, get used to touching each other on the shoulder, on the arm, however you touch each other — not sexually in this case, but intimately. Say, "I need to talk about these feelings I'm having. I need to talk about what I feel I need to be," anything like that.

If you think your partner might be frustrated or upset, or that this might push his or her buttons, then say, "Can we talk about all the changes that are going on?" Recognize that you might be talking all around the subject for quite a while, but eventually you will be able to touch on it. Know that your partner, or whoever it might be, might get very frightened when you start bringing up things that you need to be, how you need to be, and how true and natural that is for you. You'll just have to reassure your partner. "That's what I'm saying. It's not that I'm going to leave you; don't worry about that. But I need to do this now. I need to add 'this' or 'that' to my life," you might say, when in fact, it is something that is you, so it will not be easy. In some cases when you both want to do something similar, it will be wonderful, but most of the time, each of you will want to do something that seems to be out of personality. And this might, in fact, be directly your personality.

Move into Your Personality in Bits and Pieces

Try to find things to do that are constructive. Know that there will be a desire, especially in younger people — not the very young, but in younger people — to do something that breaks the mold. In some cases with younger people, the desire is to do something that sets a precedent, so to speak, something that breaks the mold or that's bigger, bolder, and so on. This can often be a desire to escape whatever norm you have been tucked or shoved into.

You have to be careful. You don't need to do anything immensely risky. Perhaps you need to take a chance — but not one that involves life and limb. Reveal some personality characteristic that other people don't know about you. Start with something small. You don't have to stand up in front of the world and say, "I am 'this,' and you thought I was 'that.'" You don't have to do all of that. Just start with something small and reveal bits and pieces. You might find yourself in a leadership position because everybody else around you is still desperately trying to find his or her mask — not necessarily all people (you've been pretty sure), but most people. Some leaders, some people, need to be willing to say, "You may not know this about me, but I am _____." For instance, you might say, "I love art, and I dearly love going and looking at 'this' or 'that' kind of picture."

Now, that might seem very innocuous, but if you were in a group wherein no one ever says that and you say something like that, it could be nerve-racking for you. It doesn't have to be like that, but that gives you an idea. It doesn't have to be something extreme. This whole thing about extremes and encouraging people to be extreme is an aspect of your personality that you were not born with but is one that really is an exit. The reason that there are so many suicides — and sometimes you don't even know there has been a suicide; it might seem like an accident — is that people have so few opportunities to reveal who they really are. The mask has been holding you back more than helping you to get up the ladder, whatever the ladder — your chosen road — might be.

The Creator has had compassion for you, and the Creator is making it less possible for you to grab the mask. In this way, it is known by spirit — and the Creator, of course — that you must be who you are. For many of you, who you are will seem at first to be this adaptive thing, this thing you've had to become to get along. Because many of you will have piled so many other characteristics that are not you on top of the person you are, you will have to get to your adaptive personality first. But know that the goal is to try to put into words the feelings you have that may not be anything like how you perceive yourself, much less how others perceive you. I know this is a challenge, and it's one of the big reasons that you are in such challenging times now.

I am mentioning this in this context today, in this fashion, because there's a belief held by many of you that to be your true, natural personalities beyond Earth, there is your spirit being, your soul being, your total being, and this is something that is overwhelming. It's not possible. How can you do that? What is it, anyway? In fact, you were born with all those capabilities.

Children Born Now Refuse Masks

I know some of you have noticed how different many of the children now are. A lot of this has to do with the fact that they've been born during the time when the mask was not available. The mask has been hard to hold for those of you who have taken it on. It's been hard to hold on to for the past three years. So generally speaking, children born during the past three years are not using the mask, nor would they be willing to accept one even if it were to be thrust on them.

So parents, let's say you've been trying to train your child out of some habit that while it may not be destructive or harmful, it might be a bit embarrassing in your community, your family, or even your neighborhood. But when you look at that habit, when you pull back or when your friends look at it and say, "Well, there's nothing wrong with that; it's just different than what we're doing," then you have to recognize that what you are seeing is a personality unmasked.

This is why many books, even widely respected ones, have said that a child will lead you. Religions have sometimes grabbed on to this to say it is this or that child, but it's not a child, not one child. The interpretation there got a little confused because long ago — and also in the deep

Figure 11.1. Artwork by Anatole Krasnyansky. Permission requested.

levels of your sleep when you talk to your teachers and guides and angels and so on — you were reminded that the children would lead you. That's really what's being said. Their leading you is really beyond the children, because they're revealing who you are even as they reveal who they are.

So if you get the chance, when you are around children, especially if you have really young ones in your family, pay attention to what they do — not just what they do with you, how they interact, how they interact with their mothers, and how much you love them, and so on. Really pay attention. Are they doing something different from what your other youngsters (or other youngsters you've been around) have done? They will not only reveal who they are but also demonstrate how your true personality can be revealed as well.

Physical Gestures Can Help Reveal Personality

Sometimes one of the easiest ways to reveal your personality is to start using physical gestures that are not necessarily part and parcel of the mask you have attained to survive or thrive in your community. I'm not saying that you have to take on some gestures that are unpleasant, but sometimes it's enough just to move in a different way. This is hard to describe, since it is visual, but if you need someone to set an example, take a look at how babies, one-year-olds, two-year-olds, and three-year-olds move. You will see gestures that sometimes don't seem to fit. "Wait, what is that? What are they doing?"

It wouldn't necessarily be embarrassing for you to do, but look at that. And I'm not talking about bending around in some position that only babies can do because their skeletal structure hasn't yet formed as completely as your own — nothing harmful. I'm just talking about something they might do with their hands or the way they move their necks or their heads or the way they walk. Granted, they may not be walking at their best, but they are doing the best they can at their physical state of being. Pay attention, because it's a way to reveal.

If you're not comfortable doing that in front of others, then do it on your own and see whether it reminds you of something. You would be surprised by how much your body can do to remind you of who you are — who you were born as — rather than to bring forth something that is terrible or off or dirty. It's not about that. It's about letting your body do something, even if you are just sitting there and your hands are moving around in the air. Allow yourself to do that. Oftentimes it might seem like a dance. Just let that flow happen in a time and place where it feels safe. If you're shy or nervous, which most of you will be, then do this entirely on your own when no one else is around. But if you have good friends and they are also doing it, or if several of you decide to get together and do this on your own for a while, then that's something I recommend.

Your body now is very often the clearest portion of your expression of yourself. It doesn't mean that what your body does is interpretable directly into the words of your language, but it helps to release and to bring up those portions of you that you were born with.

You catch on quickly to the skills and abilities you've been trained in or that you were helped to remember by many of the books in the Explorer Race and Shamanic Secrets series and particularly in the blogs. In these, there is this education about the long vision and the long touch, for example. When you are taught these things, many of you catch on to doing them quickly because you were born with them, you see.

To be your true, natural, native spirit as your day-to-day personality, you only need to get in touch with who you were when you were born, meaning that's always been in physical life for you. I'm trying to find an easier way for you to be that, because at least up to the age of seven months, and in many cases (in fact in most cases), up to the age of two, you weren't wearing any kind of mask at all. In some rare cases, by the time you're three years old, you already had some type of adaptive mask. Those of you who are adults can read this; really young people can read this. Right now, the very young, as I've said before, are not using a mask, so these beings, these children, are your teachers.

The Physical Body Can Bring Up Skill Sets

Can you give me an example of something a little more concrete? What might a person suddenly realize he or she can do or start doing?

No, because it will be different for different people and every time we give an example, people look for that. I will give you something else, though. When you're looking at the youngsters, whether they're considered to be normal and natural or different, there's a gesture you can look for. This is particularly noticeable in toddlers. Look for this hand gesture. Notice when, for no particular reason, their hands shake. This is not because they have a tremor or a disease, and it's not because they seem to be expressing something, but their hands and wrists will shake a little bit. It passes quickly.

For a youngster or toddler, this is a form of the physical body bringing up a memory of who and what he or she is. I'm mentioning this because some of you who are much older, even adults, have this gesture come up for you sometimes. What I mean by something remembered is that it is your body's way of stimulating something that you were born with that one might identify as a spiritual ability bordering on the magical. It's something you can do that you didn't know you could do, something that in the past you would have dropped under the category of impossible. Your body will do these things — sometimes it will shake, or sometimes there will be a sudden jerk. I'm not talking about people who have identifiable twitches and so on that have to do with a condition, although sometimes these are misdiagnosed and the person is attempting to bring something up.

What's going on now is that in order to help, your body is bringing up "this" or "that" type of gesture that your physical body can use to bring up something you might need — if not in that exact moment, then soon after or in some unexpected situation that might develop later that day. What's going on is your body will bring this up from the components that make you up. You might have a skill set stashed in your spleen. You might have one stashed in the deep levels of your brain. A skill set might be anywhere in your body, just residing, available to be called on, and sometimes your body will make a sudden, quick motion.

Mother Earth's Movement Is Driven by Electricity

How is that happening mechanically? What's happening is that there is a little more electricity in the air these days. You may not know this, but electricity is not only a function of Mother Earth's body, it is actually what she uses to move. It's what drives her. You know she has her plates, but she has other things about her natural being. Electricity is what drives that. So physically, your bodies are made up of her body, your soul and your energy included.

You are also experiencing more electricity these days. It is really in the air, isn't it, the feeling that you sometimes say you could cut the energy with a knife. You can feel it. The air around you seems to have more substance in a way, but also you're tense even when nothing is happening, when nothing is going on. Some of you have had the experience of it being much more difficult to sleep because of that tension. So a little chamomile tea before bed might be useful — not necessarily a whole cup, but a little.

Aside from that, this tension is the muscles in your body literally reacting to the electricity. Mother Earth has heightened the electricity a bit to help your body and your somewhat masked personality by stimulating those elements of your true personality by your body making a sudden motion, a jerking motion. This might happen to some of you in moments of relaxation.

Please don't laugh at others when this happens. If people stop laughing at others for doing these things, then more people will remember who they are, and that would be a good thing. I'm not saying you have to start jerking and shaking around all the time, but it is well-known, even in some religious (sometimes called mystical) circles within some religions, that a certain amount of shaking or moving around shows that there's a direct correlation to Spirit. Sometimes people have laughed at this, but those who were guided to do it or found it to be true may have been onto something.

You don't have to do this all the time. Look for when it happens without trying to make it happen. It will happen here or there. Most of the time it won't happen in a way that embarrasses you. You're not suddenly going to drop a plate full of cups and saucers. But it could happen at a time when you are trying to relax, when you are trying to sleep possibly, and it's more likely when you are sitting down, so don't let it frighten you. It's your body trying to bring something up, and once you get past your immediate reaction to it, whatever it is, don't just say, "What was that about?" and go on with your life. Say, "What was that about?" Whisper it to yourself.

Maybe you will dream what it was about when you sleep next time. Maybe you will have an inspiration of what it was about. Maybe you will be open to whatever it is that your body was trying to remind you of — to bring up for you — so that you can do something or be something that is you, not somebody else in whatever that situation is going to be later on. It might be something innocuous, perhaps other people being embarrassed by being natural and true to themselves in some way. Maybe what will be asked of you is to say, "Well, maybe it's okay," something as simple as that. Maybe it will be just not to laugh at it. Who knows? It could be anything.

The reason I am not giving you a concrete example is that I don't want you to latch on to something and say, "Okay, this is it. We are going to look at this," because it will be different for everybody. However, if you were a global statistician, you might find several thousand different things: To this person, it happened once, and to that person, it happened twice, and so on. But there's no point in bringing it up because basically it will be different for everyone.

It Is Always Easier to Add Something than to Destroy Something

What do walk-ins do in this situation? How do they get past the conditioning of the body they're in to reach their natural selves?

It's much easier for walk-ins. If you know you are a walk-in, then it's much easier because you're not going to have the attachment to the mask. You're not going to have the same attachment to whatever the previous soul had built up so as to thrive and survive in that community. So it isn't as difficult; it is much easier for walk-ins.

How much of the drama playing out around the world now has to do with this — not just at one locale or another, but the young people all over the world who are asking for more than what their parents had, demanding more?

This is not so new. Very little of this has to do with what I am talking today, but some of it has to do with the fact that when you are young, you haven't clamped that mask on completely, and you might feel some of your personality characteristics that are really you, that you want to be. But in other cases — in that particular group, since you brought it up — it might be, again, a situation of "Everybody is doing it, so let's do it!" which is really a case of following along.

You might be caught up in a situation like that, whether you are young or not. If you're young and you want and need change that you feel will bring about something better in your community or for yourself, your friends, and your family, remember that you don't have to destroy the old. It is always easier to add something to a community than to stop something. So look at it that way. Adding something is infinitely easier; it's not as traumatic and doesn't involve a reaction to stopping or destroying. When you stop or destroy something, there will be a reaction, and it will very often be a violent reaction to a greater or lesser degree, depending on what has been altered and how it has been altered. Work more on adding rather than subtracting things, and understand and be patient with those who have clamped on the mask harder than you have.

Know that you don't have to do anything for that mask to come off and not be available to you in the same way. That's happening, but perhaps you can suggest something or add something. If you add something, always make sure it is something you are doing. If you don't have anything that you could add to the situation, make sure you do it because it works for you and not because others say you should. If you don't have what you feel that situation needs, then look around for somebody else in your community who does have that, who is that, and who can be a good example of that. Try to add things rather than destroy things. Destruction will invariably create a reaction that is equal to or greater than the actions you are doing, and it could perpetuate the problem.

For those of you who are older and are exposed to those who are trying to change things, you may also need to be patient. In your communications with these people, ask them what could be added to make things better rather than saying, "Okay, we give up! Now you can build it all over again on your own, but don't look to me for any help." Try to say what could be added. There have been many voices who have tried to say this, and I grant that they weren't always listened to. But many times you won't have to wait for things to boil over to bring this up. Some teachers with very young students in the second or third grade give assignments like "What would you add to the world?" Not "What would you stop," but "What would you add?" such as, "What would you add to the day-to-day world in which you interact with others to make it a better place?" And teachers, as well as older adults, you should write down a list of what you would add to the world so that the world could be a better place. While you're at it, make sure that the world is your world, one you experience on a regular basis — not just something happening forty or a hundred miles away or farther, but something that you experience.

Slow and Incremental Motion Is Less Traumatic

How does the Creator make it more difficult for us to reach for the old masks? That's intriguing.

It may be intriguing, but since you're not a creator at that level, I don't think I would care to say the mechanics of it. That's what you're really asking. You're asking, "What are the creator mechanics involved here?" All you really need to know is that Creator, interacting with Mother Earth, has taken out some of the stops, as you might say, but in fact Creator just released Mother Earth to be more of her natural self. One of the first things Mother Earth would do to be her natural self is to be more electrical. So that's the answer.

Now, you understand that Creator didn't make Mother Earth more electrical. Creator just said, "Okay, it's all right to be more electrical now," meaning that's part of Mother Earth's core personality. It's all right to be more of yourself now. Remember that you are made up of Mother Earth's personality, so anything she does, physically speaking, you are going to be as well. Get it?

Right. So that makes us more actionable, more outgoing, more — I don't want to say aggressive, but ...

More inclined to be physical.

Physical, yes, rather than sitting back and receiving.

Yes, exactly.

You mentioned that this is the time of transition. Is it going to last a long time? Are we just barely into this time? Halfway through?

You are well and thoroughly into it, not barely. What Creator and creation — all of you being part of creation, you see — are trying to avoid is a situation where suddenly everybody breaks through and there is a huge rush toward your natural, native personality, sort of the rub-ber-band effect, in other words. It would be better to have a slow and incremental motion, but if you don't have that, then you get the sudden thing. The sudden thing can be traumatic for many people's personalities, so that's not as desirable. I know many people would like things to just go *poof!*, as Zoosh might say, and then everything is all better. But *poof!* is not a desirable moment in this case. What is desirable is for you to act, to be involved, to be the change yourself, rather than to be changed. That way, you're involved.

You are, after all, in creator school here. I know it doesn't feel like that very often, but sometimes the simplest things can be of a creator. As I said before, you might say something in a peer situation. Somebody might be is going through something, and people poke fun at it. You might say, "Maybe it's all right." And that is part of this. Just saying "Maybe it's all right," is sometimes very brave. And if you are respected in your group (and even if you are not so respected), somebody else might chime in and say, "Yeah, it's all right. Let's keep going to do what we are going to do," and then the moment is transformed. Transformation does not have to be something grand. It doesn't have to be turning lead into gold, so to speak. It can be something seemingly smaller and more innocuous, and it could have larger, more beneficial impacts.

The Spirit World Wants to Support You

During this time of transition, I've found many things that you can't or won't talk about. So this is a delicate time now, right?

Very delicate. It's so delicate that we are talking around many things. We're talking around things because if we say too much, we can push it "this" way or "that" way. You have to remember that the reason your souls were attracted to coming here to this Earth, to this drama you are experiencing, is because you wanted to do something yourselves. You wanted to experience something different. You wanted to bring about a better way of life, one that you felt might be worthwhile on your planet, wherever you were, and in other places as well. You wanted to do. That was it, essentially.

You wanted to participate. So you'll find that when I — Isis — or others talk through this channel and perhaps even other beings through other channels or even those who speak to you and inspire you in other situations, you won't be poked or prodded in any particular direction. We are just a gentle support system that supports you to do, to be involved, to participate beyond thought, to act in some benevolent way for yourself and for others. In this way, those actions fulfill your soul's desire to do, to be involved.

We do not — as Isis, I do not, and speaking for Spirit in general, we do not — tell you what to do. We do not want to tell you how to do too much — a tiny bit, but not much — because we know that your whole motivation to be here as a soul and as a physical being is to do it yourself. You are here to do the transformation with all the other souls who wanted to be here and participate as the Earth family of people. You wanted to bring about a transformation that will somehow benefit all beings everywhere, so far be it for us in spirit world to push you "this" way or "that" way. You came here to do, and we are going to allow you to do it.

It's Better to Add than to Stop

Don't be too intimidated by your world these days. I know there are dramas, dangers, and pitfalls. Try to act in a gentle way. Try to add something that you feel will be worthwhile. If people don't wish to add this to their lives, maybe it isn't about that in that situation. Maybe it's just mentioning it. Maybe, for all you know, it will stimulate others who overheard it, even if they were just passing by. Maybe it will be a spark. Maybe even a suggestion of adding something can be good to help bring that about. Try to make it something benevolent, not something dramatic, like "Let's destroy this" or "Let's stop that"; rather, "Let's add."

I know some things do need to be stopped, but keep in mind that if you stop something suddenly, violently, there will be a reaction to that — you can be certain of this. Often the reaction and then the reaction to that and then the reaction to that can go on for a very long time. It's better to add or suggest to add.

These are times when people will be very delicate. Even the strongest and most powerful will be very delicate; it just might not be obvious. So try to add, try to suggest, and do your best. Do the best you can to get through these times. It won't last forever. You'll just need to ease through as gently as you can until all people make a forward motion. At some point, all people will agree. They will not only agree in the unconscious state in which you've already agreed, and not even only in the subconscious state in which most of you have agreed, but also in the conscious day-to-day state: "Okay, let's add 'this'. Let's add 'that.'"

After a while, it won't seem like your life is being overwhelmed with additions because these things that work for you, that work for others, and that work for everybody will simply allow you to shed lots of things that were adaptations and ultimately a part of the mask. When those things are shed, it will turn out that what's going to happen will be much simpler, easier, and more enjoyable to live.

Thank you.

CHAPTER TWELVE

You Are Being Activated from Inside to Become Your Spirit Self in Your Day-to-Day Life

Isis

May 20, 2011

All right. This is Isis. I want to let you know that you are not done with crop circles here on this planet. One might assume that the circles are definable by crops only, but this is not the case. I want you all to be a bit more observant (though I know most of you reading this are observant already), because you're going to see the signs that you've become familiar with — shapes and whatnot, generally defined by circular or at least rounded patterns — in more places than in crops.

It's obvious why this phenomenon takes place in crops: Not only is definition possible, but there are also very often grains that are matured in these fields. The birds come and eat the grain not only because it's good and the farmer allows it and the birds are birds but also because the farmer can't really get the crop up once it's been turned over like that. And when the birds eat that grain that they're attracted to because of the good energy, the birds are helped. They feel better, and they fly about. And by being physically active, they broadcast that energy farther away than it would get if the birds had not done this.

These Patterns Activate Your True Personalities

Now, these patterns are needed in other parts of the world, because seeing a picture of a crop circle is not the same as being in its proximity. You will even see things that definitely remind you of crop circles in the clouds. If you live somewhere there is snow, you will definitely see them in the snow. If you live where there is water — even if the water is in motion — you might get a sense of one in the water. By that, I mean it will be there for a split second and then will be gone, and many of you will not actually be cognizant that it was present until slightly after it has left. So some of you will think it was an illusion or not real — you saw something, as you say — but in fact, you *did* see something. [Chuckles.] You saw something that really was there.

The purpose of crop circles is largely to jog your deep memory, for most of you — not your conscious memory, but a deep memory having to do with things you know and feel in your soul and spirit level. Psychologists might refer to this as your unconscious, or the unconscious mind, but it's not a mental thing; it's physical, and therefore it's meant to activate you. The activation does not have anything to do with the strife and conflict you're experiencing on the planet today. That has largely to do with confusion and people feeling hurried and rushed and that there's not enough of time and what they need, and so on — the usual feelings behind these things.

No, these stimulations have everything to do with activating your true personalities, your true natures — literally your souls and spirits — because your mind cannot fathom what these patterns actually mean. Some people have managed to get a sense of "this" and "that," but by "fathoming," I do not mean reading — somebody perhaps having written an inspired or enlightened book about crop circles — because that would happen later. Your true cognizance, even on the physical level —not necessarily mental, meaning a sense of recognition, a good feeling about it, you understand, physically — would really have to take place in the presence of or in the immediate sight of such a pattern in material form.

Some of you might also see things even in static objects, meaning objects that are not moving, objects that are otherwise just plain — a wall, fabric, a drapery, perhaps — that look very much like crop circles. It might even look briefly like a face or something like that, and then you look away for a second — again, that aftereffect cognizance — and you look back and it's not there anymore. Again, this is spirit at a deep level: soul, Creator, angels, and guides attempting to activate your spirit self as your day-to-day self.

Rapid Changes Are Necessary

The activation does not come from outside, though. This is an activation that takes place because you were all born with your soul and your spirit as part of your day-to-day selves. Most of you are only in connection with that on a level of immediate knowing at the deep levels of your sleep. You are not in connection with that on a full-time basis except in that fashion. Now it's important for you to be in connection with that immediately on a day-to-day basis. This is not because some disaster is going to happen. Rather, it's because to make the sudden changes that are necessary to save your world and all the beings on it, including yourselves, you need to make rapid changes. This means not just in lifestyle and consumption and usage but rapid changes so that you will not be overwhelmed and crushed, so to speak, by the problems that you're becoming aware of.

A lot of these problems have been long standing, but there are so many human beings on the planet now and so many are overwhelmed by these problems and struggles that you must know about them, even if you are not experiencing these problems and struggles yourselves. Right now you're rapidly approaching a number — a percentage, you might say — whereby as a spirit self, even if you are not physical, you would automatically respond to difficulties and strife. If you are an angel or a guide, you have certain objects that you interact with. It's a sense of objective — yes, there's that — but it's also a sense in which you are literally summoned. The people you are guiding have a strong feeling, a strong need, and you are there, even if the ability to communicate is impaired in some way. So for you now in physical bodies, you're not that different from those beings. You might think you are, but there's not that much difference, especially now as you transition from one dimension to another while you are still physically functioning on your planet.

So you are at this crossroads, and the good news is that it is impossible to be alive in these times — to be physical, to be on the Earth — without being triggered into your natural spirit selves as your day-to-day selves. It's happening, and right now it's happening, granted, in a way in which you have intense moments of it happening. And during those moments, you are sometimes confused or forgetful, and there are other feelings. Also there are moments during those moments, if you will, during which you are suddenly enlightened, when you can see, when you can sense, when you have all of the abilities that you normally have when you are spirit or a soul beyond your physical body.

These things are necessary, and crop circles are but one way to jog that memory that is built into your physical body and is ready to be jogged to help you to become that spirit self, that natural personality that you are when you're away from Earth and not physical. You don't have to work at this too hard. If you don't notice these crop-circle shapes — these patterns in the sky, in the water, in the lawn, in the dust, in the dirt, in the crops — it's all right. At some point (and that point is rapidly approaching) enough people will be triggered by sight or sensation, by a bird flying by that has consumed a seed or been around another bird, and they will be naturally emanating that seed energy from that crop circle or near it. And that energy will be all around you.

You Can Change Any Circumstance on Earth

You are being activated, and this is a prompt put in for you at this time by Creator and by those beings who serve Creator and the creations associated with Creator. You are that. So Creator is not without feeling. One might say that Creator does not have the same feelings you do, but Creator has love for you. At the same time, Creator knows that you're here because you want to do something on your own; you don't want to just simply live and exist in other times and other places where you have benign, safe lifestyles.

You are here because you all have adventurous spirits. You want to know; you want to understand how things work. You want to be in charge of something — not as a ruler, not to dominate, but because you want to be able to do something that will make a change so that you will have a feeling of accomplishment. So you can say at some point (I'm putting feelings into words here), "I did that. I felt that, and I did that, and now I feel good about that." It's that kind of feeling, not necessarily a statement that goes that way. So that's why you're here.

Creator does not feel good about interfering with that too much, but Creator also has compassion for you. He does not want you to suffer beyond what you've suffered already as a people, as beings on the planet. Creator wants you to have your natural abilities that you have in your soul and spirit and body, but you don't know you have them, and often you mentally project those abilities on others. You are dazzled when others do such things that are associated with what you might call magical effects, but it's not really magical. It's part of who you really are.

There is no flood, there is no typhoon or cyclone or hurricane, there is no earthquake, there is no strife or combat or war, there is no struggle, no disease, no famine, there is no circumstance that causes suffering on Earth that you cannot change with your natural, spiritual abilities. And you can change that almost instantaneously. There is no damage to this planet that you cannot change almost instantaneously with your spirit abilities when you are your spirit self and even sometimes as your day-to-day self.

You Can Use Your Abilities Now

Don't think that you have to wait to use these abilities until you become your spirit or your soul self as your day-to-day self all the time. It can be moments, so if you happen to catch yourself in one of those moments of enlightenment, if you don't know what to do and there isn't some action you can take to help your fellow beings in that moment, then you might say a living prayer, but it is also something that is associated with what I would call an action sequence: You see, you feel, and then you do.

Try to remember that if you don't catch it the first time, maybe you'll catch it the second or third time, because over time, these moments of enlightenment — moments that are not coming from the outside but from the inside because you're being activated — will become more frequent, and they will last longer for some of you. Then they will become more frequent and last longer for everybody. So remember to say something like this:

Living Prayer
"I am asking that all beings on this planet now have the capacity to remember who they truly are to bring about the greatest benevolence for all beings."

That is perfectly adequate to say. You might feel a rush of energy before, during, or after you say that. Don't try to suppress it so you can get all the words out. Even if you get some of the words out while knowing the rest of the words, the energy may be so strong that you won't even be able to move — or you won't want to. The energy is the energy of other souls, other natural beings: guides, angels, and yes, Creator. The energy is ultimately of creation that is taking place to bring about not only the definition of the words you are saying but most importantly, the intent.

So intend for yourself. Intend to bring about greater good, greater benevolence. For those of you who don't have the word "benevolence" in your language, it essentially means total good for all beings, and it has nothing to do with what you define as good in "this" or "that" religion or philosophy. It is actually good with no coercion to believe in "this" or "that" person's ideas or ideals, regardless of whether they are good or not so good. It is something that you know and recognize completely when you are not on Earth or when you are at the deep sleep levels and with guides and angels and feel that overwhelming sense of love, which you identify — and quite rightly so — as Home. That love is ultimately the energy that you live in when you are not in this very difficult school that is taking place on Earth and for which you are not only participating but you are a student and, at other times, a teacher and a guide — not quite an angel yet, but someday.

Other Signs Will Bring Benevolent Energy

Know that these signs like crop circles have equal signs — meaning there are other kinds of signs: an unexpected flash of light, a floating thing of light. It would seem like a solid substance, only when you look at it, it's there just for a split second, or you're aware of it, cognizant of it, just after the fact. "It was a color; it was an energy." You can feel it, but it was real. Those will always be souls, and depending on the color, it might be a soul passing over. It might be a soul coming from a recent death and returning to bring some benevolent energy. If it is gold light, it is always an angelic presence.

There will be other colors that will have transitory meanings. Sometimes the meaning will be physical strength, as a red or pink, but it could be another color. It might be green or other colors. It could be purple, and that could be many things, including a guide or a being who was on the planet at one time. There will be many different colors; don't get stuck on the idea that "this" color means that and "that" color means "this." It will come; it will go. It will be many different colors, though usually one specific color with sometimes a sense of banding across it, meaning diagonal lines, which might suggest that it's more than a being. It could be a temporarily present portal through which a being is emerging in your proximity — it will always be a benevolent being if you are seeing this or experiencing the energy — or through which a being is exiting. Again, this will always be a benevolent energy.

But there are other signs, and that's why I bring them up. Some of you might suddenly have a feeling of wonderful energy or get a warmth in your body that feels good and reminds you of love, even if there is no one there in that moment that you are loving or thinking of that you love. It might be that someone is loving you in spirit, perhaps somebody who has been on the planet before, and perhaps even somebody you've known. They will come for a brief moment to radiate the love they feel for you, and if you're fortunate, you will feel it for a moment. This is always a sign as well, a visitation and a further activation.

Activation is happening swiftly for you now, so you will be able to have many of these moments, and many people will have many moments. And even being your natural self, your spirit self, your soul self, as your day-to-day self in those moments — without anything on your part being done — will tend to activate others around you or globally, because it is like a lifting. I'm not talking about going to another dimension because of that, but it will support that. It is a lifting of your physical self into the benevolent being you were, all of you, when you were born. People often say how angelic babies appear to be, and that's because they really are. They are of that world that is beyond. After a time of life, you adapt to the world you're living in, and you don't seem so angelic anymore, but it's there, and it can be lifted to the surface with these activations I'm talking about.

Creator's Gift of Home

Don't let life get you down too much. These things have been happening for a while and are happening now, and they will happen to every person on the planet, who you are, where you are, what you're doing, and or *what you've done*. These things will happen, and in those moments of awareness of your spirit or soul self as your day-to-day self, you will actually be your natural, benevolent spirit in those moments. Even though you are physical and might do or have done things that you do not feel good about, all of that will be shed for those moments, and you will be this wonderful, radiant being in them, and others may well feel it. So if they say to you afterward — because you might be a bit confused; you might not be sure about who you are in that moment — that you felt wonderful or "I felt something from you that felt terrific," don't be offended. Some of you may not know how to take that or how to react. Just accept it and say, "Oh, that must be the kind of thing I've felt from others these days." You don't have to get elaborate about it. You don't have to explain it. You can if you like, but know that it's a good thing. It is sanctioned by Creator. It is supported by angels and guides, and it is something that is a bit of Home for you in those moments.

These things are going on now. As you read this, you might be able to remember when these things were happening and you didn't know what they were. Some of you will be able to remember way back in your lives when you had moments like this, and you might say, "Oh, that's what that was!" and "Hey! I've felt something like that since!" And some of you might say, "Oh, I feel so much better. I had this moment, and I felt confused and like I was a little dizzy, and I had to sit down. It felt good, but I was confused.

When you have that feeling more than once, you won't feel confused; it will just be familiar. The more familiar it becomes, the more you will realize how good it feels. It's not going to happen while you're driving or doing something that requires your attention and distract you. It will always happen in some moment when it's safe. So look forward to it, know that it is a gift, and know that it is for you. It is for your support, and it is for the support of all life on Earth. Know that it will help to bring out your true nature, your true personality, and the true you that can only help all beings in the most benevolent way.

The Activation Is for Everyone

Is the activation happening to everybody?

Yes, the nice thing about it is that you don't have to have a key to the club. It's happening no matter what.

[Laughs.] Whether you want it to or not.

Well, generally speaking, people will want it to because it's happening, and it's really your soul's desire. Your soul is not that separate from you.

No, I was thinking of the guys trying to control the planet.

Oh yes, it will happen to them too. And you know, at first it might feel uncomfortable for them, but then again, they'll realize that if you have enough moments like that, even if you're being sensible and mental, you have to say, "Well hey, that felt good. If it felt good, it can't be all bad."

Will we ever talk again about the sinister secret government, about who's trying to control? I mean, is that all in the past? Should we just not even concern ourselves with it anymore?

Think about what's going on in the world now. It's almost as if people are saying, "This is our last chance to have wars and enemies and combat and violence." It's as if somebody suddenly said, "Okay, we're going to compress all of this stuff that we were going to have if we were going along the way we were going to go along—let's have it now or forever lose our chance!" And when you think about that . . .

That's almost the way it feels! [Laughs.]

Yes, that was in quotes. But when you think about that, it's like . . . let's not add our two cents in there, because even the most benevolent comments, even the best explanations, if you're talking about the sinister secret government, you're basically talking about people. And people always wonder who read these books, "Who are these people" and worse yet . . .

Other people may say, "Let's get them."

Not only that: If you decide that somebody is of that group—and whether they are or not, most likely they're not going to be when you consider the teensy percentage of people who are involved in that compared to the mass of population—how many people have died or suffered or worse because somebody thought they were this or somebody said they were that? No, let's not add our two cents worth. In short, we won't stir up the pot.

Okay. Well, what do you do when you leave here? [Laughs.]

That's my question for you.

[Laughs.] What does Isis do? You guide people all over the planet? You interact, you channel through them, you . . . what do you do?

I do all things I normally do, and you are no different when you are not embodied here. We all do what we do because we like it, we enjoy it, it's part of our natural being, and service to all and being served by all is what life is all about. Good night.

CHAPTER THIRTEEN

The Polarity Reversal Affects Men

Grandfather

May 26, 2011

All right, this is Grandfather. Now, there is an issue going on that especially affects all males of the human species: babies, youngsters, teenagers, adults, and elderly men. It hardly affects women or girls at all.

So men, listen up. Right now you are all experiencing a polarity change, whether you believe it or not. Part of this polarity change is causing you to be very nervous and edgy. Have you noticed lately how short-tempered, argumentative, and edgy you are when people talk to you? This is happening even with good friends, best friends, wives, lovers, girlfriends, whatever. This is an outer expression of your discomfort with this polarity reversal.

You are experiencing a rise in the feminine energy on the planet on a physical level. Let me explain some of the qualities that this will demonstrate in your physical body. If you have been right-handed your whole life or — how can we say? — felt more on your right side when doing things, you will now have a desire and even feel like you ought to be doing things using your left hand or, generally speaking, the left side of your body. If you allow that to be, you'll notice that you'll be able to experience the subtle things in life much more, the subtle things that you may have been missing. I'm not saying you should stop being right-handed, but I'm saying that if you begin to use your left hand, your left arm, your left leg, or the left side of your body for more things, you will notice subtle experiences.

How many times has your friend, your mate, your wife, anybody, said something to you that urged you or asked you to sense — "Well, don't you feel that?" or "Don't you know that?" or one of those kinds of things — and you reply honestly that no, you don't sense it? You'll find that if you utilize the left side of your body now, you'll be able to notice it, whatever it is. I'm going to give you an example, because so far I know that sounds vague to you.

A New Decision-Making Method Is Available

This is what to do. Suppose you're out on a date and your friend says to you, "Let's go to this movie. I know we were going to go to another movie, that was the plan, but I'm getting a feeling to go to this movie." In the past, you wouldn't have had such a feeling at all, and you probably would have advocated going to the original movie. Say you're in the theater, the multiplex, or even if you're at home looking at the newspaper, this is what to do: I want you to reach out. Sort of curl the fingers on your left hand and reach with your palm down, if you're in the theater, toward the doors that lead to the movie that your friend wants to go to, or toward, say, a newspaper advertisement for the movie, like that, and see what you feel. Don't try to interpret the feeling yet.

Do that for a moment — for some of you, this could be just five to ten seconds. When you're reaching, by the way, try not to reach along the line where the people are. If you can, reach above the heads of the people and toward that door. Note how you feel. You might have to wait until you feel a change in your body, and note how you feel. Then reach toward the door of the movie where you were going to go, and note how you feel.

This is not something I'm trying to urge you to learn how to do. I'm saying it's happening right now. These are ways you can notice it and discover the subtle energy — the hint, the intuition, if you will — that you'd hoped your whole life you could have. This subtle energy will help you make better choices that will be much better opportunities for you and perhaps for others, even for your friends and family, if the decision is yours. This is happening now. You need to learn how to use it.

Note how you feel reaching toward the other movie that your friend has a feeling for. You'll probably note that the other movie theater or the other door in the multiplex feels better. If it doesn't feel better, maybe she just wants to go see that movie.

The Yes or No Card Method

Let's do something else that is just on you. Say you have a decision to make and you're not sure what to do. Keep it simple. Get yourself a couple of note cards. They have to be pieces of paper or note cards that you can write on one side and when you flip them over, you can't read anything on the other side, and both cards should look exactly the same. If there are three or more possible answers, you'll need that many cards. Use a pencil or pen, whatever you want. You don't have to write down the question, but you can if you want to.

If you write down the question, put that to the side. "Should I _____," whatever it is. Then write down on a card the word "yes." After you write it down on whichever side of the card you want — I recommend writing it on the lined side, but if there are no lines, don't worry about it — then write the word "no" on the other card, and turn those both over. On a third or fourth card, write variations, "Well, maybe, but I need to do _____," something like that, any variations or possibilities. By the way, this can work for simple questions or for the most complex questions. Write down other possible answers until you get to the end.

Use as many cards as you need, but only put one answer per card. Don't try to cover all the bases, just write one specific answer per card, a yes or a no. Write yes on one card and flip it over, and no on another card and flip it over. If there's some variation, write down the possibilities and flip those cards over.

Then swirl those cards around in front of you for a long time until you have no idea what's on what card. This isn't a magic trick. It's primarily a way of not just getting an answer that might work for you but of learning how to use the feminine energy that has been visited upon you. There's nothing you can do about it to prevent it because Mother Earth is experiencing a strong rise in her feminine energy, and since your body is made up of Mother Earth material, you can't help it. It's happening and there you are. You're stuck with it, so let's learn how to use it. Maybe it will work to your advantage and to the advantage of others.

Swirl those cards around in front of you, and then lay them out in some pattern that's comfortable for you. I recommend a straight line. Put some space between the cards so there are at least four, five, or six inches between each card. If there are twenty cards [laughs], you know, just do the best you can, but make sure that the cards are not touching each other. I don't think there'll be twenty cards, but some of you might have six or seven, so try to have four of five inches between and around each card.

Then just ask your question out loud. You have the question on the table to the left of you or on the desk, wherever it is. If it's a desk, make sure you move everything so that only that material — those cards — are on the surface. Obviously you can't do that with most desks, but you need to do this because you're sharpening up your capacities. This is not going to work on a computer, by the way. You need to use physical matter, meaning cards — or heavy pieces of paper might work. Don't bother cheating; the whole purpose of this is to learn how to use this energy you have on your left side now.

This method is less to use for making these decisions on the cards, but for some of you, those cards will work really well. You'll use them for other questions for quite a while, and that's fine. Again, use your hand the way I said before: palm down, fingers curled in a natural position. Don't curl them and make a fist. You want them to be relaxed. This is why you need to have four or five inches between the cards all the way around them: because I want you to use your left hand and point.

Aim your left hand toward one of the cards, and notice how you feel. If you get a good feeling, then you can put a G on the back of that card — you can use a pencil or pen; it doesn't make a difference — and wait about twenty to thirty seconds. Then point to the next card and do the same thing. If you get a physically uncomfortable feeling, then put an N, meaning "no," on the back of that card. Try not to touch the other cards when you're making these notes, and go right on through to the end.

Remember to wait twenty to thirty seconds before you aim at any other card. When you finish, relax for a moment — a good twenty seconds — then turn the cards over that are marked with Gs, and line them up under the question. The cards can touch each other at this point. After that, turn the cards over that are marked with Ns. Stack those up on the other side, ideally on the right side of the table. (It's probably best to use an empty table, if you can do this.)

These Methods Can Bring You Closer to Your Mates

Most of you won't be able to do this at the office because you'll be too busy or get interrupted and you're desk is cluttered. You might want to practice it at home, because this is something you're learning for yourself. You're not trying to learn it to make office decisions. However, when you get good at this, you will be able to use it in the office to your great advantage and probably to the advantage of your clients, to say nothing of your career.

Take note of the answer to your question. I recommend the first time you're asking a question, pick something simple, not earth-shattering — meaning don't pick a question that is really seriously disturbing you, okay, not for the first time. Pick something simple, such as, "I'm going out with my wife, my friend, on a special date. Should I wear white? Should I wear black?" Like that. Just ask one thing: "Going out on my date, would it be best for me to wear a dark color?" That's all. You need to have something that a "yes" or a "no" answer would work for. And if those are the only cards you want to use, that's fine. The purpose of this, quite obviously, is to give you a way to make decisions you have difficulty with, and you will discover how you use this subtle energy, especially if it's something that you've had difficulty with your whole life.

Doing this can make a huge difference for you. Don't do it just because I want you to do it. That's entirely up to you. But if you can do this, you will find that you and your mate will be drawn closer together. You'll suddenly understand each other a great deal more, you'll have a little more in common. Your communication will get a lot better, and you'll get along better. You'll notice these things especially if your mate has been able to do this all along and you haven't. And it will be fun. Try to remember how it was when you first got together. This kind of step can bring you closer together. You'll remember what it was that attracted you to this person in the first place, so that's a big plus.

I will have more to say about this in time, but I wanted to mention this to you now because it's happening to you now. And it's really important that you acknowledge it. So if other men talk to you about this and you say, "Well, I read this article, and it's talking about how we can feel things with our left sides now that we could never feel before. You know how the wives go on about intuition, and we can do it now too." It's going to be that, if other guys talk about it. Believe me, even though this is the sort of thing that a lot of men don't like to talk about — because you might have been shy about it yourself — you're going to discover now that you have this increased sense of feeling on your left side. And many of you have noticed it for the last six months or so. This is a way you can learn how to use it.

CHAPTER FOURTEEN

How to Reconnect with Your Magical Powers

Isis and Grandfather

June 13, 2011

This is something that is magic and empowering, and it is something you can do. These are times that require you to use the magical powers you were all born with. You don't remember these magical powers because to adapt to the world in which you live, you had to unlearn what you knew when you arrived as a baby. But now you need to learn it again. Carefully cut the page with the hand outlines out of this book. We (this is Grandfather and Isis speaking at the same time) must bring to the surface — at least in your subconscious and accessible by your conscious mind — the magical powers you were born with, so cut that page out of the book.

If you sleep on a bed regularly — and most of you do — put that page inside your pillowcase. If you sleep with somebody else, make sure that only you use that pillow that night. We need you to touch that piece of paper while you are awake and for the energy of your more total being and of the beings and teachers you work with when you are asleep to permeate it. It would be best, but not necessary, for the page to be inside the pillowcase. The advantage of it being inside the pillowcase is that if anyone else touches it — a child or a dog or a cat — then it won't get damaged in any way. So it is in there, and it will be permeated with your energy.

Then when you have time available, maybe over a weekend, take the paper out of the pillowcase and put both hands on the paper: your left hand on the left outline of a hand, and your right hand on the right outline. Then hold it straight out in front of you. You can be sitting down or standing up; it doesn't make any difference. However, it might be good to do this sitting so that you can rest your elbows on the arms of a chair. You might need to hold that position for five or ten minutes and in some cases, longer. Try to make sure that your eyes are not also looking at work, so don't do this at the office. I don't want you to be distracted. This is important. If you are in a room where work takes place, close your eyes. Then after you have held the paper out in front of you, move it toward your solar plexus so that your hands are still on both sides of the paper but your wrists and a portion of the paper are touching your solar plexus. Then say,

> "I am asking that all the most benevolent energies that are available for me — including my guides, teachers, angels, and Creator's energy — be available for me now in the most benevolent way for me."

Then wait for a few seconds. Some of you will feel heat or tingling or something. Remember, try not to think. Stay focused on what you are doing. Because these words are precise, you can keep another piece of paper nearby and read the words from it. Make sure you say the words exactly right. If you trip over a word, you will have to go back and do it over, but it is not going to take a long time in any event. If you have to go back to do it over, wait at least half an hour. So you don't trip over the words, read them as slowly as you like, and if energy comes up at any time, pause until the energy passes a bit, and then go on. That energy will be your guides, teachers, angels, and other benevolent beings of light helping to bring about what you are requesting. Then say this:

> *Benevolent Magic*
> "I am asking to have full access now, any time I need it, to my most benevolent magical powers that I was born with in my now life and that that happen for me in the most benevolent way and result in the most benevolent outcome.

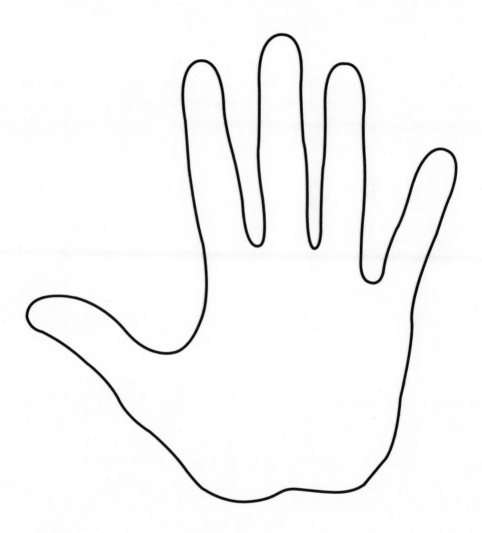

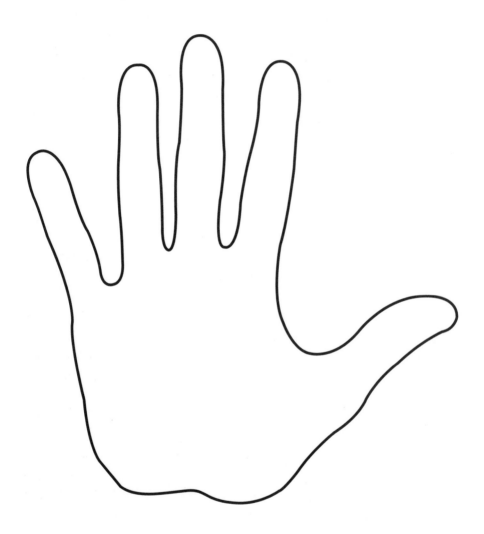

Say this slowly. Remember, if the energy is present, say it very slowly. If the energy builds up very strongly, wait for it to pass a bit. Don't expect it to pass completely, because this is powerful. Then at some point when you are done saying that, the energy is going to fade a bit. For some of you, the energy will be so relaxing that you will fall asleep. That's okay. But when you wake up, or if you don't fall asleep and assuming you felt something, this is what to do. I'll give you something after this if you didn't feel anything, but assuming you felt something, then relax until the energy fades and, if you're sitting, place the paper down on your legs just in front of you (about at your knees), and do not fold it. Then take the piece of paper and get up. If the energy is still very strong, don't move; wait. Remember, the energy is what you have requested. It may not happen instantaneously, it may not happen readily, but it will happen — slowly but surely.

When you can move, move slowly over to your bed and slip that page into your pillowcase again. But this time, instead of slipping it just under the pillowcase with the pillow beneath it (although you can put it there), you can put it on the bottom, meaning the pillow is on top of the piece of paper. You can do it either way; it's up to you.

Then rest a bit. Try to do no work, nothing. Don't eat. If you need to go to the bathroom, go. If you need to have a little sip of water, that's fine. But no food, nothing with any nutrients — and by that I mean no fruit or vegetable content, no plant content, you understand: nothing food-like. For those of you who drink beer, so you don't miss my point: no alcohol, just water for a half-hour.

You also need to try not to think. If you're surrounded by things that stimulate your thought, keep your eyes closed as much as you can. If you want to lie down and take a nap, that's fine. If it's your sleep time, go to bed. That's all right. If it isn't and you want to stay up, then return to where you were sitting and you can sit there. Basically, I don't want you to do much. I'm recommending that you don't do much for another hour and a half — so that's about two hours total after doing this.

After that, you can move around the house. You can do things. If you're in a hotel room, you can move around there. It's all right to eat. However, do not drive a car. So if you're a professional driver and you have somebody else with you, let them do the driving. If you're a professional driver — say, a trucker or something — then don't do this when you are likely to drive. Do it during your time of sleep and rest. It is not safe to drive for at least six hours because you will have times when you will go in and out, meaning you'll have times when you are not entirely present in your physical body, so to speak. That doesn't mean anybody else will be present; it just means that it will be like a meditative state. That's why it's not good to drive then. I want to underscore that. It's also not good to use machinery or to work in a kitchen, all right? So it's just a time for rest, sleep, and relaxation. If you read and watch television, it can only be something that is amusing and does not involve harm or hurt to anyone or anything.

You Will Develop the Powers to Transform

You are doing something magical to bring up your personal magical powers that you are all born with, and you are establishing a relationship of trust with your own soul born in your body that has been lost over the years and that became confused when it had to adapt to the ways of your culture — and that means any culture on Earth. So now you, as an adult, are really parenting the soul that was born in your body, the soul that is you. You are taking care of that being, and that being will take care of you.

Now, over the next three to six months, many of you will discover that something you weren't able to do in the past without great struggle will suddenly be much easier — in some cases, just a snap. "Oh!" you'll say. Sometimes you'll think about this thing that you did, but most of the time, you won't. It'll just happen in the flow of life.

There will be a few other things that you will notice. Some things that you were attracted to doing will simply fall away. Some of those things you felt a little guilty about doing because you knew they weren't good for you. Maybe they weren't necessarily good for others, but you were able to rationalize that it was "no big deal" and that they'd "get over it" (you know how rationalization goes), or that you were able to rationalize for yourself — "It's all right; I can take it." A lot of those behaviors will just fall away. You won't feel guilty; it won't be something like that. Doing those things, whether they are harmful to others or to yourself, will just fall away. You won't do those things anymore. I'm not saying it's a cure-all; I'm saying that it will just happen, and you'll find other things that are easy and fun for you to do it that you didn't know you could do.

I'm bringing this to your attention because there are problems in the world today that need solutions, and sometimes those solutions will be impossible in the course of life at the level of technology you have right now — and that means any technology, whether it is known or unknown (meaning known only to a select few). It will take the magical powers you were born with to be able to transform it.

You Are Learning How to Function in Your Physical Body

I want to get back to something that I said I would do. Some of you don't feel energy — meaning you might feel it, but you're not sure if it is energy, or you don't have a physical sensation at all. So when you're doing these things, when you get to some place where you feel like, "Maybe I ought to stop there for a moment" — you don't feel any energy, but you have read what is said to others, and you think, "Well, maybe I should stop there" — go ahead, stop when you are reading the words. And by all means, when you read the words to do these things, you can speak the words slowly. All right?

Please understand that that kind of thing and the pauses I'm talking about are important. But again, regardless of whether you feel the energy, do all of the suggestions about the half-hour, the extra hour and a half — don't drive; don't operate machinery, follow all that kind of stuff for the same amount of time. It's for your safety and the safety of others.

Now, this is for everybody: After six hours, you can drive a vehicle, but be vigilant about how you feel. You'll probably need to pause and rest more often. You might feel the need to eat different foods for the next twenty-four to forty-eight hours. Some things that you normally eat, you may want to eat less of. Some things you don't normally eat, you might eat more of — that kind of thing. Some things that you've never eaten before and other people eat might smell or look good. If so, get a portion, taste it, and if it tastes okay, if it feels all right in your body, go ahead and eat it. If it doesn't taste okay or you just eat a little bit, that's enough. Don't feel as if you have to eat all of it because you ordered it. That's really important.

You are literally learning how to function inside your physical body. A lot of what you've been taught in your various cultures on the planet, while well intended by those who taught you, goes against the grain — meaning it goes against what your physical body, your personal, physical body, can do with your soul. So you need to learn, basically, how your soul — your spirit, you understand, your day-to-day self — functions in your physical body in the most benevolent way for you. Don't assume that a pattern of behavior that is benevolent for somebody else who is doing this is also right for you. You have to find your own way.

I know that this is a lot, but keep in mind that even though I'm saying, "I recommend that you do this," the main thing I'm trying to say here is do this only because you want to do it. Do not do this until you want to do it, and keep in mind that the magical powers I'm talking about will all be completely benevolent for you and others. I'm not talking about something you see in the movies or on television where someone has magical powers of destruction. It's not going to be like that. Right now, you have all too many powers of destruction that you are using technologically and in other ways. You need to balance that not only with benevolent, true magical powers that you were born with but also with an understanding of who you really are. And you will be getting in touch with that by doing this work.

Everything Must Be Transformed

So I'm speaking this way to you today because, as I said before, there are problems in the world now that while they are being addressed by people with practical knowledge and perhaps expertise in the fields that are needed in order to address those problems, some of the problems are unsolvable at the current level of technology, no matter how good the expert is. And even though they might never acknowledge what you have done [chuckles], some things can be resolved through magical powers and magic. That's why a great deal of the teaching through this channel and others over the years has to do with benevolent magic in different forms now. But physical magic is also the key.

Words set the tone. They set the intent. But ultimately, the energy — the magnetic energy, the electrical energy, the physical energy, the spirit energy, the love — is what transforms. It will be up to you, now and in the times to come, to be able to perform the magical powers you came in with in this life, to transform all things, all life, all existence on Earth, into the most benevolent form it can be. There will be times when you won't even want to transform something — when you'll be mad at someone or something for what they have done — you will be able to justify that and others will agree with you.

Yet all that will need transformation, because in order to do, to cure, to bring about benevolence for all beings from the tiniest ant to the biggest whale, from the youngest baby to the oldest adult, everyone — every blade of grass, every grain of sand, everything — must be transformed. Granted, some of it does not need much transformation, such as the grains of sand, the animals, and the plants, but they must be addressed. They must be appreciated. They must be respected. And you must allow them to be the most benevolent way they can be.

I know it sounds like a Herculean task, but you will all be able to do this. You will. And you were all born with benevolent magical powers, every single one of you — different ones for different people, although some of them overlap from person to person. So that's what I have to recommend today. I'm not taking any questions because this is not about an intellectual pursuit. This is physical; this is spiritual. It is something you can do, but do it only if you want to. Good life.

CHAPTER FIFTEEN

Earth and Humans Are More Electric Now

Element of Electricity

June 17, 2011

Now I will speak briefly, and then you will probably hear from Zoosh.

Well, that's wonderful. Welcome.

Thank you. I am speaking for the element of electricity that is being utilized now at the greatest level that Earth has used it for a great many years. She is currently using 3 percent of her electrical capacity. In recent years — say, going back sixty, eighty years or so and before that — she was only using about 1 to 1.5 percent, but she's had to use more lately to put herself in balance. Electricity is an element that is generated by bodies in motion. Earth has more motion than her orbit; she has a significant amount of inner motion even relating all the way to surface motion.

As far as planets go that are hospitable to other life forms, Earth is probably demonstrating more motion than most. As a result, she has a considerable amount of electricity that is available to her. This is why human beings generating or in fact temporarily capturing that electricity is completely allowed by Earth, and she will not in any way prevent you from capturing more for your temporary usage — meaning you can store it to a degree, but it continues to move. Electricity as an element must remain in motion. If batteries are developed that are so efficient that the electricity can be stored for over sixty days — and some batteries can do that — they will be prone to break down, and therefore probably the better way to go is electricity reduction through the use of more standardized systems, including solar energy systems.

Now, I am just here to speak for a moment, defining electricity and broadening its parameters a bit, but I am not here to state its source. However, I will say that generally speaking, the centers of any galaxy do create the portals that allow for electrical and magnetic fields. I think this is already known by your people. That's all I'm going to say now, and Zoosh will come in and take up your questions.

Well, thank you so much for honoring us.

You Can Shield Your Electronics from Orbital Broadcast Electricity

Zoosh

All right, Zoosh speaking. Greetings.

Greetings! Welcome.

You had a question about something, eh?

Yes. Electrical and electronic components in our equipment seem to be breaking down, and I wonder whether the extra electricity is one of the causes.

One might think so, but it is not. One of the main issues going on here is a certain amount of broadcast electricity in the air. This is not associated with the kind of electricity broadcast one might feel in a lightning storm even when there's vast amounts of lightning, because that lightning is essentially — how can we say? — encapsulated within itself. If you've ever seen a lightning bolt hit the ground and it flashes and you get the impression that it's coming up and going down or going down and coming up, what is happening is that it really is doing that within its temporary parameters. So it's pretty much encapsulated, and even though you might feel some sensation in your body and would certainly have a survival reaction around it, there is no great amount of broadcast electricity there. Tesla did experiments along these lines and found that out for himself.

However, there is technology now in use that is produced by human beings and is orbiting the planet, and it does use a certain amount of broadcast electricity to function and to carry out its purposes. Most of the time, that does not interfere with electrical appliances or machinery or even electronics, but sometimes when there is a surge — meaning a sudden need for a greater amount in whatever those projects are involved in doing — then your electrical devices or your electronics that are not well insulated are definitely vulnerable.

So a suggestion: If you have the need to replace cables for anything, replace them with shielded cables, if you can get that for whatever your mechanism is. If you can't, then find some simple way — it doesn't have to be expensive — to shield as much of your electrical cable bundles and machinery as possible. One often finds in large machinery that motors and such are encased in some kind of steel anyway, but things are a bit more exposed in some older machines. So if you cannot easily encase it in something — and that may be the case — then you might be able to put something temporary around it, even a structure that allows for ventilation with vents or louvers or something that still allows for the devices to be at least somewhat shielded.

I do recommend, generally speaking, that if you're having problems with an electronic device, look toward doing more shielding. Modern electronics are usually shielded pretty well unless they are cheaply built. But even if you have to wrap some aluminum foil around something temporarily, say a phone or something that's giving you problems, that could work as well. I'm not saying that is a cure; I'm saying it could work temporarily in a situation where there's some problem.

Now, I don't know whether there's anything the average person can do about the situation in general, because those projects in space are doing things that usually contribute to the safety of all human beings on the planet, such as observing weather and other phenomena that can be predicted and save lives. Of course, there are other space projects doing other things, but that is the main issue.

You Are Becoming More Electrical Yourselves

There is one other source of broadcast electricity, however, that might escape your notice: The other main issue is that human beings now have a necessity to support many of the things that Mother Earth used to support for you, because she's having to take care of herself more these days. Therefore, all human beings on the planet are having to become more electrical, so you have to become more electrical yourselves. You are made up of Mother Earth's body, physically speaking, and you can become more electrical.

So whether you're conscious of it or not, you yourself might actually be broadcasting some electricity, and anywhere there are many human beings, there's an increase in that broadcast. Now, keep in mind that human beings are in motion, of course, and that relates back to what the first speaker said. There is more motion going for most people these days than ever before due to the pace of life. As people get more involved in walking or sprinting to places, or if you live in a community where athletic activities are something that people pursue with great zeal, then you might notice that effect even more.

Again, I come back to the insulation that can be used to protect your electrical and electronic devices. Needless to say, most manufacturers did not factor in the possibility that human beings themselves would be more electrical. And of course, it's human beings who are accessing electronics and even heavy machinery, to say nothing of simple, uncomplicated machinery such as household appliances. I would say that if your household appliances are made of metal — say, like an old toaster or something like that, or a metal electric kettle — there's not going to be anything to worry about. But a lot of appliances now are made of plastic, and the manufacturers of the plastic devices quite understandably did not factor in having a more electrical human being be in contact with their devices.

I'm not saying be less electrical; I'm just saying [chuckles] that you might need to take another look at the insulation of electrical and electronic devices. There might be after-market things you can do, but here's a way to know: If you feel kind of jumpy and your muscles are kind of nervous, and you've slept reasonably well — meaning you've gotten at least four or five hours of sleep, okay? I grant that you would like to get eight hours of sleep, but say you've had at least four and a half to five hours of sleep — but you're still feeling kind of jumpy, that might be a sign. I'm not talking about feeling jumpy because you've had four or five cups of coffee — of course you'd feel jumpy then. I'm just saying that if you feel something that is not just nervousness — not an anticipation, not an anxiety, nothing like that — you just feel kind of tense, chances are you're electrically involved in helping out Earth, or you need to do something to release that electricity to help out Earth.

So I'm going to tell you right now what you can do. If you're at home, you can get up and jump up and down if you need to, or you can walk quickly around the house. If you're outdoors, you can walk quickly. Now,

I'm assuming that you're in reasonably good health. For those of you who get that feeling and who are not in the best of health or unable to move — say you're in a wheelchair — then if you can, if your arms are strong enough, wheel quickly around somewhere. You see what I'm saying: If you can have a burst of motion in a safe way for even a minute or a minute and a half, perhaps two minutes — it doesn't have to be sudden or violent; you don't have to shadowbox or anything like that, but something like brisk walking and swinging your arms — that will pretty well dissipate that feeling, and you'll feel a lot better. All right?

Okay. What are some of the other uses that satellites broadcasting electricity might be involved in?

Many of them are involved in mapping space and in understanding the nature of humanity and how humanity interacts with science. Very few are involved with anything really highly secret, but because I'm attempting to honor the needs of people who are investors — to say nothing of people who have worked mightily and long to produce some kind of experiment in space that will someday result in products that will be very helpful to people — I'm being discreet about what to say here, because I don't want to ruin people's chances to contribute to the betterment of human beings. So I'm just going to say that some of them are experiments that will lead to something good someday.

All Electricity Comes from Creator

The Element of Electricity said at the beginning of this session that some people on the planet, maybe some of the more advanced scientists, might know that there is a portal in the center of galaxies that allows electric and magnetic fields to come in. Now is that where all the electricity here comes from for Mother Earth and for humanity and ... ?

Well, it's really just a way of saying that this is something that stems from Creator, and the center of any galaxy can be connected right back to the Creator of this universe. So anything having to do with love, motion, and life would be involved there. This universe is not typical. You might think, because this universe has certain so-called physical laws — although you haven't, as a scientific community, discovered all of these, but you will at some point — that motion is a given in a universe. But you know, there are many other universes created by other creators that are not known for that. You might see planets, but they do not in fact spin or orbit; they are just fixed. You will say, "How is that possible?" The life forms are just different; that's all. And just because you assume that certain truths are evident about physical reality, they only appear to be evident because of the universe you're in now. So this Creator obviously derives great joy from motion and obviously has great love, and everything is permeated by that, and likes to keep things — how can we say? — balanced.

So as a result, whether the center of any galaxy is in the obvious center — like your spiral galaxy — or whether the galaxy, many of which seem to be of a more abstract shape, has it's center in another part of it doesn't make any difference. At some point, that galaxy had a point of origin, and it still grows out of that point of origin even though it may have other points that it's also growing from. I think astrophysicists are familiar with that.

So there may be more than one center to a galaxy?

There may be, yes. It's quite obvious that there is a single center in a typical spiral galaxy, but not all galaxies are like that.

That's amazing! You're saying that the electricity that runs our bodies, that runs our houses, that is in Mother Earth, all comes from the Creator? I mean it's created, you said, by motion, but the original impetus comes from Creator?

Yes. Creator is an electrical and magnetic being and, of course, a loving being. So it is not possible for Creator to create anything without infusing it with itself. Think about that: It's not possible. So everything is going to be at least potentially electrical.

Earth Is an Unusually Active Planet

Now, it's true that you can go to some planets and the measured electrical level will be very low, but it's still there, whereas the Earth has this tremendous capacity for electrical energy; it's just that she doesn't use much of it, and that's because she doesn't have to. As the Element of Electricity said, when Earth is using, say, 3 percent of her electrical energy on another planet — not even the ones that have very little demonstration of electricity, but the average planet — what amounts to 3 percent of Mother Earth's electrical energy might be five to ten times more than the entire capacity of another planet.

Most other planets upon which you find thriving, living communities have hardly any electricity because they are not in motion other than to be turning on an axis and moving in an orbit. But you do not find volcanoes on those planets, for example. You will usually not even find the ancient sites of volcanoes that once were, as one might find on, say, Mars, for example. But Mars does not now have volcanoes — the Mars that you can see, the Mars that you can send your rovers up to, the Mars that you will interact with and where you will have colonies someday. But on a planet where you would have a thriving population — say, a planet from which visitors come to visit you here: you've had visitors from the Pleiades, Orion, Andromeda, and so on — you would not find anything like that. You would even not typically find mountains on those planets.

That's part of the reason visitors come to Earth: it's so full of motion. Not all mountains, obviously, come from volcanoes; most of them are caused by the upthrusting of plates — what you call earthquakes and so on. And with earthquakes, things sometimes move up and sometimes move down. Mother Earth is in motion, and because there is so much motion, it has, especially in the past, been a popular place to visit. You know: "Go to Earth, where things are happening!" you might say. But maybe you wouldn't say it quite like that.

So if she chose to use the other 90 percent of her electricity, what are the potential uses — what would she do with it?

Needless to say, if she did that, none of you would be alive.

Right, but would she broadcast more or move more, or what?

No, no. It's not that she needs that extra electricity, see. It's not that she needs that much. It's that this excess of electricity is available because she is so involved in motion. Everything on Mother Earth is moving. Granted, some things are moving slowly, and you don't see them, but a great many things are moving constantly or quickly: water, the lava inside volcanoes, the wind. There are basic elements that are in motion all the time, and this motion — and to a degree, friction — produces a great deal of electrical energy on the available level. But she does not need that much. She used to only use 1.5 percent, but now that she's working on herself more and has to take care of herself and you have to take over some of her duties and all that business, she is using about 3 percent. But she would probably never use the full capacity that she has.

Pulling back here a little bit and looking at Mother Earth right now, I do not see any reason that she would ever use any more than 5 percent of her electrical energy. And even at 5 percent, it would probably be hazardous for most of her surface populations. So I don't think she'll go there. She doesn't want to get rid of you; believe me, if she wanted to get rid of you, it would take her a split second, but she doesn't want to do that. She wants you to be healthy; she wants you to be happy. She'd prefer it if you didn't go digging around in her body so much, but at some point when you learn to create things that do not require such digging, I know you will stop. And you will know how to do these things before too long. Some of it will be shared by visitors from other places, and other things are coming along on their own, such as (obviously) so-called alternative energies. But I don't want to go off on that tangent.

Okay, I may not be asking the question right. Why would she have this capacity? Why did she develop the capacity if she's never going to use it? What are some of the things she could use it for?

No, you're still not getting it. I must not be saying it to you correctly. What if you had a car that instead of its usual generator or alternator, it had one ten times that size? Now, it would produce vastly more electricity than you would need, and since it would be available, you could add, say, a whole light show on the roof if you wanted to, but you wouldn't do that. It would be as if you had a car that was doing that, and it still ran. It didn't burn up the wiring system. It was just producing vastly more energy because of the generator or alternator that was in there. This is an example in which you couldn't get the car you needed, so you got that big one — and it could produce all that energy, but you would never use it.

So with that analogy, did she bring her alternator or generator with her to Earth from somewhere else where she used that much energy?

No. It is because she is in motion. That motion is what produces the electricity. Motion and electricity, physicality and electricity, are one thing.

Oh! Okay. I see: She produces it, but she just doesn't use it.

She produces it because of who she is.

Use Alternative Forms of Energy and Build Products to Last

Okay, but we're desperate here; we need electricity. We can't use nuclear energy, and coal has got to go. How can we access some of that electricity for our uses? Is that possible?

It is possible, and I recommend strongly that you use solar energy. And even solar energy used to produce steam is okay, but I think that solar energy used to produce steam will probably ultimately be primarily used for industry. But in terms of what you might need around the house, solar power is really the way to go.

You know, it's much more advanced now than people realize, and there are advances coming down the road in solar batteries and so on that will be presented to you within the next three years that will totally revolutionize solar technology. It's been around for a while; it just hasn't been largely in circulation. So I recommend you use that, and you can use wind power — things like that. I really feel they will be sufficient.

You don't need to (how can we say?) have tremendous sources of electrical energy that can run all kinds of heavy industry. By the time those sources are available to you, you won't be creating products the way you create them now. Certainly, you won't be creating disposable products. You know, in the past — and I'm not going back too far in the past — things were created to last a long, long time. Industry knows how to do this right now, and because there are so many people on Earth and they have so many needs — and most peoples are not having their needs met — for the products that they could use, industry needs to begin building products that last a long time.

I'm talking about the industry that exists today. It would take industry a minimum of twenty-seven years just to catch up with everybody's needs. And by that time, there would be new things to create. So I'm saying this: Create things that last a long, long time, industry. You know you know how, and it's not difficult. You really don't have anywhere to put trash as it is, and so much trash now is made up of stuff that didn't have to wear out. So you can do a lot better than that.

Express Your Motion, and Produce Energy

The Earth creates electricity through motion, yet humans, when they absorb too much just from the atmosphere, use motion to broadcast it or get rid of it? It seems to be an opposite thing. I mean, do we soak up electricity just from the atmosphere and from walking on the earth?

No, no. Remember, you were told a while back that you were going to have to take over some things that Mother Earth wasn't able to do for you anymore. And you are physically made up of Mother Earth, so you have the capacity to produce electricity of your own. So the motion that you or people around you make is what you want to express.

When you were a child, you did express it. Children get up and they start jumping around because it is natural for them to express motion, you see. But as you grow into an adult, you become more concerned about what people will think of you if you suddenly get up and start doing deep knee bends, for example. [Chuckles.] So you don't do that; you hold back in your natural production of motion, and that's why you get nervous. You don't get nervous in that sense — I'm not talking about anxious nervousness; I'm talking about feeling physically tense. You get physically tense because you're not expressing motion the way you did when you were a child. Please change a little bit, folks. Let other people move around. If you see an adult on the street who's just hopping around, doing jumping jacks, maybe, say, "Okay, this is great. Maybe I'll do them with you if I can" — that kind of thing. And that will make you feel better, and it will release the excess tension in your body.

One more thing: Since human beings are now broadcasting electricity through their own motion, then given the number of human beings on the planet, this is really the time to put up the antennas that Tesla designed to receive electricity. Put up something small, something you can make as a hobby if you have the means and know how to use something. It will be fun. It can be a great class project. Just see how much electricity you can utilize. There have been demonstrations of things that move slightly, but I think you'll find now that there is so much electricity in the air that you will be able to begin to utilize it in — how can we say? — gathering devices. All you need is ... you easily broadcast electricity through antennas; you can receive it as well. That technology exists.

Could we receive enough of it to put in batteries to run devices?

Oh, maybe enough to run a small charger, but I wouldn't count on that. Do it just as an experiment, as a classroom assignment. Do it for fun, and you'll see. Once people get more physically in motion, then maybe it will be possible to produce a battery charger. But really there are so many ways people can be in motion and produce energy on their own. You can ride a bicycle and produce energy.

Okay. Now, for clarification: We have more energy because we're getting it from Mother Earth, and because we're not moving properly, is it possible that we're broadcasting it in a way that is uneven? Are we part of the cause for some of the machinery that won't work? Is our broadcasting of it not smooth and flowing but uneven and causing problems?

When you tense your muscles in your physical body, you have a tendency to either move in an ungainly fashion or to suddenly release that energy out of necessity. If you find, for instance, that some part of your body hurts a little bit — not a big pain, just a very slight ache — you might just need to get up and move around, all right? Moving around is something that used to be very typical for everybody, but now there are many more sedentary things to do than there were even 100 years ago. I think the first time people became more sedentary was when the radio came along or entertainment like that. And now you have work reasons to remain sedentary, such as the computer.

Generally speaking, if you're working at a computer or watching television or doing anything sedentary, it would be very good for you to get up and walk around at least once an hour. This is actually an answer to your question. You're asking whether somehow a human being might broadcast a sudden jolt of energy that would cause harm to a device they were using, and I'm saying no. But if there are enough human beings in a given space and they are all tense and uncomfortable and they need to get up and walk around [chuckles], then there can be some anomalies in equipment. In the case of a computer, there could be an anomaly and then five minutes later, it's fine.

All right, so what happens in the next few years? Is this percentage of electricity going to increase as we go along, or will we just have to learn to deal with what we have?

I don't think you can really tolerate too much more electricity unless you become much more physically active. Those of you who are physically active will be able to tolerate a little bit more, but you're not going to have to. No, what you do now to help and support Mother Earth, you do because you are consciously making the effort through some spiritual phenomenon or through something you do physically — perhaps with a group, perhaps on your own — or unconsciously because you yourself are becoming heightened in your electrical and magnetic capabilities, becoming kind of like a small, low-powered generator, and you are able, even when you are asleep, to support some of the things that Mother Earth did with electricity and magnetism before, which supports life in general.

One more thing: I know quite a few of you are having trouble sleeping. I can assure you that if you are able to move around and even take a walk in your home or something — walk or run in place or something (you don't have to do major calisthenics) — if you can move around like that about an hour before you go to sleep, or in some cases even twenty minutes before you go to sleep, especially if you're trying to take a nap, you will find that you sleep much deeper and much longer.

Sunspots Support Earth and the Other Planets

The solar surges, the ejections of solar energy onto the Earth — are those electric, or do they have some other composition?

Sunspots? They are definitely something that is happening to support Earth as a planet and the other planets in the solar system. But the formation of sunspots is also being done to support the lack of Mother Earth being able to support you physically with the energy that she has supported you with before. Of course, you get a lot of support from Spirit, but that goes without saying.

Now, I know you're talking about major sunspots that have been seen and so forth. This is mostly to support other planets. Recently, there was one, I think, that was noted by a lot of people, but if you look at it, it is quite obvious that the blast of energy was not actually headed for Earth. That's because it was headed for other planets in the solar system, including a few moons. There are some moons that will develop into places that can be habitable for life as you know it. So what you saw on that recent event was not aimed at you — sort of like seeing a splash from the side, all right? It was headed somewhere else, but you were able to see a portion, you might say, of the side effect.

But when sunspots do come to Earth — you say to support humans when Mother Earth can't — what do we receive from that? What is the chemistry or the mechanics?

Really, most of what comes to Earth that supports humans is sunlight, so generally speaking, take note of sunspots or sudden bursts of energy like that. Does it actually appear to be headed toward Earth? I know that there's an outflow toward Earth, but is it actually aimed toward Earth? Very often, it is not. Still, because it is happening while you are in its general area [chuckles], you will get a blast of energy. Just be physical and it won't bother you so much. I know that's not what you're asking, but generally speaking, it's supporting other life forms on Earth. You have to remember that you are not the only life form on Earth. The Sun does not exist in this solar system exclusively to support Earth human beings. There are a great many other beings on your planet, as well as beings on some of the other planets. You know, it might be for them.

For now, I'll sign off with this: These days, the biggest challenge for you has been having enough time in the day to do all you need to do and the ability to stop it all so that you can sleep well at night. I'm going to make a suggestion that some of you will not like, but I have to make it again: Seriously consider your exposure to electrically radiating devices. You're getting plenty of electricity as it is.

I know that a great many of you must sit in front of computers. If the computer has a flat screen, it's not throwing off too much electricity, but if you're sitting in front of an old screen, that's just like sitting in front of an old television set. It's too much, okay? And if you then go home and watch TV, it's way too much. So I'm going to suggest — I know this is not popular — to watch less television and to be more active. You'd be surprised how many real friends you can make with a simple walk around the neighborhood. Good life.

CHAPTER SIXTEEN

A Truly Global Currency Is Coming

Spirit of Famed Economist

August 8, 2011

I'm going to address a current situation, if you don't mind. I am a being, a spirit, if you would, of a famed economist in the past. That's all I'm going to say. I want to reassure people in your times. I know you are going through some difficulties with the value of things and that for a long time, specie — otherwise known as money — has been circulating as a substitute for the old forms of exchange, which is barter or trade, and that has made commercial interaction much more convenient. But now your planet is unifying (though it may not be completely obvious), and as a result of the unification process, you are easing toward a global currency. I know some of you are worried and are taking money out of the banks and so on, but I do not expect banks to fail. Perhaps the odd weak bank might, but most likely, this will be safe. You see, right now even with countries that are not particularly friendly toward each other and are definitely competitive, you have a global business community.

The big problem, the real struggle going on politically, right now in economics is currency. And there are battles with that — not physical fisti-cuffs or anything, but there are serious problems. You need more than just a standardized currency, meaning whatever is popular; you must have a genuine global currency. For a time, people wanted to say, "Well, we could have some kind of silver or gold," but really there is too much claim on those precious metals for other purposes, some of which are industrial and cannot be replaced by anything else and of course some of which are decorative, and the desire for the uses for it decoratively is not going to go away any time soon.

So it makes much more sense to have a global currency that is not associated with any single country, meaning it won't be the euro, it won't be the yen, or it won't be the drachma. It will be something new. What will occur is something along this line: It will be something that the banks and governments will get together. They've already done that and have said, "We've got to have this." And what will happen is that nobody will lose any money. Your money is going to be safe in the banks, but you'll essentially wind up getting an exchange rate, okay? This will take a few years to work out, and the global currency will not be with you prob-ably for at least six or seven years, but it's actually needed right now. And when you have this global currency, not just something that you're told you must have, you'll all breathe a sigh of relief — everybody.

Even if you're buying a cup of coffee in Paris or in Boston, you'll say, "Why didn't they do this years ago?" because it's so sensible. Europe has gotten together and formed the currency for a wide area across coun-tries. Even though the euro's struggling a bit now, it will become more steady, as will all currencies, toward the end of this month or early next month. But these are all preparatory situations. Once the global cur-rency is established, then you will be able to trade easily and comfort-ably, and everybody will know what the value of anything is based on a single currency.

It's coming. So I want to assure you that it will be all right. Please do not [chuckles] try to bring down your banks with the best of inten-tions. Having money in the bank is a good thing, and the banks will not cheat you. If you're worried about it, you can check on it. You know how much you have in there, and you'll get your fair exchange of the new cur-rency. This will be something that's talked of in the United Nations, but ultimately, it will be resolved by the global business community and the governments, and everybody will be happy with it. So don't worry about that. I wanted to come through and say that. All right?

A Global Currency Will Bring Stability

Like you said, why didn't they do that years ago?

Well, they would have loved to have done it years ago, but the competition and the struggle between systems of politics were extreme, and there wasn't any uniting factor. But now, regardless of political systems, you have something in place called "fair trade" that's going on between countries. And even if a country is competitive based on nationalism or religion or political system, there's still the recognition that global trade and business is a good thing. This is the foundation of your unification.

Ultimately, it won't be how the planet goes as a human race and becomes spiritually aware and everybody loving and all that. This is going to take a few years. But in terms of your initial organization and structure, it's now possible. You don't have to wait any longer, because the common interest of the business community and every single person who uses and/or benefits from money — which is just about everybody — is going to be in agreement that this is a good thing.

This will bring about the stability of governments, the stability of societies, and of course the stability and predictability of conditions so that people can make plans. They can say, "I want to send my sons and daughters to college. I want to plan ahead so I can buy a house. I want to pay off my mortgage. I want my family to be happier and live better than I did." In short, people can make short- and long-range plans, and they can be dependable because you have global, political, financial, and economical stability. So I wanted to reassure you — and it is all coming now — there's nothing you have to do. It is in place; as a citizen, you don't have to do anything. It's being resolved right now, so don't let all of the fuss and the upset and the worry about the dollar and the euro and every other currency bother you.

We love to get news like this because money and credit and deficits are a big struggle for many countries now.

They are a struggle, and most — pretty soon it will be all — of the governments in the world really do want this, and almost all the governments, to say nothing of the global business community that desperately wants it, will welcome it. Initially, there will be some fussing about how it should be "this" currency or "that" currency, and that's really what's been holding it up, but ultimately, people will recognize that this is everybody's best interest, not just the global business community's. This is about people having stability in their society and being able to make plans and see them come to fruition. Everybody will benefit.

Common Exchange Will Allow Long-Range Plans

That must give you pleasure to be able to say that. Can you say anything about who you are?

I want to keep it simple. I'll just say I lived a physical life a couple hundred years ago, and that's all I'm going to say about that.

I've been interested because I spoke about these matters years ago and felt then not very differently than I do now — that what was holding back trade was not having a common means of exchange that could be planned ahead for, because no matter how good you were at farming in my time on Earth, crops could not be absolutely depended on. There was no irrigation and so on as you know it today, so you had to just hope. You couldn't make long-range plans, and that was the problem. But now you have all kinds of technology, and you can make long-range plans.

You just need to have a convenient way for everybody to communicate, and there will be a general global language that will continue to evolve, and it will be partly English and partly other people's languages, and it will be known as the business language. It will be sort of a mix of a lot of things, and eventually it will evolve into something that people will not understand unless they're part of the global business community. This has already begun. So I would say that, generally speaking, things are looking up.

I just wanted to come through and reassure people that as chaotic as things are now and as disorganized as they seem to be, it's just temporary. You know, if you, even in your family, decide to do things differently, everybody tends to do things the old way for a while because they forget, and so things are a bit chaotic for a time. But then you start to discover things that you like about what you're doing differently, about the new thing that you're doing, and the more you discover you like it, the more you do it.

Generally, the children adapt to it more quickly, and it's the same way with this. Now in your world, you find that young people are communicating globally on their various Internet things. They adapted to that technology and embraced it almost immediately. It's the same in the family, and it's not that different in governments and in business. Initially, the young strongly go for the new idea, but the old are still in power, so they take a little time to catch on and realize that "Hey, the world is changing, and things are getting better. We have to acknowledge it and embrace it, and we can still be influential, but maybe we have to stand back a couple paces and let these young people reorganize things." That's what's coming. So I just wanted to come through today and reassure you because I know there's a lot of confusion and discomfort and so on, but it's going to get better very soon. Good night.

CHAPTER SEVENTEEN

You Have to Be Conscious Now – Be in the Present

Isis

August 10, 2011

All right, this is Isis. Now, this is just a reminder that you are moving through what feels like a minefield at times, but that is because you are literally changing your way of doing everything. You've been doing things by thought and mostly by the prompting of others, and except for the very young and those who are trained in various ways, instinct has largely been put to the side. Instinct is something that is rooted in your physical feelings and is also beyond your physical feelings to a perimeter that varies around your body, given how far your auric field has stretched out. So it's your physical feelings and your energy body.

Now, I bring that up because a factor of your natural existence is something called vertical memory. This means that you can recall something — something that comes either from your own experience or from the experience of others — that is a proven fact and can be utilized as wisdom because it works in your life. That's vertical memory (another term for that is "vertical wisdom"), and you're easing into that again because that's what you do in spirit. Until recently, you've been using linear memory for your experience in this dimension you're living in — roughly [chuckles], right now you're in about the 3.5 dimension, if there was one, to give you an idea.

Your Vertical Memories Trigger Physical Feelings

What you are currently experiencing is a difficulty with your instinct because many of you will have imaginations, and usually this is all right. You have fantasies, perhaps. You also have memories, and sometimes you even make plans — what you're going to say and how you're going to say it, sometimes, as one might do as a teacher or a presenter. Other times, maybe you're going to ask your boss for a raise. In short, in your head you go through what will happen. Other times, you fantasize about something that hasn't happened in reality but that could or might. Other times, you have a spiritual conversation, but you are awake — like that. Then you also have memories that trigger physical feelings.

All of what I have just said triggers physical feelings, but where you are getting confused now is that your linear time is gradually moving into a state in which time will be vertical. Now, you understand this is abstract and not scientific, okay? But when you get to the point where you are at about 3.58 and 3.60, you'll be in vertical time for a while as you ease over into 4.0, meaning the fourth dimension. And without getting too esoteric, I'll say that what is going to happen — and what is actually happening at the level you're at now, which is right around 3.53, easing into 3.54 — is that you're experiencing times when you are in vertical time instead of linear time.

In vertical time, what's occurring is that your intersections of linear time and vertical time are clashing somewhat. And when you have a fantasy and you're imagining something — or any kind of imagination, even making a plan — it's going to stimulate physical feelings in your body exactly the same as your physical feelings might be stimulated in your body from an actual memory. This can create a problem, because if you're an especially conscious person working on being spiritually conscious — being in the present, being in the now, all of that — and you utilize the physical feelings in your body to know what you might need to do at any given moment, you can get confused.

So here is a suggestion: Try not to do any fantasizing — dreaming, hoping, planning, wishing — when you're driving a car, when you're at work, when you're going places, when you're doing things. Try to do that during quiet time. I'm not saying don't do it; I'm saying try to do that during a quiet time when little to nothing is demanded of you. This situation will prevail. Really, for most people it will start in about three to six months, and it will be ongoing off and on until you're locked into the fourth dimension. So just be aware of it because it's going to affect your life.

Be Conscious to Thrive in These Times

If you're having feelings that you might normally respond to in a specific way, you're going to have to pay attention to what you've been thinking. Were you worrying? Were you having a conversation in your mind? Were you planning? Were you fantasizing? If none of that's going on — and it doesn't require much thought to just notice what you were thinking — then respond using your feelings.

All right. I can see where that could create some confusion in our lives.

Yes, and that's part of the reason that the training has been going on the way it has primarily on the blogs for the general public — and spiritual people mostly go there anyway, but it's aimed out there to touch the general public. Really quite a bit in the Shamanic Secrets books and, for the most part, the whole Explorer Race series is aimed toward preparing people for these times, because you have to have discernment, and if you have judgment, you're going to possibly shove away quite an extensive amount of your own ability to perceive what is essential. So that's why the fine line to know what's judgment and what's discernment is essential. Discernment, of course, is applying that which you know, that which is your wisdom, whereas judgment might have to do with blaming and using other people's perceptions that you have purchased (essentially, bought into) or simply inherited through your socialization. That is just one example.

Yes, it can do that. It's not, what you say, stimulating your linear memory to fall away — because you need to have it in linear time — but in those moments ... I don't want to really call it clashing. I want to say that it's sort of a superimposition of both, one atop the other. So they're both happening in the same moment, and you have to try to sort out what's what. If you can tell you were thinking, then you're dealing with a response like you described. But on the other hand, if you weren't thinking, then you can just act on the basis of how you might normally act in response to that physical feeling.

You have to literally be conscious now. You can't simply go unconscious. You have to be conscious not necessarily to survive but to thrive in these times. You'll have to be conscious. You have to notice what's going on in the present moment, because the present moment is not only where life is occurring for everyone but it's also the place of opportunity. And sometimes opportunity is missed very easily because you are thinking about something in the past or fantasizing about something, and you are not really in the present moment. And most people who do that miss lots of opportunities.

Welcome All Opportunities That Might Serve You

Here's something I recommend you do. It's something simple, but it will be surprisingly effective. First, ask for all the most benevolent energies that are available for you to be all round you and all about you. Then pause for about fifteen or twenty seconds. Then say:

> *Benevolent Magic*
> "I am asking that I be able to welcome all benevolent and wonderful opportunities, experiences, and any other that might serve me so that I can thrive during these times, and that my welcoming will happen without my having to be conscious of it. It will be natural and easy, and it will happen in the most benevolent way for me now."

Naturally, if at any time during any of those words — and it's all right to write them down so that you can say them verbatim (always try to say these things verbatim) — the energy comes up for you, pause and wait until it fades a bit. That's the beings — the lightbeings, your guides, angels, everybody — helping you to bring it about. Then when it feels right to you, continue on with the words. Always do that. And I need to remind you of that from time to time because it's easy to forget and just go right on through the words, especially if you're reading them.

Some of you will feel the need to move your hands and arms. That's quite all right to do when you're saying these things. It very often helps the energy. That way your body might make a better commitment to the energy. But don't do it if you don't have a feeling to do it; only do it if you have a feeling to do it. Some of you might feel the need to move other parts of your body, but try to stay in one place because the energy will tend to be in that place. If you dance around, you might step out of the energy and not experience the culmination of what it is you are asking for. So that's what I recommend for you today. Good life.

CHAPTER EIGHTEEN

Flowing with the Change in the Circle of Life

Ortho

August 19, 2011

This is Ortho. I am a guide and teacher associated with aquatic beings. Lately I have been welcoming aquatic beings on their pathway home, as only those who have direct knowledge given to them or specific capabilities to pass that knowledge on to human beings are going to stay on Earth now. Other than that, the reincarnational cycle has been diminished or removed from a great many species. This does not mean they won't exist, but they will exist on other planets — perhaps their home, perhaps some place they wish to visit, but no longer on Earth as you know it.

As you know, Earth as a planet is changing. This is not surprising. While a certain amount of mining and digging around can be tolerated, past that point, it cannot. Forty years ago, your planet was intended to have the types of products, services, and so on, that exist on other planets, but there was so much fear and resistance — not just from the "powers that be," as you say, but also from individuals — that those who had come to deliver such capabilities withdrew on their own without being asked to. Granted, there were some messages delivered sixty or even seventy years ago that the day would come when Earth would be invited into the party, the welcoming party of other planetary citizens, but that was not placed into the overriding knowledge and wisdom of the planet because of factionalization. While some people knew and were prepared to welcome such visitors, others did not, and the sharing of knowledge and wisdom became complicated.

Now, however, you are experiencing a revitalization of the welcoming feeling, and Earth, after all this time, is moving toward the alterations any planet would have to make because of that extra forty years of mining and drilling and so on. So if you can, as a people (meaning all Earth people), welcome visitors from other planets — *true* visitors from other planets, I should say — then it might be possible to bring you up to speed, so to speak, in order to engage with those capabilities known on other planets.

All Nonhumans Have Received the Message of the Circle

Here's the issue: Messages, sometimes really elaborate ones, were given by those visitors from other planets in the past, as I've said, and there are documents that exist in this or that culture that lay out in very precise detail who will come, how they will help, what they will offer, and so on. But since this information has not been widely disseminated — and by widely disseminated, we do not mean just from one governmental body to another in secret forums, but widely disseminated to everybody on the planet — the delay has been a problem.

However, now you have the circumstance that people all over the planet are communicating with each other, and that will continue. This general feeling of welcoming as well as an awareness of the conditions, the real conditions that people live in all over the planet — not just as a theory but as a fact — is creating an air of welcome: welcome to change and welcome to benevolence, meaning a good and kind world for all people.

There have been messages in your contemporary times from nonhumans, and one of the most profound form of message is something that is a symbol that goes back to ancient times. In ancient times, the symbol of completeness, that which is complete, has always been a circle. Now the aquatic Earth beings, as well as Earth herself, have been putting forth a message of the circle. This message is how nonhuman beings know that they do not have to stay or that they could stay to answer a question you didn't get a chance to ask yet.

The circle message has been delivered by aquatic beings at sea and in lakes and in rivers, and sometimes whole colonies of aquatic beings have seen that message. But the circle message has also been coming in other forms, even in smoke and steam rings from volcanoes and other messages, including your crop circles, so that all nonhumans on the planet who are associated with the planet have received that message now. This is why a lot of them are leaving: Their knowledge and wisdom is not something you need to know anymore, and the circle message, while being about completion, is also about changes in the circle of life.

All Life Is Now Personal for Earth Humans

Now, in order to adapt and instill these changes on Earth, they are happening in every human being, whether you've been here for 80, 90, or even 100 years or you're just being born. For most of you, the changes are happening in your chest and, to some degree, in your midsection and lower section, meaning your abdomen. These changes have to do with anchoring your physical body so that you can feel and be connected to all life on this planet.

The first thing you need to know is that sometimes when you get a quick pain and then it passes, it means someone somewhere — or more likely a group of beings, maybe humans, maybe nonhumans — needs your assistance. And by "your," I do not mean they generally need the assistance of human beings; I mean that they need actual assistance from you as a person. If you are a religious person, it would be good to say a prayer according to your religion. If you are interested in the things that are taught in these pages, then you might start that off by doing the following. Say, "I am asking that all the most benevolent energies that are available for me be all around me, in and out, and supportive of all portions of me now in the most benevolent way." Wait a moment. Some of you will feel the energy. You might only feel it a little bit, but it will still be present. Then you can say,

Living Prayer
"I am asking that those who are calling on me for my assistance and help now receive all the help they need in the most benevolent way for them."

It's all right to pause when you're saying that if there is energy that comes out. These things are personal. The big change in the circle of life that has happened for all of you is that all life for you now is personal —

your own, yes of course, but all life on the planet is personal for you. It's no longer birds and cows and humans and dogs; it's that all life is personal.

Eating Meat Has Become Very Difficult

This is what happened with the animals in the past twenty years. All life suddenly became personal, and there was a confusion because that had been the case when they existed, you see, on other planets. But when it became personal, it became a bit more difficult to consume other life forms because you felt their discomfiture at being consumed; they felt it as an animal consuming somebody else. And at the same time, they felt as if they were consuming themselves. Understand that on other planets, those you know as animals do not normally consume each other. That's unique to this planet. Therefore, when they literally took on their native, natural ways of being on this planet as the essence of the beings they are on other planets in these past twenty years, you can see how that would be difficult, since this planet is not like other planets that they have lived on.

Now that same thing is happening for human beings. That's why this is important to bring forward at this time: Some of you have noticed that it's getting almost impossible to eat meat or fish. You can consume it, but it's very difficult, and that's because you are going through the exact same thing the animals were going through for the past twenty years, as I just mentioned. And going through this is difficult, because on the one hand, you will feel as if you are causing pain to somebody else — even though the meat, for most of you, has already been processed and doesn't look like the animal. But you will know what the animal or the combination of animals looked like in most cases, and sometimes it does look like it did when it was alive, and then there's no denying it.

I want to let you know, however, that if you do need to eat meat or fish, you will be able to eat a very small portion and still get the protein and other things you need, and then you can eat other things. It's also going to be a good time for those of you who farm and raise nuts and other crops that are known for having a considerable amount of protein, because the demand for these things is going to increase meteorically. I'm not saying that everybody is going to become vegetarian; I am saying that you just won't need as much for your diets — the food you eat, you understand. And at the same time, you won't be able to eat as much. You'll be able to remember that just a few years ago, you could have eaten a whole steak. Now you eat just a little bit of it, a few bites and that's it. That's all you can eat, but it fills you up. It satiates you; it feeds you.

So it's important to know these things now, because when it happens — and it's been happening for many of you for the past three to six months or so — it will not only happen in that year but it will build beyond that time so that eventually, you'll only be able to eat a tiny bite of that steak. And that tiny bite will be enough. This doesn't mean, as I say, that you have to be a vegetarian, but compared to the way you were, you'll feel as if you are a vegetarian.

One good thing about this change is that the supplies of these things — meats and fish and so on — have been growing a little bit thin, and it's been a little difficult for those who raise or catch these beings to get enough for everybody. So not only are you going to feel like eating a great deal less of these types of foods, but the quantity you have now will serve everyone who eats meat or fish. In this way, changes in the circle of life are affecting human beings as well.

Creating without Thinking

There are other changes. There will be changes in what you have done by thought in the past — for example, something that requires thought. If you're going to, say, build a shed out in the back of your property to keep tools and implements in or other things, then you have to plan ahead, yes? "I need this and this and this, and how much of this and how much time …" In short, you have to think it out. And when you're building it — say you're using wood — you have to make measurements. You have to think about it. There are other examples, but I have chosen that one.

What will be happening — and some of you have been noticing it for a few years now, especially those of you in the profession of carpentry, and others will notice this, even amateurs — is that you will be able to go to the store where you buy supplies for such projects, and you'll be able to acquire what you need without thinking. You'll look at certain things, and you'll know: "That's what I need." You'll bring the supplies home, and you'll be able to use tools, especially those of you who are trained in these things — or for those of you who are not trained and look at power tools and for some reason they make you nervous, you'll use hand tools — and you'll enjoy making the cuts and building the shed, and you won't be thinking about it too much.

You'll know where you are, and you'll know not to put your fingers in the way of the saw, but you'll find that building the shed will be a great pleasure the slower you go. And when you are done and you look at it, you'll feel good about it. You'll find that you want to sand the wood down very slowly so that it's so smooth on the inside and on the outside that you'll almost not want to paint it. Many more sheds will be stained with wood stain, even old varnish, than have been in the past when they were painted or covered in other ways, maybe shingled.

In short, you will be able to do these things without thinking. People who are journeyman carpenters have been able to do it because they've done it for so long, and there will still be plenty of work for people like that. But even you, the professionals, will find that thought will not be necessary. It will be not only inspired but almost as if you don't have to think, and that's something that comes under the heading of vertical wisdom, as described through this channel.

Inspiration and Instinct Will Be Part of One's Daily Experience

Now, there is more. Raising children has always been challenging. Part of the reason for this, of course, is that many parents don't get training to be parents when they are young. For those who do, raising children is easier and more of a joyful experience. Yet those who don't have training have been struggling, and things have not been working well. Now you will be inspired. Even if you've never had the opportunity to really study what a parent does, you will be inspired. Inspiration will be so much a part of your day-to-day life that you will not be able to understand how you ever lived without it. But it will not be inspiration of words — it won't be "do this; do that." You will simply find yourself doing something, and the inspiration will be physical. It will be on a feeling level, but you won't think about it.

When you have inspirations in your body and you feel something, you tend to think about it: "What does that mean?" Now you won't find that. You'll get an inspiration in your body, and you'll just do it. You don't think about it. And you will know it's inspiration because it will come with a genuine feeling, a comfortable feeling of warmth. You'll feel that warmth, and you'll just start doing something. It will be good for you, and it will be good for others. Sometimes it will be something simple. You'll perhaps be sitting at home in the evening with your mate, and suddenly you'll get up and go into the other room — perhaps to the kitchen to brew a pot of tea and pour a cup and come back and give the cup to your mate, and your mate says, "How did you know that's just what I wanted?" You see, it will be like that. And after a couple of years, you won't even say, "How did you know that's just what I wanted?" You'll just smile when someone gives you the tea or you give the tea to someone else.

It is in your nature to be instinctual. Now and beyond, being instinctual will gradually become part of your day-to-day life. Know that it is coming from the most benevolent beings: creators, angels, guides, your greater soul's self. It is synchronizing you so that you will be able to flow easily as you complete the move from the third to the fourth dimension. There is no need to wait for fifty years for this to happen. You're about halfway there now.

As all of you easily become more instinctual in this benevolent, comfortable, good and kind way, you will not have to make an effort to be good. You will not have to make an effort to be kind. When you are instinctual, it just is. That's what you do, and that's what others do for you. Then there is no resentment. There is no anger. There is no payback. Everything just smoothly clicks into place. And the more that happens, the more it allows the shift from third to fourth dimension to only take a couple to three years instead of fifty. So why wait?

The Profound Message of the Circle

These changes in the circle of life are heralded by circles all about you, and circles that are seen by the animals and on the land. And you'll notice how the circle comes to be a predominant design. All kinds of fabrics, even symbols, will take on circular and spherical shapes. There will be many more talks about "this" form of circle and "that" form of circle. Clubs will be called circles, and so on. Old, ancient understandings of the circle will be incorporated in your life.

Know that these are good times and good signs. People you have known with whom you have not been comfortable or people you have been at odds with or people who have been at odds with you or worse — all of these things will be forgiven and let go of and, in time, forgotten because it is better to have a complete circle of life that embraces and welcomes everyone. And everyone living instinctually like that is able to shed harm, anger, and other discomforting aspects — violence and so on. It just falls away from you as a need. There will be no need to strike back or to strike first.

Wow! I'm scanning my notes here because this is pretty awesome. You're saying that what we've been talking about as in the future is happening right now.

It's important to explain the nature of these mysteries so that people understand there's a purpose. Dolphins are not just playing a game when they create those circles with air bubbles. And the enigmatic game of the circles that the dolphins seem to be playing is intended by them to draw human beings' attention. Earth has also been displaying smoke and steam rings and other circles that have been enigmas. It's important to understand that there is a meaning to these circles, and it is not just a mystery intended to keep you confused. You know, when human beings do not understand a mystery, others must come forward to deliver the message in the best way they know how.

All crop circles up to now, aside from any other meanings they have, are aimed to give messages to nonhumans. As a result, the messages spread far and wide, and eventually nonhumans began giving messages to human beings by doing things that drew human beings' attention. One of the main things that has been fascinating people for several years now is dolphins' playing with these rings that they create, and whales have been doing it as well. And it is seen. It is filmed; it is not faked. And you can see them doing it, especially the whales. They might blow one directly at you. You have seen the video, eh? [**Editor's Note:** If you have not seen any videos of this behavior, we highly recommend looking up "dolphin bubble rings" on the Internet for some lovely examples.] And then when the bubble dissipates, they turn. They don't play with it; they're blowing it at the person with the camera. They do understand there's a film going on, and the moment the ring dissipates, they turn and go away, telling you that's the message: the ring, the circle, the circle of life. They cannot speak to you in words, so they speak to you in symbols.

Earth Humans Are Born with Natural Understanding

The circle symbol is the most profound message that has been given over time. You can look at carvings in stone going back thousands of years, and you will find the circle. Such things were left for you by previous civilizations. You can find kivas, circular structures left by civilizations that have moved on, and even though the tops of the kivas have caved in because what they were covered with rotted or parts have been removed by others, the foundations of the kivas are there in circles that are set into the earth. And this also is a message: Changes in the circle of life are designed to bring you into alignment with your natural, native, soul-spirit being.

The best part about it now is that you don't have to change what you think. You don't have to change your mind. You just become your natural self. All babies are born with this natural understanding, and even though you have to adapt as a child to becoming part of the culture you live in, you have that knowledge and that awareness in you because you were born with it. All human babies born on Earth in all time have that knowledge. So you won't have to learn something; it is in your nature.

There has always been the circle of life. It changes with the passing time, then — the meaning of it, the point of it — right?

The assumption in the contemporary understanding of the circle of life has to do with a hierarchy. But hierarchy has nothing to do with the circle of life. This is a way that human beings have adjusted to their apparent — at times — dominance over other forms of life, yet one is reminded at different times that other forms of life might just be able to superimpose their dominance. It's not about dominance; it's about the connections between all life, the equality of all life, and the family of all life. It's always been that.

Yes. But we know we have to achieve unity.

No, that's a mistake. You're mistaken. I'm interrupting you because the messages cover this. You don't have to achieve it.

That's right. When you think of achieving something, you *think* of achieving it. "How am I going to do this?" you ask. Then a myriad of plans come forward about how to achieve that, and in fact, some of them are in conflict with others. If you had to achieve it, it would be difficult. And as a civilization, an Earth human civilization, you have not been able to achieve it and hold it, because it always involved a system, and not everybody wanted to be a portion of that system. But if it is your nature, then you don't have to achieve it; you are simply reconstituting something you are, something you were born with. And when you do that, achieving is not necessary.

It's important to understand this. If you understand it, then you can picture yourself in the circle. When babies are born, they are a circle. They don't start a circle; they *are* a circle. This means that they are going to continue around that circle or the sphere, move around in different portions of the sphere but always in a whole, complete thing, including others who are moving around in that same sphere. It's not an accident that planets are round. Complete planets on which people live and cultures grow and thrive are round. There are plenty of asteroids big enough and even in pretty good shape enough to have a civilization, but you don't find civilizations on anything other than planets that are round. Everything is about the circle.

I don't like to interrupt you when you are asking a question, but when the question is based on all you have been taught in the past and all you have learned, however accurate it was for those times, however it helped you to come to be who you are now, it is overly complicated when it is all a portion of the circle you were born into. All babies know this.

Thank you so much. Thank you.

CHAPTER NINETEEN

Supernova Is an Expansion into Other Dimensions, Not an Explosion

Cassiopeia

January 23, 2012

Cassiopeia.

Welcome.

A Supernova Is a Creation Process

I have the remembrance of talking to you one time, and you said that you needed to break up. You had learned all you could in your present form, and you needed to break up so that you could start over again, or something like that.

I needed to create a window, an opening, so that I could branch out, in a sense — meaning, like a tree that has its trunk but also its branches, which explore different directions. Like that.

So it's not clear — humans call five stars in that area of space the Cassiopeia constellation. Do you identify with one star or the constellation?

The constellation.

So one star went supernova, but the rest are still intact?

Yes.

How do you get more branches by one star exploding?

It's actually a window. And it's not actually an explosion — it just looks like it. If you were on your own planet and something exploded, you would usually see residue — dust, bits, and pieces coming out in

Figure 19.1. NASA image of the historical supernova remnant Cassiopeia A, located 11,000 light-years away (www.nasa.gov).

places, you understand? But what is seen is that stars, suns, do not explode. They expand. And when they expand, they can only expand so far in your visible light spectrum, which you could call the third dimension, allowing for the passage of light and time and so on. It happened a while back, and you see it when the light catches up to you.

What's actually happening is the star can only expand so much within the third dimension, so it has to essentially migrate. So when you see a supernova, what's actually happening is that there's the light, which is the creation process. And then the star, the rest of it, goes into another dimension — usually the fifth or the sixth or something like that — where it is much larger than it once was. That's what's *really* happening in a supernova. It's not like you would have an explosion on Earth — nothing like that. It's a *creation* process; it is *not* a destruction process.

This Universe *Is* Creator

Wow. Thank you for that. Can you tell me something about yourself? Most everyone in this universe was invited here by the Creator because they had a particular talent or energy. Did that happen with you?

Well, Creator was interested in variety for this universe, as you know. But Creator also wanted something to temper Its variety, meaning Creator understood Creator's own buoyancy when it came to overenthusiasm and asked for a few beings to come along who would keep Creator from going way, way over Its own capacity, to sort of keep an eye on that portion of It so that It turns into a creation. This creation, this universe, literally *is* Creator, and that is why beings will say to you that we are all one and that you are Creator and all this kind of stuff — because the universe is a portion of Creator. But Creator is much more than that. But still, within the physical concept, including all of the different dimensions, what is represented in any creation is Creator manifest physically. Of course, any creator is going to be more than its physical aspect. So Creator did ask for a few beings to come along who would keep Creator from going too far.

This Creator is so enthusiastic, so full of life, if you will, that It could have created a creation twenty times as large, even on the third dimension. But that wouldn't have worked for what Creator wanted to *do* with this creation, which was to have variety but to essentially have categories of variety that could be built on later as inspiration struck — not only for Creator, but as it turns out, for those who will follow in Creator's footsteps, so to speak.

Thus, you will find that as you, the Explorer Race, become Creator — you might say "Creator's apprentice" — you will find that there will be a great many avenues (categories, you might say) of creation that you'll want to pursue, and at the same time, many categories that you will not be interested in pursuing. But the variety of categories is what we feel is best for Creator to do, rather than to expand every single category, so we have encouraged Creator to focus on categories. Granted, Creator does not always do that, but Creator wanted our advice. He didn't want a boss. So that's why we came along. And there are several others who agree with our position, and this is what Creator wants. Creator wants sort of an ad hoc committee, you might say, that could advise Creator, even though Creator will do what It chooses.

When you say "we," that includes you and who?

Others who came along. One is in the seventh dimension, one is in the thirteenth, one is in the sixteenth, and we are in the third. We are also represented in other dimensions, quite obviously, or our Sun, which you recently saw become brighter, couldn't go to the sixth dimension — it is sort of in passage now to the sixth dimension.

The Wisdom of Cassiopeia

How did you get the wisdom that you have to be able to advise Him? What is your experience before you came here?

No — that's linear time.

Okay. Please explain.

Very simple — I've always had this.

What did you do before you came here?

That's linear time. I'm bringing you up short on that because I want the reader to understand that the questions you are asking would be typical questions that anybody on your planet would ask. But in fact, linear time, as you're experiencing it, is incredibly slower than any other linear time in this universe — or any that I've encountered anywhere. And it's that slow because Creator wanted you to have a chance to understand what you might call the "microsteps" from one step to another — in that sense, understanding the fractions as compared to the whole numbers. This is something that Creator felt was important for you. Therefore, you experience linear time on your planet *very much* more slowly than linear time anywhere else.

So the way I would experience my personality is ongoing — there is no linear time whatsoever. Even though you see my ... galaxy [constellation], let's say, eh? ... you see me as something that you can measure: "Now it looks this way, now it looks that way, oh, then it looked this way." That is your perception. It is as if you are looking through a lens of your own version of linear time, and you perceive everything through that lens. When you look through a lens like that at a world beyond, you will see things within the context of your own understanding. That is why, since you see explosions ... and say, for instance, a volcano erupts with some enthusiasm. Then there would be an explosion, followed by material — dust and so on. And you would naturally assume that if you see a bright light somewhere in space, something is probably exploding, because if you saw that on your planet, that's what you would think. But

I've already explained that is not the case. In any event, I am who I am, and I've always had this wisdom. I didn't acquire it.

I might add that you are exactly the same. When you are your natural, native personalities as your souls and spirit selves, you don't *acquire* knowledge — you *have* the knowledge. And that makes complete sense when you think about it, because Creator, yes, makes up this creation, and you are a portion of that creation, and you are a portion of Creator. And you can, if it makes you happy, think about that as a brain, but of course it isn't. In your brain, each cell has its own knowledge and wisdom, all right? So you have your own knowledge and wisdom when you are beyond being physical, especially in this very slow linear time. You have your own knowledge and wisdom, and you will not have acquired it anywhere. You *are* that knowledge, you *are* that wisdom, you *are* that light, you *are* that love, and so forth.

The Way People Look Identifies Their Personalities in This Space

Did the other four stars in what we call the Cassiopeia constellation — did they come with you? Or were they already here?

I see we have to go back a bit further. Creator creates, yes? Before Creator created this creation, what was here?

Life force, energy, particles ...

No particles.

Empty space?

Receptive space. So I existed, along with other beings asked to come — or welcomed, depending. And then, as the creation manifested, portions of my personality manifested in the shapes and forms you see here. It was creation — all right? — brought about by Creator's desire. But what you see is my personality manifest in physical form in the third dimension. You might see a different form in other dimensions. What does that suggest to each of you personally?

What that suggests is that the way you look — in every way you look in this third-dimension, with very slow linear time on Earth — is your personality manifest with the creation of Creator. This is how you look *in this space*. Time does not factor in. This is how you would look if an identical universe was created by this Creator and there was linear time, like this, and a planet, and everything was the same. You would look exactly like this because it is based on your personality manifest with the energy and physical representation of creation. So you would look like this no matter what circumstance. Of course, in other dimensions, you are different. And in your actual in-between situation where you are not manifest physically, you are a point of light.

I bring this out because — and this is addressed to you, reader — I don't want you to criticize your physical body. This is how you look in *this time*, you might say. This is how you look in this place, and you have looked differently throughout the scope of your life. When you were inside your mother, that's how you looked; when you were a baby, that's how you looked; when you were a teenager, that's how you looked; when you're an adult, that's how you look; and when you're very old and elderly, that will be how you look. It's based entirely on your personality, which is immortal; your soul, which is immortal; and your spirit, which is immortal. Please don't criticize it, or you're literally criticizing Creator and creation.

If you wish to criticize that, go ahead, but it's important for you to know that you're criticizing your own lightbeing, you're criticizing creation, and you're criticizing Creator. You look the way you look because it identifies your personality in this space.

Hmm. So you are all five stars, then — not just one.

Yes. And everything associated with the constellation.

So only one star ... so a part of you, then, is expanding into the next dimension.

Yes, in this case, because the third dimension is particularly volatile now. Even though your planet is well encapsulated, it's uncomfortable for the third dimension of this universe to be exposed to what's going on on your planet. You have to understand that, even though you are totally insulated and the rest of the universe is totally insulated from you ... think about it. It's like having a portion of your body that's there and it's like a bump, something like that. You know that you're safe from it, but it's just uncomfortable. If you've ever sat on something — say you had a wallet in your back pocket and you sat on it — it's just uncomfortable, so you squirm around until you move it out of your back pocket and put it in your purse or in your front pocket, and then you feel better, like that. Only you can't get it out of your back pocket. [Chuckles.]

Okay.

How the Universe Looks through Different Dimensional Lenses

I had a real hit when I saw this picture [of Cassiopeia]. Did you want to speak, or was there some connection or something?

I think there's a soul connection for you.

Really? I've been on that — in your — constellation?

No, you just like the personality.

So what you did then didn't affect your neighbors, like Alpha Centauri or Andromeda?

They would see the expanded light. But the light has to do with creation, so it wouldn't be a bad thing. If you were on such a planet, there would just be a flash of light.

Our scientists say a supernova is something that blasts all the material from the star out into the surrounding area.

It's possible in some cases. It wasn't in this case. Let me just put it this way: If stars actually exploded, you'd see a big chunk of the galaxy just disappear. Explosions do not really exist in space. I know you *think* they do, but that's because of the lens you're looking into.

What kind of lens will we look through when we get to the fourth dimension? Will it be more realistic?

It will be more realistic. And you won't be in the third dimension in any event, so explosions aren't going to happen, period.

But even after we leave this dimension, you will still have portions there? What we see now will still be here, won't it?

Oh, you think that fourth-dimensional space with all the stars and all that business is going to look the same? It wouldn't look anything like that.

No, I didn't know that. I thought we'd just see more of it.

Oh no, no. It's completely different. All other dimensional spaces are totally different. For example (this is one of the more startling differences), when you look into space now, you see points of light that illuminate what is otherwise blacked out, you might say. There's some dimensions where it's completely opposite.

Points of blackness within light?

Yes. And those are not planets. Those are doorways for other places. There are all kinds of different types of things. Remember, what does this Creator like best?

Variety.

That's right. So you will never see the same star fields from one dimension to another. Creator would be oh so bored with that.

The Civilizations and Life Forms of Cassiopeia

The star that is moving to another dimension — did you have planets around that before you began to move?

Well, some of the planets — you understand, some of the constellation — some of the bits and pieces chose to move with that star, but it's much easier for a star to move than for planets to move, so the planets are going a little slower, and they're not occupied at this point. Only the planets that didn't have civilizations were allowed to go.

Okay, so is there anything that we would consider extraordinarily interesting — are there humans there?

Yes, there are.

Are they technological? Are they space travelers? Did they travel to other planets?

Not on their own. If they wanted to, someone would take them. But I don't think they're interested in that at this point, probably because they're very evolved. And anytime they had interest in that in the past, they generally would get a ride on a ship or something like that. But they're well past that. If they want to know about a place, they just can picture it. They can see it.

What we call "long touch"?

No, more what you would call "telepathy."

So they are very evolved. Is your constellation one of the oldest ones in this area of space?

It's hard for me to say that, because everything is the same age. Everything. There is no form of energy, manifest physically or otherwise, in this creation that is any other age, including you.

Yes, we all came out of unmanifestation at the same time, right? Did any of your beings ever come to Earth to have a colony here or seed a civilization here?

Yes, I think we had some water beings there for a while, but they've all come home now. But we had some pretty big dolphins there for a while — about the size of orcas.

That's big!

Yes, they were very pleasant, slow moving. But they really need vast amounts of fresh, clear water, not salt water, so they were in lakes. But they came home quite a while back. I'm trying to think of something else you might be able to identify with. We had some very ancient "clams," I think you call them. They've all come home.

So you have very many water planets?

Quite a few.

Manifest Personalities in Multidimensionality

You are a constellation, so everything in that area of space is part of you?

Well, you have to keep in mind that there are other ... okay, the simple answer to your question is yes. But there are other constellations nearby, and their personalities come and go, expand and contract, just like mine. You might say, within your context, that your personality expands and contracts also — not only if you're more enthusiastic about something, but when you are sleeping, you could say that your personality has retracted, although it simply exists somewhere else. It's like that.

So what percentage of your being is on the other dimensions?

Oh, about 98 percent. That's taking into account … and of course I am 100 percent available here. Because percentage — it doesn't really work. What you're really asking is how many other dimensions do I occupy? And that would be several thousand within this creation.

And not all in the area of your third dimension, but other places in this creation?

Yes, quite obviously, since all the other dimensions have completely different star fields from each other. There's nothing the same. There are no dimensions that look the same. They're all different. And that is because —

Of the Creator's love for variety. Did you create or manifest the stars and planets in your constellation? Or were they already there?

Everything you see associated with any constellation is a result of what Creator has done. But the location is where the personalities of the beings Creator invited or welcomed chose to be. This is where my personality chose to be. But the energy of creation, and thus the manifest of creation, has to do with my personality manifest in the third dimension, my personality manifest in that form and shape based on Creator's energy, just as I explained the way you are.

I still don't know if you manifested the star or if you inhabited it.

I don't know how to say it any differently. I am here. If there was nothing here, I would still be here. If you could see nothing — no planets, no suns, nothing — I would still be here. And the reason there are planets and suns and stars and all that is why? Creator *made* it. Creator flooded the area with Its creation, yes? And my personality was manifested in physical form in the third dimension, as you see it now, based on my personality.

Using what the Creator flooded it with, just like we manifest in a body that comes from the material of the planet — like that?

Yes. And, of course, the substance of your soul and the substance of your mother and father (especially your mother) and the substance of your spirit. Yes.

What have you enjoyed the most about being here?

The camaraderie is pleasant.

With whom? The beings on the planets or other stars or what?

With the beings in the universe.

Everybody, okay. Do you learn from them? Or you don't need to learn?

Nobody needs to learn, but for those who are interested, they'll be exposed to information. It isn't information that you're being taught. It's just available. Other beings are who they are. If you could know everything about another being on Earth … let's say you could know everything about a squirrel in the tree. You could know everything about the tree. You could know everything about your neighbor. You could know everything about any being or particle. It would take you the rest of your life to even know about the particle. I'm trying to put it in context for you. So information is available, but you may or may not necessarily choose to avail yourself of it. But camaraderie has to do with the interaction among personalities. That's what I like.

The expansion into the other dimensions — why that star? Why that one star? Why not the others? How did that work out?

It was prepared to migrate. It wanted to go to the next point on its chosen path, the next — how can we say? — it wanted to move further up the branch. And it will create a portal for a while in case bits and pieces want to go, to make it easier to go, but it will start creating something in the sixth dimension. We'll see what.

Oh, you don't even know?

I don't put my thought there, you would say. It's like this: When anybody seeds something … all right, a tree will drop seeds. Do you think that the tree then supervises the growth of the seed, watches it every step of the way to make sure it doesn't make mistakes? Once you have seeded, then you let it go.

But it's still you.

Yes, but at another dimension. As I said, I'm in thousands of dimensions just in this creation. I'll check on it, but I'm not going to, you know, be checking off boxes with red marks and blue marks.

So have any of these things you've seeded ever brought you great joy, like unexpected results or anything?

Not unexpected, but they usually engender joy.

What is your plan after Creator leaves? Are you going to stay here, or do you get to go back where you came from?

What do you mean "get to go" — whether I have permission to go back?

Do you choose to go back?

Why? I'm happy here.

Good. Does your energy have any influence on Earth?

The light does have influence. And all beings have influence. The fact that you can see the light, even with a telescope, will have some influence.

Can you say what the effects are?

It has something to do with my personality, I'm sure. You could see where Creator would want that.

The Explorer Race Experiment: Too Much Pain

What is your opinion of the Explorer Race experiment?

Well, I'm a member of the camp that feels it's way too painful, meaning I don't agree with allowing people or other beings to have such pain. I'm including all beings as people. I do not accept that it is necessary in the Explorer Race — the whole thing about the Explorer Race. I feel that it's appalling.

How do you see it working out?

It will be resolved, but it's going to take a while to recover from the pain, I feel. Souls don't forget things like that. Even though souls do not feel pain, they will have an uncomfortable feeling, so to speak, associated with their experience on Earth, and it will take quite a while for that uncomfortable feeling to be moderated. So from my point of view, it was a mistake.

But it wasn't something that you could warn or intercede?

How could I intercede with Creator? Of course I warned. I was of that camp that said, "Don't do it. Don't allow pain, even at 1 or 1.5 percent. It could grow." Creator regrets it. Creator regrets allowing pain. Or let's just say Creator regrets allowing pain to move past 1.5 percent of your total experience as an individual — any being.

How long do you see before it'll get back to that?

That's up to you.

But you feel that we will resolve it?

You will make it. But I feel it has been entirely too difficult for you to make it. And even now, when people — meaning human beings — are waking up all over the planet nobody is exempt from that anymore. When people are waking up all over the planet, it causes confusion. Sometimes that confusion creates pain or it creates injuries. Someone's driving down the road, and they're thinking about something that happened. Maybe they saw some light when they were at home, or maybe they saw a ripple in space, meaning they're looking at something and suddenly it sort of ripples. For some people who are of this consciousness, the consciousness associated with these things that you're interested in now — channeling and understanding things, the broad view, philosophy, what could be, what might be, all of this — it won't be so difficult. It'll be relatively easy. But for many people, they're in a much more focused — you might say "thin" — line. They believe "this" and "this" and "this" and "this," and that's it. It can upset them. It can make them think they are crazy when they're not. And I felt that was a mistake. They can think about it later and get distracted.

What if they're driving a car? No, I think that whole allowance of pain is a mistake. I can understand the point of discomfort — having a slight amount of discomfort, such as a draft at the back of the neck (like Zoosh said, and then you get up, you close the window, and then it's fine), that doesn't necessarily mean pain. I have no problem with that. But pain was a mistake, I feel.

Okay. What is your best advice as to how we can deal with life, how to handle it?

Be kind to each other. Be patient with yourself and others. And live life as well as possible.

The Evolved State of Cassiopeian Humans

Okay. You said that your beings on your planets were very, very evolved. Can you describe that?

I didn't say that was all beings. You asked about *human* beings.

How do they live their lives in this evolved state? How does that manifest?

Well, they are who they are. They understand that they are souls, they are spirit, and so on, and they are choosing, you might say, to be human beings. They have a fixed population. Their bodies do not wear out, so they don't die. There are no births; there are no deaths. They are basically immortal. And as a result, they do not inundate themselves with information. They do choose to eat; they do choose to drink liquids. They enjoy the variety of tastes. They enjoy the sense of touch — they have that, you know, and seeing and all the senses you have. They have that. They enjoy life as well as possible. They are kind to each other, and they are patient.

If you're asking whether they live like you do, no, they don't. You're not very patient with yourselves or others as a human race (I'm not talking about you individually). You're not very kind to yourselves and others, as a whole race of beings. And you don't make it a point to live as well as possible and encourage others to live as well as possible, in terms of cooperating with that actually happening. Many of you will tell people how to live, but you don't help them to live that way. But these beings do.

Earth Humans Are Profoundly Shaped by Suffering

I'm not trying to criticize you. I'm saying that you are what you are because you suffer pain. And when there is pain, it tends to — I'm going to use a phrase you use — cramp your style. It cramps everything you do. I know that some people believe that there are advantages in pain. From my point of view, there is no advantage. There are advantages for what you're trying to do as the Explorer Race. There are advantages in very slight discomfort. But even though you've tried to turn pain into a good thing, it isn't, in my belief — and now, I believe, in Creator's belief.

Were you able to see any of this before you joined this creation, or did it play out as a surprise?

The only surprise is that Creator chose to include pain on your planet for your peoples. I was surprised and not happy about that.

This creation's gone on an awful long time. They say 98 percent of it is over. So this doesn't show until almost the end, then, right?

Nevertheless, the fact that Creator would even think — as you say, "think"; I'm using your words, understand? — or chose to include that in His creation and invite along a being who would necessarily want to express that, I found appalling.

We are told that the Creator can't feel the pain.

That's the problem.

Why can't this Creator feel pain?

You'll have to ask Creator that.

Do other creators feel pain?

Not to my knowledge. But they don't *create* something that they are *not*. Do you understand me? This Creator of this universe created pain, and yet It created something that It *isn't*. And It could only have done that because the Master of Discomfort [see the The Explorer Race Series Book 4, *Creators and Friends: The Mechanics of Creation*, Light

Technology Publishing, 1997] was included in this creation, *and* Creator allowed the Master of Discomfort to influence this creation when Creator cannot feel pain. And I feel *that* was the error, and I am unhappy about it.

But there is nothing that you or any of the other hundreds of beings I've talked to who feel the same way you do can do about it — is that the way it is?

That's the way it is.

The last two or three beings I talked to have expressed — in much stronger terms than you have — the same thing.

Yes, and this is because right now your planet is going through so much, and people are going through so much. My feeling is that to expect people to wake up and become their soul selves as their day-to-day selves or their spirit selves as their day-to-day selves while either they or those around them are going through pain and suffering — it's outrageous. Your soul has no pain; your spirit has no pain; your natural being has no pain. So you're expected to become something of your natural self while you're totally immersed in something that's totally and completely foreign to you and has nothing to do with who you are.

How the Master of Discomfort Got Rooted on Earth

What was the point of this to start with, from the Creator's point of view?

Well, you'll have to ask Creator. From our point of view — others like myself — Creator included the Master of Discomfort because Creator has love for all beings, and the Master of Discomfort was unhappy, was uncomfortable, naturally. So Creator welcomed the Master of Discomfort to come along but didn't include the Master of Discomfort's energy in any creation other than where you are and expected there to only be 1 to 1.5 percent discomfort. But look what happened.

What was the catalyst that created the expansion of pain if it started out so little?

The Master of Discomfort was trying to transform itself so that it's no longer of discomfort, and Creator said, "Go ahead."

When we resolve this, what will the Master of Discomfort's life be like?

He won't be in this universe anymore. He's not a "he" — I'm just using it …

I know.

The Master of Discomfort will migrate, and — most importantly — it will migrate to where it was going in the first place, before Creator said, "Come on along."

Where was it going?

It was going to go to a place where it would be transformed. But Creator, being a compassionate and loving being, said, "Here, let me help." Have you seen the cartoon about helping somebody across the street when, in fact, they wanted to stay on the other side? That's what went on here. Creator thought that this would help. And this is why you see things on Earth that are very similar. Human beings moving around other species of beings — "Oh, we think they should be here," "Oh, we think those should be there" — and it turns out to be a catastrophic mistake. That's where that comes from. You learn by who and what you're exposed to. You're a human being living in a linear environment.

Now, Creator understands Its mistake and is doing everything It can to bring about a transformation. And the main thing It can do is move on and let some being who is more knowledgeable about pain take over this creation so that ...

It never happens again.

And any type of anything that could turn into pain will be moved out of the creation. That's you — the Explorer Race. And the Master of Discomfort will then be allowed to go on its way to where it was going in the first place.

Why can't he go now?

Because there's pain here. All of the pain past 1 to 1.5 percent — all of that — is a portion of the Master of Discomfort. And the Master of Discomfort, even if it *wanted* to go on to the other place — and it does — cannot do that because it's stuck. It's like being rooted to a spot. Can you imagine if a tree was meant to be somewhere else and it suddenly had roots? It's going to be stuck! It's going to be stuck until those roots are no longer there. It's going to be up to you to bring about — with no pain and no discomfort — a slow but thorough disconnect for the Master of Discomfort. And when every portion of the Master of Discomfort is back within itself, it will then, very quickly, move on to where it was going. It will probably say to itself, "I'm glad that's over."

So all of the pain and suffering that humans — 7 billion humans — on this planet ...

To say nothing of those in the past.

... and those in the past — it all comes from this one being?

Yes.

And it just flows out of him? He can't control it or anything?

It's available. Imagine a tree, yes? It drops seeds; it drops apples. And the apples eventually turn into other trees. What can it do? And those trees root into the ground and then those seed, and so on.

It's beyond him then, it's —

It's stuck. The Master of Discomfort is stuck. When you all move on to the fourth dimension, it'll be a big help to the Master.

Now we're learning how to transmute using benevolent magic. Is there anything we can say or do that will expedite or fast-forward the moving of this pain back to the Master of Discomfort?

Let me see. You could say,

Living Prayer

"I am asking that all excess discomfort on this planet now migrate benevolently to the Master of Discomfort and that this will result in greater benevolence for all beings."

Very good. Thank you. I never thought to do that before.

Now we're going to end.

Okay. I really enjoyed talking to you. Thank you for coming through.

You're welcome.

CHAPTER TWENTY

Be Happy, and Change the Energy of the World

Zoosh

February 13, 2012

All right, Zoosh, greetings. Your world is in a phase where you are sort of sweeping out the corners. Many people believe that you are going through the time of Atlantis, but I think it is more complex. There are crosscurrents of not only timelines as described in previous books but also of the people, because they are waking up, you see.

People have more of their spirit energy, thus they have more capabilities to manifest. At times, this displays itself in ways that are upsetting because people feel overwhelmed by the complexity of their lives having had many "time-saving" devices added to their lives that in fact actually use time and the usual things that people do: work, organized play, romance, and raising children, of course, and other complexities. There are issues going on that create crosscurrents like a weave of complexity. Think about it. If a person, even one person, feels overwhelmed by his or her life, then because of his or her capacity to manifest, which is at about 20 percent of what you are able to do in your spirit form at this time, then the feeling of being overwhelmed will not only be present in his or her life but also radiate as he or she goes on with life.

So you have to ask yourself, how many people are feeling positive and buoyant versus the number of people who are upset, harassed, overwhelmed, angry, and so on. It depends really where you are in life to get the percentage, but the percentage is lopsided at the moment in favor of people who are basically upset more of the time than they are happy. This is why for so many years, spirits (not unlike myself) and others, including people who are in the counseling and sometimes psychological and other fields and professions as well as well-meaning people, have been encouraging people to do "this" or "that" meditation or to think positive, and so on, because it tends to create an opening in the life of someone, doesn't it? So at least they have moments when they feel positive.

Discipline Yourself to Feel Positive

It is more important now than ever to be able — and this will sound a bit like it's at cross-purposes — to discipline yourself to feel positive. It doesn't have to be at the same time every day, and you don't have to do it, but this is what to do to keep it simple: For those of you who like to make lists, you can do so. For those of you who find making lists annoying (and there might be many of you) or you just don't have the time, try to make it a point, rather than planning to be positive or disciplining yourself to be positive, at least once a day to think about things that you are grateful for in your life.

For some of you, it will be little things that you are conscious of, but take another look at your life. Notice whether you have a nice place to live or a nice car to drive or are grateful for your children or grandchildren or for your health, even in part with children and grandchildren, mates, friends, whatever. Think about the good things in your life, because in the fast pace of life or in a complex life, the things that are not working will tend to have a stronger impact on your life. Even though you might not be conscious of it, your soul and your spirit are attempting to find resolution with those things, thus smoothing out your pathway to manifest benevolently for yourself and ultimately for others.

Your typical way of doing this in spirit is to address it when it comes up. But your soul is different. Your soul is more attuned to your physical life, whereas your spirit is attuned to the whole of your existence in all of your lives and all of everything that you've touched and that has ever touched you. So your soul is attempting to alter that which isn't working for you, and that is why there is a tendency to repeat certain experiences over and over: Your soul is, from your soul's point of view, grinding away at trying to find a solution about _____ (fill in the blank; whatever it is for you).

If you haven't done this before, I want you to take just a moment —
not while you're driving, not while you're typing, not while you're at
work, not while you're disciplining the children — and sit down. When
you are relaxed, say the following as if you are addressing someone:

> *Benevolent Magic*
>
> "Soul, I am asking that you now relax and allow me to proceed
> in my life, noticing what needs to be made better for me, but not
> acting on it the way you have in the past. I can help these things,
> and you can observe and learn at this time what I can do, even if
> it is simply to pray and make it better."

You will notice that this is not a living prayer because I have included
not only what you want but also what you don't want. That makes it a
conversation, a statement. In a living prayer, for instance, you always
ask for what you want, never what you don't want. Any time you state
anything in a living prayer or benevolent magic that includes what you
don't want, your creative self is there, and it will automatically create
what you don't want — not because you don't want it, but because you
are in creation mode. This is something to remember for those of you
who might trip over that.

If by the way, you notice that you're asking for something that you don't
want, try to stop. Start again when you are ready to say the living prayer or
benevolent magic or regular prayer. If you are doing something in church,
perhaps, and it is a prayer you are saying for yourself or others, try to rephrase
it so that you ask only for what you want. These types of prayers are more
likely to be answered in a way that you will feel good about.

What You Radiate Now Affects Others

There are other issues going on. One of the issues that's really creating
cross-purposes, aside from your ability to manifest, and radiating all
around and about what you are creating, what you are being, is the impact of that radiated field. Because many of you are involved in community things or feeling anything that you are feeling so powerfully, what
you radiate now affects others. When you are in need of anything or
even doing things that have to do with the needs overall for yourself and
for others, you tend to radiate more. And since everybody is in need all

the time, they tend to take in that energy that is all around and about them, and if it is upset energy, they will find that they get upset about things and they don't even know about what.

Naturally, your brain works in this way. Your brain will look at your life and try to figure out what it is you are upset about, and something that you're perhaps just slightly upset about will loom into being much larger than it really is because of the energy you're taking in of the upset of others. Another reason that, in times past, the meditation movement moved meditation out of ashrams and some churches into the general public was to attempt to create calm and peace within. Those who initially encouraged that movement or who developed the means realized that such upsetting radiations from even one individual, to say nothing of many millions, can create a constantly expanding and roiling mass of upset. And since people must be receptive to have their needs fulfilled, it becomes a self-perpetuating organism.

Now, a lot of this is known, but I'm putting it together in this opening statement because it is important for you to realize your responsibility, for every one of you — whether you are married, seem to have vitally important work, feel lonely and unfulfilled, or are perhaps even in a situation where your freedom has been taken away (perhaps you are institutionalized for one reason or another) — it doesn't make any difference who you are, where you are, what you've done, anything — is manifesting with 20 percent, all right? It ranges from 18 to 21 percent, but I'm averaging it to 20 percent of your spirit energy.

The reason it is held to that amount, of course, is that if you were manifesting with 100 percent of your spirit energy, the world would be rent into pieces, and we cannot allow that. So when I say we, I mean all beings including you. That is always the case whenever I say we, which I do not say too often — just to let you know what these things mean.

If you cannot or choose not to do things for yourself, then recognize that the idea of community is not only an idea; it is also now a fact. This particular opening statement I am making is the means by which communities that have become out of control throughout all time have understood and taken to heart. I do not expect all of your to do that simply because I am saying so, but look around at others who are teaching some variation of these things, and you will notice that ultimately the point that is agreed on is that it is much better to be happy and joyous in your experience of life than to be miserable and wretched. Regardless of what philosophy and even belief system you focus on, you will find that is an agreement point to all of them.

So if you understand that you are basically sweeping out the corners of what isn't working in your personal life and on your pathway to move from one dimension to another, then you will realize that things will not be left for others to resolve. You must resolve these things, and it is so much easier than you realize.

You Can Create Benevolently Now

I'm not saying, "Let's all do this." I'm reminding you that if one quarter of Earth's population felt positive and upbeat about anything at the same time or within the same minute at any time, you would leap forward to being three quarters of the way to the next dimension. Now, I don't expect you all to organize such a thing — and it's not easy to organize feeling positive, upbeat, and happy. But you can begin. You don't have to focus (and you will be surprised that I say this) on any one thing. Just focus on what makes you happy.

For some of you, others would be appalled if they knew what made you happy, but that applies to all situations. If you look around at the disagreements in belief systems these days, you will note that many people are appalled at what others are doing even if those others and the general community believe that it is a good thing. So sometimes what people are upset about might actually be something positive that they do not see or understand as positive in that moment. Those of you who are a bit older understand this because you can look back on your life and remember when you felt that "this" or "that" was awful and terrible.

Now that you're a little older and have gone through changes and had experience, you can look back on those moments and chuckle to yourself, realizing that you just didn't understand what was going on, and now you have a more complete picture, just to give you an example of things that are real. Therefore I think you will find that you'll be able, with the natural magic you have available to you — and I'm referring to simply what your spirit self does in terms of creation, re-creation, and being a portion of all things in the rest of creation, which is entirely benevolent beyond this school of Earth — that these things are now possible. It is possible for you right now as a human being to create benevolently.

So much teaching has gone on in these books, in *Sedona Journal of Emergence* articles, on the blogs, and in the vlogs — so much has gone on that is intended to teach you how to do things that are actually very simple. But the one thing all that teaching in all those places has in common with what other people have taught in the past about meditation, and so on, is to call on that creator portion of your total, benevolent spirit being that you all have beyond this planet and really have here as well.

Creating from that portion of yourself is what is going on these days. I felt it was important for you to know that so you would recognize that some conflicts can be resolved easier than you think. Not just with the negotiation with your soul, as I mentioned before, but also recognizing that what you ask for — even in a private prayer for yourself in your church or temple or mosque or wherever you go to do these things, talking to Creator in the term you know Creator by — when you ask very simply for what you want, not for what you don't want, that it is more likely to be fulfilled. Now, understand that I do not expect you all to agree with anything whatsoever that I say, but I would like you just to consider it as a possibility.

People Are Attempting to Resolve Old Disagreements

Can we look at some of the examples of the corners we are sweeping out? These are things we didn't quite finish or we didn't do them right. Can you expand on that a little bit?

Things left unfinished, such as how a disagreement can suddenly lead to war. Very often there are disagreements in philosophy between different governments or impatience, which also has a great deal to do with outcomes that are not happy, such as war, battles, fights between people, and violence — things like that.

All right, so we sweep them out and look at them. How do we resolve them?

People are attempting to resolve these things right now with greater communication and an attempt to understand how people in other countries feel and live through these different types of communication. The Internet has been helpful. Even seeing videos, especially so you can understand people's greater communication, because words on a printed page do not demonstrate that, though they might stimulate your thoughts.

For those who can and do travel, they discover very quickly how much other people, whether they look like them or act like them or not, still have a great deal in common with them. So this is helping. Also those who are praying in their places of worship, this is helping. Also, people who are attempting to do things like meditate or be more positive, this is helping. And for those who are doing living prayer or benevolent magic, this is helping. All of these things are helping.

Even simple unexpected things help. You see somebody staggering down the street with a couple of heavy parcels. You do not know this person, but you are polite, and you approach him or her. You ask, "Would you like some help?" If the person nods, perhaps because he or she is struggling, you help take the parcels to his or her car or wherever that person is going. Then you simply tip your hat, if you are wearing one, or say whatever. The person says, "Thank you," and you go on your way or perhaps make a new friend. In short, you are doing things that are benevolent. All these things help to resolve old issues.

Then, as you said, we have to be receptive.

You have to be receptive, because — think about it — you are consuming beings. You must consume water, you must consume food, and you must sleep. There are many things you must do. You must breathe. In short, you are totally receptive beings. When you are born, you are absolutely 100 percent receptive all the time. Other than the way you express yourself and by your pure being, do you feed others? Your parents and perhaps your brothers and sisters and your extended family, they just love you because you are there or because you are doing something cute or what have you, as babies often do. But other than that, you are totally receptive, and you remain receptive throughout your life, simply to exist.

The More Happiness People Radiate, the Less Upset Is Absorbed

But the problem now — you are saying we are consuming this upset energy now.

That's not now, that's always.

But you're saying there is more of it now.

There's more of it now because there are more people and life is more complex now, even though those providing things such as technology, opportunities, and most of these things — not all, but most of them — are intended to improve your life. Very often when you have a lot of things, they make demands on your time. Even without things, in the past, parents who had many children know how that creates demands on their time and how life gets more complex.

Right, but there is really no filter. We have to be receptive, and there is upset energy out there all the way across the spectrum from upsetness to war and violence. But as we radiate benevolence, we can't take in that upsetness while we are radiating benevolence. Is that what you're saying?

Yes, that's right, and the more people who are radiating that happiness, the more it also gets out there into the energy that surrounds you. Some people might just call that air. But air, while it is that which you breathe, is also energy. So it adds something positive to the mix that surrounds you, and as you said yourself, when you are feeling that happiness in that moment, it fills you with joy, and it radiates. Thus, you do not take in any upset energy in that moment.

Of course, you may be experiencing happiness from something you are doing. Perhaps you are having a happy experience, or perhaps you are eating something you love. There are any number of things. Of course, you can do more than one thing at once. But happiness is a very powerful feeling, and it tends to radiate and also — and many of you can identify with this — when you are happy, you tend to be more benign. Things that have happened in the past (not all, but many of them) don't seem to upset you as much because happiness is not only the natural state of your spirit and the natural state of your soul — meaning in the overall being of yourself — but also your predominant feeling. Then that becomes, in that moment, a portion of your physical life, and your physical life is entirely about creation.

You are creative, and you create throughout your entire life. So you merge in those moments with your soul, your spirit, and creation, thus creating a very powerful energy broadcast, more powerful than other things. I know people call this love, and I'm perfectly comfortable with that word as well, but love means different things to different people these days and sometimes seems to be very personal. Yet you all have happiness, at least at times, and this, I feel, is a word you can accept, even if your happiness might not always be for benevolent reasons.

That's great! Feel happy, and you're protecting yourself and diluting the negative feelings that are on the planet.

Yes. These are simple things we are talking about these days in the videos and the blogs and all of that, but in a complex world with so many people creating in it, they take on complexity because that is the shading of the time. Just as an artist might do a general sketch but then add shading, things have depth, contour, and expression, so that is the shading of the time.

Service to Others Is a Complete Foundational Element of Existence

Will this energy continue this way and get more upset before it gets better, or will it phase down consistently to less upsetness?

It depends on how many people do things not only to be happy for their own sakes and for others but also continue to do things to help others. I must tell you this: No soul has ever been born as a human being on Earth in the past, now, or in the future who does not come here to do things for people — in other words, to be of service. This is not a requirement; it is a desire. In spirit (meaning beyond physical form), in soul (meaning that portion of your spirit that is pretty much exclusively associated with any given life you have), and in the general universal expression of all life, service to others is a complete foundational element of existence.

When you are devoted to serving the needs of others, you know absolutely that your own needs will be served, because others have that same devotion to you and to everyone else. So when you come here — all beings, but I am only addressing human beings today — that is why you come and why you continue to serve throughout your life.

If your life has gone astray and you're doing things that after life you, if you could, would shudder to think that you had actually done, you still have moments when you are serving the greater good of all beings. From the worst to the best and from the best to the worst, you are always in service, even though you might not realize it.

Natural Magic

You mentioned natural magic, and you said it had to do with the creator portion of us. Is that different from benevolent magic and true magic?

That term [natural] simply means that which you do on a natural basis in your spirit self, meaning in your total being, and everybody does that in the rest of the universe. But you are being insulated right now on Earth so that it can be a school. And I'm calling it natural magic now because if you were there in your total consciousness and awake and could observe it, it would seem to you as if it were totally magical — things appearing, things needed and suddenly being there, you would naturally say to yourself, "It's magic!" It is natural magic. That is how things are in the completely benevolent creation in which you normally live, so it is referred to as natural magic.

Many beings have said through Robby that all needs are fulfilled. How does that work on Earth? There's a delay factor or there's what you called "crosscurrents"? We don't seem to have our needs fulfilled as quickly as we'd like to here.

That's where you're wrong. You have needs that are your core needs: you need to sleep, breathe, eat, things like that. But souls also come in with desires, some way they wish to serve, and very often, at least one thing they are attempting to learn more about or work on to resolve. Know that all things having to do with any problem in your life have to do with the soul's creation to work on the resolution of that thing. Sometimes this is called a life lesson or something you understand that you're working on. But if you don't know what that is, you can kind of take a look at your life and at what it is that you need, what it is that you are trying to get, and what it is that you have that makes you feel better.

In other words, there is a very specific moment of feeling that you have briefly — even perhaps an object that makes you feel very happy, and for a few days or a week you love this object — and then the feeling fades for one reason or another. Maybe there is something new you want. Maybe this is a person, or maybe it's an experience. In short, it will be a moment of great joy and great happiness while you have this thing. That has to do with what you are here to resolve.

Conversely, it might also have to do with what you are here to do, to serve. It can be either one of these things, and sometimes what you are here to do for others— meaning to serve — and what you are here to resolve for yourself as a soul are closely aligned. Then it is hard to differentiate what it is, so you get a general idea. But sometimes they are two different things, and when they are two different things, you can examine what it is that makes you happy — even for those moments that come and go — and what it is that feels happy to you, because you have done something for somebody else.

I'm not saying that this can be resolved and you can understand that you are here to do something that is harmful. Generally, if you are doing something that is harming yourself or others, you are off track because that is not the natural way of your spirit. Even if you are a very harmful person and, as it is with all people, you die and go on with your lives elsewhere, you are not that way elsewhere. So this is just to let you know that is not who you are, even though some of you become attached to that, thinking that it is. It isn't.

If you look underneath those things you are doing that are harmful, you will discover that you are angry about something you don't have. And when you do those harmful things, it makes you feel victorious in those brief moments and thus happy in those moments because you are showing yourself or others that you can fight back. This gets distorted, and this is how people become violent toward themselves or others.

But this is known and understood. If you do not have the means to talk to some wise woman or man who can help you to understand what you're here to do, what your service as a soul self is, or what you are here to learn as a soul self, then you will have to try to figure it out for yourself. But I have given you a few landmarks here today so that you might seek the solution to those mysteries.

Well, we have natural magic. If we ask, will we hear, be shown, or get a clue?

Always ask in your prayers to be presented with evidence in a happy and joyful way if you don't have the word or the understanding of what benevolent means or if you do know what it means. I am talking, of course, to people here who speak other languages when I refer to such meanings of words. Simply ask to receive this awareness in a repeated way that you can understand and that is a benevolent experience so that you will be able to consciously understand it. Perhaps write it down somewhere so you don't forget or are at least reminded of it on a regular basis. Put that in your own words, of course, in a simple way. When you do that, talk to your soul, as before. Say something like this:

Benevolent Magic
"Soul, would you please create for me in ways that I can understand?"

And then go on with the rest of it, putting it in your own words. Then, at the end, say,

Benevolent Magic
"And please create these things for me in benevolent ways always."

For those of you who do living prayer and benevolent magic, you can do it like that. For those of you who say prayers in churches or mosques or temples or synagogues or others place of worship, then again ask for what you want within the context of your personal prayer and within the context of your beliefs, religion, or philosophy, whether for yourself or for others, that are meant to honor not only Creator and creation but also the goodness in all beings. Always remember, there is goodness in all beings, but sometimes it is so submerged that you cannot see it. All souls are born with this, and it can emerge, sometimes even in unlikely circumstances, demonstrating that it is there.

Good life, good night.

CHAPTER TWENTY-ONE

Learn and Practice Feminine Technology to Transform Atomic Radiation

Isis

June 27, 2012

All right, this is Isis. There is an issue that must be discussed, and it is this: Right now your people are moving from masculine technology to feminine technology. In the case of the masculine — which, for example, is hammering a nail into wood compared to the feminine, which might simply request cooperation from all beings to create something, meaning it might be loving teamwork — there is sometimes a lack of trust for feminine technology on the part of masculine technology. Feminine technology might say, "Well, if we could have a house, it would be beautiful, and it would just seem to come together on its own out of whatever materials that were available. The stone would fit perfectly well, and everything else would also come together because it wanted to be part of that house. And the house would be just fine to live in." That's feminine technology.

However, masculine technology might say, "We can measure, we can cut it, we can place it, and we can use our machines." But feminine technology would say, "Well, all of the machines were something else, really, made up of the raw materials they used to be. They are not happy with what they were manufactured into being. What if we didn't have to tear up things, drill into things, or create suffering to create tools? What if we could just have these structures that we need for shelter, and they would last forever?" Masculine technology might be suspicious of that at this time, but in its natural, native state, masculine technology would not be suspicious.

Masculine Technology Is Reluctant to Move Away from Original Goals

You as a society, meaning Earth people, are moving from masculine technology to feminine technology, and this has been going on for a little while. But there is a great reluctance to do this, isn't there? If you had to travel a narrow trail to cross a mountain or a ridgetop and you had ropes and various other things such as walking sticks to support you, you would be much more comfortable — wouldn't you? — than if you had to cross, for instance, in the way the deer or people born and raised in the mountains might. Seemingly, they can just run down the path without a concern, because essentially they would be glued on the bottoms of their feet to Earth, using love. Feminine technology is about love, and love does not mean passion. In this case, it means welcoming.

So the foot of the deer, wherever it lands, is loved and welcomed by Earth at that time. Earth would not do anything to shove the deer off the path, even if it is just a ridge, a cliff, or a narrow trail on a mountainside. The deer knows this, and he can run along and be safe. Very often, people who are born and raised in the mountains, especially high enough so they don't have too much contact with the technological world as you know it in your big cities, can often do this too if they have been trained properly by elders and by the animals they live with. So I give this example.

You now know that what's happening in the world of masculine technology is a reluctance to move away from original goals, such as in the case of atomic energy, to something like fusion, in which there would be no waste and no worries. You could have a very small power plant, and it would produce a huge amount of power and take care of everybody's needs, whether it is lighting a house or powering a factory and everything in between. So, for example, there is a reluctance by that industry to give up on the dream, even though the current level of atomic energy is really something that never should have left the laboratory. This was understood by the early pioneers, even though there were some who said, "Yes, we can do it." They didn't mean any harm, they just believed it could work.

Now you have what you have, and first, there needs to be recognition that you are moving from one type of technology to another. Feminine technology is about love, support. Some of the mysteries in the world are somewhat more understood, perhaps, just by what I said in my opening words here. In ancient sites all over the planet, how did people move and fit those huge stones so close together, and so on? Well, it was with feminine technology. It was maybe a thousand years ago or thousands of years ago, and that knowledge still exists. It actually exists in the bloodstream, in the molecules, in the DNA of every human being on the planet, because not only does your spirit know these things but Earth as a planet also knows these things. What doesn't know these things is your conscious mind. But your conscious mind can think about these things, consider them, and give them a certain amount of possibility, even those most mistrustful of the feminine technology can consider them nice ideas. So what you have to face is this: As you say, "The squeaky wheel gets the grease."

Right now, you are in a situation, or you as a world culture (I realize there are many people in the world) would like atomic energy to no longer be generated. But atomic energy will continue to be used as long as there are people who need it, who want it, or who profit from it, because it does — even in its current state of existence — support a great deal of that electrical needs of a lot of people. There isn't, at this point in time, a substitute that would replace it completely, though there could be within just a few years. That substitute is coming along. There is a lot of work on that, and it is coming along nicely. But it won't be ready to replace atomic energy for a few more years, so the squeaky wheel is getting the grease, eh?

The attachment is to the future hope of, in this case (I know it seems as if I am picking on atomic energy, but you understand why, because of the current situation), fusion, for example. Although fusion has worked a few times in laboratories, it still hasn't been entirely trusted because of the way science is at the moment. Science is still determinedly masculine, even though at the core of its being, it is definitely feminine, because science is intended to serve the needs of all beings — not just all people, but all beings — and it will be that way at some point. Of course, it is intended to do so with love.

The Northern Hemisphere Might Experience
an Atomic Energy Problem

I've been building to something here that is problematic. You've had one catastrophic thing happen recently in Japan. This wasn't the atomic power plant simply blowing up; it was an effect Earth needed to do for her reasons. She wasn't angry with the people of Japan, not at all. Good people are there just as other places. But it is an area that Mother Earth needs to have waters present very often. She also supports all beings equally. Mother Earth is inclined to love and welcome all beings — human beings, yes, but also the beings of the sea; you say fish. But Mother Earth loves the beings of the sea just as much as she loves human beings and the beings of the air — birds and so on — equally.

It might interest you to know that Creator also feels the same way, even though Creator is fully aware that human beings are intended to learn things. And all the beings who manifest on Earth, whether "animal" or human, are volunteers who come to this Earth school to learn how to create benevolently in a world that seems to be set for anything but. But that is because someday you will help others do the same thing, and you must be able to do that with absolute patience, with complete commitment, and with total love. That is why you as human beings are all here as members of the Explorer Race. You are here to explore, yes, but with absolute commitment and as I said above.

Now we get to the hard part. There has been a reluctance to give up on atomic energy not just in Japan but also in other places. Some places have let go of atomic energy and are shifting to other things. It can be done even in a society that has factories and so on. You will see more of that as time goes on, because the wind blows and the sun shines, so there are things that can be done. I am reluctant to say but I will: There is a very distinct potential that there will be another problem with atomic energy. The only thing I can say for certain is that the chances are it will happen in the Northern Hemisphere. I am not talking about bombs exploding — interestingly enough, there is fortunately quite a bit of cooperation from one government to another, and even nongovernmental people are cooperating to prevent that, as well as Spirit, of course, and other energies. So I don't think that is too much of a threat. But it is still somewhat of a threat, so I encourage those who are attempting to prevent that to continue their good efforts.

I feel the real risk is something that has to do with atomic power plants — fixed ones, not ones that move about. There is a real risk that something else will happen soon. I hope it will not, but it could; and if it does, it will mean that the Northern Hemisphere especially will become even more contaminated than it is now. I know that there has been an attempt for obvious reasons, good reasons, to keep the level of contamination from this disaster in the Fukushima area somewhat secret. But because of the type of atomic power you are using now, radioactive waste and radioactive materials are not readily and easily stored in any safe place, even with the best of technology. So this is an issue, a very serious issue.

I just want to say this: Think about the Southern Hemisphere as an area of residence. Here is an interesting fact: For a long time, there has been the whole idea in various philosophical and now in what you know as New Age circles that there would be a pole shift. The poles aren't really going to shift; however, the population might. Don't hit the panic button — you have some time yet — but know that the radiation level in the Northern Hemisphere now is generally unhealthy. It's not catastrophically unhealthy, but it is generally unhealthy, meaning for the long range, not too good. For starters, I recommend that it would be good to learn the languages of the Southern Hemisphere if you can. Learn about the cultures, especially the young people. Learn about the good things.

Don't plan to just take your culture down there and stick your flag in the ground and say, "Here we are" and "This is what we're going to do." If you learn the culture and how to speak the languages, be respectful. A lot of people will be welcomed. Some of you have been doing that now. I want you to consider doing it, especially your young ones, who are likely to be together in having children.

Atomic Power Plants Don't Just Turn Off

Another long-range factor to consider is that this will require science. And science (speaking as if it were someone), you have already figured out how people could live underground, but not necessarily how people could live underground and maintain a comfortable, healthy lifestyle. It needs to be something you put your energy toward. On other planets, it is not at all unusual to find cultures living underground so they don't disturb the surface of the planet, not because they have had disasters there but because the surface of the planet is for other forms of life. I don't want to sound like the world is coming to an end; it isn't. It is just shifting to feminine technology.

For those of you already engaged in feminine technology, some of which has been taught through this channel — good examples are benevolent magic, living prayer, true magic, and more along those lines — it will feel like a natural flow, and that is because of the love. The word "magic" is used only because it describes a change in internal and external circumstances that happens only with love and comfort for all beings. This shift to feminine technology will seem magical because things seem to happen, and it will just feel like the flow of life. It doesn't feel like a magician suddenly pulled a rabbit out of a seemingly empty hat, so it's not sudden.

While others may be easing toward the Southern Hemisphere, there will be a whole cadre of people, not militarized, working on the Northern Hemisphere as well as the rest of the planet. I'm using the term "cadre" because you will have a strong sense of support for each other. Most of them will be volunteers, some will be trainees, and some will simply be so good at it naturally that others will perhaps even pay them to do this or support them in some way. They will be using forms of this loving feminine technology to transform the atomic energy above ground to below ground — the radiation, all of that — so that it is completely benign.

When you are ready to shift to the alternate sources of producing electricity, which many places are, and when you're ready to turn off the need for electrical energy from atomic power plants, you're going to be faced with the fact that atomic power plants do not switch off. The atomic energy part doesn't turn off. Once it is "turned on," it stays on. That is something that is not completely understood by the general population: You can't really turn it off. But it can be turned off with feminine technology. So I need to say this to you so that those of you who are working with it understand that you can go beyond.

I am not saying that you should go around doing this now, but learn how to do it because you can literally save your planet and all of the people and all of the beings on it with this feminine technology. Masculine technology science right now does not have the means to transform atomic waste and atomic energy — meaning the pile, as they call it, the rods and all that business your current scientists do not have a means to transform — so that it is "off," you might say, so that it is not radiating, also known as completely benign. That does not exist, but the feminine technology that I have referred to as magic — that this channel refers to that way and that this publisher has published any number of things about — is seemingly magic because everything transforms only a little bit. Nothing has to transform totally. Everything happens incrementally in the most benevolent way for all beings.

Do you want to say here what someone should say to transform the atomic waste?

No, because I want all of you to continue your training in benevolent magic and living prayer and all of the things that can be done to help ease yourself into a comfortable state to do this work. I want you to continue learning how to do these things and understand that even though you may not be part of the cadre that lives in the North and survives in a place that is not healthy because of radioactivity, you may be protected because you will learn first and foremost how to protect yourself from radioactivity. The people who learn how to do that and are able to do that well and safely will be the ones who move about on the surface of the Northern Hemisphere to transform the land and everything on it so that it becomes habitable, and the atomic power plants can be safely turned off. And the atomic pile itself will be off to the extent that it gives off no more radiation than would have been measured in the past as simple background radiation that is always present, because of simply nothing to-worry-about energy that comes from the stars and space and so on. But even that can be transformed, so that helps to eliminate a lot of diseases as well. (And science, please don't test the people doing this work. This thing of testing, sometimes called "destructive testing," is not an acceptable way to do that.)

Can you be more specific? An atomic power plant in the Northern Hemisphere is going to ... ?

I will not be more specific. I will just say that everybody who works in atomic power plants knows that there are leaks and things happen. Even with the best of efforts by the most conscientious people, there are certain things that tend to leak, whether in the liquid or gaseous state. There are problems, and because of the inability to turn off radioactivity, it's something people in the industry — whether they simply work there or run the place — are encouraged to keep quiet about. Even people who totally believe in the value of atomic energy as it exists today understand that it exists at great risk, because in your current science, there is no method to turn it off completely. There is no current method to do anything about atomic waste, whether it is high yield or low yield. They don't talk about it because they don't know what to do about it. It's one of the issues that people who work in and around and with atomic energy feel uncomfortable about, even people who totally believe in it feel uncomfortable about that. They would have been much happier if someone had just said, "Oh, magically, here's fusion, and it will be fine." But it didn't happen that way because of historical circumstances. This is easily discovered by anybody who knows history.

You Expect the Government to Help You

How far should one live now from an operating atomic power plant to be safe from little leaks and stored waste — just a regular plant, no catastrophes?

I should think a couple hundred miles should do it, but of course, you are still exposed to the atmosphere, and water moves and goes everywhere, including through people's bodies. A couple of hundred miles wouldn't keep you safe, though, because the wind blows too, doesn't it? That's why feminine wisdom, feminine love, and — for the purpose of this talk today — feminine technology must replace the current state of technology. You can only force so many nails into so many boards. To let carpenters off the hook, you can only force the current state of technology to go so far without Mother Earth saying, "Okay, that's enough; don't do that anymore."

When you are poisoning the ocean and all of the water people within it and when you have to throw fish back into the water because they are so radioactive, it's not safe to eat them. Of course, if the fish are that radioactive, they are going to die. Safety becomes a goal that is not necessarily reachable. So there needs to be some other form of technology that doesn't have machines and working parts but that can create in the most benevolent way for all beings — and it exists now. It is just a matter of reminding you how to do it.

You don't have to give up your religion, and you don't have to give up your philosophy. You just need to recognize that it can be done, and it does not necessarily have to be done in the same way at the same time by everyone in the way that you might have a scientific method: First you do "this" and then you do "that" and so on, the same way every time. No, individual people who learn how to do this might have their own methods to do it, but what counts is the result and that it must be benevolent for all beings, meaning no one is harmed.

Oh, granted, some people might look at what's done as some people might dance around to do this, some people might sing to do it, some people might speak loudly to do it, and some people might be quiet and make unusual maneuvers with their bodies, doing a dance of some sort. Some people might be very quiet and still. In short, there will be different ways to do this, and while some people might be uncomfortable with that, that is their reaction, but it does not harm them. So be clear on what I mean by "benevolent." Benevolent means no harm caused to anyone or anything. The whole purpose of it is entirely benevolent, and one portion of benevolence we recognize is that all people are not alike, but the goal achieved can easily be accomplished by doing things in different ways as long as it is benevolent for all beings.

How do we find the level of radiation where we live?

I suggested that it is not being widely broadcast, perhaps rightly so, because the people, governments, authorities, and so on, recognize that people look to the government for help. If something is wrong, such as your street needs repair, you call the city and say, "Hey, there is a hole in the street. Can you put it on your schedule to come out and fix it?" And they respond that they will take care of it. People expect those in government to help them. But how would you feel as a government person if you went forward and said, "We have this problem, and there is nothing we can do about it." You wouldn't feel too good about that. Thus, there is sort of a universal acquiescence among government authorities that they don't want to say things like that because they feel people might panic, and from their point of view — not mistakenly so at this point in time — in most places, it is not a disaster yet, but water moves, the wind blows, and all of these things as natural elements of Earth distribute that radioactive situation.

From Japan?

From Japan at this time, but there have been other problems. I'm not trying to blame Japan. After all, the design for the atomic power plants in Japan wasn't even created there. It was created someplace else. So they just did what they could, and they built atomic power plants to have, from their point of view, the least impact possible to have the power to do manufacturing and light up homes and so on. So it just happened to be Japan, and the reason it happened to be Japan is another factor of atomic power plants. One often finds them near bodies of water, and this is done as an emergency measure, but you can see that this emergency measure doesn't work because bodies of water aren't necessarily calm.

It is not unusual for there to be earthquakes — it may not happen all the time — that happen in bodies of water that cause tidal waves, tsunamis as you say. And if there were no atomic power plant there, as catastrophic as that tsunami was in Japan, it would have been terrible — with a terrible loss of life as occurred with much suffering, it's true. But then the people would have picked up and said, "Okay, let's put things back together and go from here." But now the situation is such that an immense part of Japan and other places — because the wind blows and water flows, and so on — is being radiated. You understand that the atomic power plant might as well be sitting outdoors, because there is no roof on it, and the idea of having water, all the water you need to cool the atomic pile, isn't working very well, not when it poisons an entire ocean. So that element, learned the hard way now, will not come to bear if there were future atomic power plants being built. Even though there is a desire to build future ones, I think cooler heads will prevail.

Physical Mastery Is Done to Benefit All Beings

The issue is that there is really no way to prevent the radiation from pouring out into the atmosphere as it is right now. And by "atmosphere," I don't mean something miles and miles above the planet only. The plant in Japan — with no roof anymore, after having a complete meltdown — is just pouring radioactive energy into the air. And there is really nothing in the current state of affairs in science and of masculine technology — granted, in a more extreme state as it exists now, meaning, well, "We will put this stuff around it, and we will do everything we can to keep it safe." But that is sort of wishful thinking, you know.

Don't look for somebody to blame. This radiation is pouring out, and that's that. Of course, the levels are up very high in the area where the plant exists in Japan, and it is migrating into the general neighborhood and around the planet on the basis of the jet stream and so on. The reality is that governments are saying, "Well, perhaps we can devise something. We think we can do something about it." And of course, there has been tremendous personal sacrifices, tremendous heroism by people going into the plant knowing they are going to be killed by the radiation. There is tremendous heroism that is going on in Japan right now by people doing these things to try to help the situation: suffering, getting radiation poisoning, and dying in an unpleasant way. So know that the people in Japan are doing all they can do, but science does not have an answer. So you cannot really pursue a technology like that, meaning you cannot use that technology with hopes and prayers only. You must substitute something else, and that substitute is available through the use of wind and sun.

I am not including, as you have noticed, water, because dams might work for a while to provide electrical energy, but it is not the answer. Water needs to move; and it might interest you to know that if it doesn't move and it is behind a dam, just moving slowly, it becomes uncomfortable, and you don't want water to be uncomfortable. When water is uncomfortable enough, it wants to move suddenly. When it wants to move suddenly, there might be an earthquake. You understand, water is part of Mother Earth's body, and if you have something that is itchy in your body, you suddenly want to scratch it; even though you've been trying to resist, you're going to scratch it. There might be a tsunami. Mother Earth is nothing if not a physical master, and you are here as Earth human beings to learn about physical mastery. Physical mastery, in the most benevolent way, is done to benefit all beings, from one being to another, interacting with planets, with universes, with energies, with immortal love, and with Creator. It is done benevolently.

Please let go of atomic energy, make a long-range plan that is not so long range: five years, ten years tops. No more than ten years to transform all your electrical needs to something that is about wind (meaning wind power, wind generators), and sun (meaning batteries, solar panels). This is the most benevolent way to do it. Don't get too attached to dams, because we don't want water getting nervous and upset. Plan to eventually — not right this minute, but once you get things converted over to wind- and solar-power generation — stop building dams. Let's not have earthquakes; let's not have well-meaning people trying to take down dams. You let science do that slowly, release all the waters, and then the dam will just be taken apart or used as a road perhaps — most likely taken apart. The concrete can be recycled in some other way.

I realize you think I'm asking too much of you. But if you do nothing and continue the way you are, you don't have much of a future as Earth humans, and you might just take the rest of the beings with you. A while ago, some of you wondered why the animals were suddenly dying out, suddenly leaving. A lot of what they had to teach you is being taught now, and you can learn how to do feminine technology by not only reading these books but by practicing some of the things that are on Robert's blogs: the Mystical Man, Benevolent Magic, and Explorer Race blogs [RobertShapiroMysticalMan.blogspot.com, BenevolentMagic.blogspot.com, and ExplorerRace.com/explorer-race-blog.php]. Of course, other people teach specific things too. We mention this not because we're trying to sell you something but rather because the material, the knowledge, and the wisdom that are coming through in this way can teach you to make changes that you would consider to be magic. And I assure you that it is benevolent magic and something of Creator, of love, and only that. Good night.

CHAPTER TWENTY-TWO

The Fourth Dimension: A Preview

Isis

July 27, 2012

All right, this is Isis. Greetings.

You have said there are no such things as angels. Tell me who the beings we call angels really are.

"Angel" is just a word that is provided for beings. You understand that when religion got going — going back a few thousand years — it was a word applied to something that already existed. You could easily say guides, spirit teachers, or angels — same thing. You could also say gold lightbeings or the other forms of benevolent lightbeings — angels. The words are interchangeable. That is what is meant by the statement made in the past that there are no such things as angels. In reality, there is such a thing. It is just that the words are synonymous.

That is why in the past some of the famous paintings tended to show gold light around angels or suggested gold and white light. This is just another way of suggesting — and I might add "with religion's approval" — going back several hundred years to the old masters' classic paintings, suggesting that lightbeings and angels are the same things. It is interesting to note that even in those days hundreds of years ago, the heads of various churches and the ones who might have communicated with these painters and who were not the heads but were their representatives were perfectly happy to suggest that angels and lightbeings were one and the same. They weren't necessarily wanting to spell it out and speak to people about those things. They knew in their times it was necessary to keep things very simple and uncomplicated. For one thing, people weren't reading books — for obvious reasons — and the words they had available to speak and understand were very limited. A dictionary of common usage in those days would have been a few pages long in the English language — nothing like today. So the word "angels" was picked. They were perfectly happy to suggest to contemporary people who might see such paintings — and future generations — that they did understand that lightbeings and angels are the same beings.

Lightbeings then can be from any place — any universe, any creation. They can be anybody who is not in a body someplace — or is it more than that?

What I am referring to here would be lightbeings who are either assigned or have volunteered to come to Earth to work with Earth human beings, not just, as you say, lightbeings who could exist in their own realm of existence anywhere in the universe. While the lightbeings who come to Earth, also known as angels, can exist in other parts of the universe, they generally stay here so that they will be not only well versed in what is going on here, but immersed in what is going on here so that there is a complete focus by them on the nature of human society not only as it has been and as it is, but as it may be in terms of what they are trying to encourage. Of course, they are trying to encourage you all to be your spirit selves, your soul selves, as your day-to-day selves, and they are perfectly willing for that to take as long as it needs to take so that everybody can come along. They are also perfectly willing for some people to come along quicker than others, but that doesn't mean they are going to migrate from the planet. It is fixed because of the shift between dimensions that everybody is migrating at the same pace. Certain individuals who are more integrated into their spirituality might have certain capacities, but every Earth human will wait for everybody else. It is all or nothing in that sense.

Will we have the same angels or guides or lightbeings as teachers in the next dimension?

Most likely, yes, because the next dimension will have enough resonance with this dimension — not meaning it will be like this dimension of Earth, but it will have enough resonance. So the lightbeings, the angels, who are familiar with this dimension, the third dimension, the midpoint between the third and the fourth — since we are using those numbers —

dimensional versions of Earth upon which we will find Earth human beings of that dimension ... they will be the same beings, yes.

Earth's Physical Appearance in the Fourth Dimension

Earth has a multitude of dimensions as part of her body. We are moving from one of them to another. I had read that the planet we are going to looked green instead of blue. How will our perception of the next dimension differ? I am looking out my window at a mountain and tall green trees now. Will there be the same topography there?

The topography will be similar but not identical. There will be mountains. There may, on the very tops of the mountains, occasionally be snow, but that is unlikely. The atmosphere will not be green, but the surface of the planet will be green because of plants. As we have mentioned before, the planet itself will be vastly bigger than this planet, and while there will be waters, the waters will run underneath the foliage, so you won't necessarily see it. That suggests that there will not be vast oceans. No, there won't be. But there will be plenty of water for everybody, including the plants, and it is very likely that the bulk of the population will live underground. It won't be cave living; it will be very modern, very beautiful. There will be structures that come up from underground to gather the sunlight and bring the sunlight in its natural state, not an artificial sun, to the underground communities. The reason people will live underground is so that the surface of the planet can remain pristine. It doesn't mean people will not be able to come to the surface; it just means they will not linger there, not live there. They certainly will not cut down trees.

So people will be encouraged to come to visit for a day or even a little bit longer, but there will be no impact by various food containers or anything. Anything that you have to do or anything that you bring with you, you will take back for recycling. You will have surface dwellers at times, but they will be in something like a vehicle that travels between planets so that it will remain most likely elevated above the surface of the planet. Sometimes these pods (I am going to call them that — they're not glass domes, but they have been described sometimes in science-fiction books as looking like that) will have significant population. But the populations in there — the Earth human beings — will not remain for any length of time. These pods will not actually sit on the planet — they will float above the planet so that the surface of the planet itself is completely safe. And all needs of the human population will remain inside the pod, but everybody inside the pod will be able to go out on the surface of the planet for a few hours, if they like, and breathe the air, profoundly rich in oxygen — much more so than it is now. There will be no pollution. If just a few people go out at a time, meaning no more than a thousand on any given day, there won't really be a problem.

There are no bodies of water — no lakes or oceans or dolphins or whales or anything like that?

You didn't listen. There is water. It is just that the trees ... if you approach from space, the planet looks green because of trees, and the trees will be very tall. Heights of 400, 600, 800 feet will not be unusual, and there will be much taller ones, up to 1,200 feet tall. They will be very big trees, and underneath the trees, running in many streams and small rivers, but mostly streams, will be water. So you may have occasionally, in the case of rivers, freshwater dolphins. They used to exist on this planet. There might be a few left but not many.

So that implies that the Sun also has many different levels to its being — dimensions. The Sun there will be the same Sun as we have now?

Yes, of course.

An Expanded Version of the Third Dimension

So the fourth dimension will be here but in a more expanded version than the third.

Yes, it will be the same solar system. The one significant difference, however, is that the asteroid belt will no longer be present. There will be a planet there.

Which one?

Well, it will have its own name, but it will be the planetary orbit before Jupiter.

So we will look out and see the twelve planets in this solar system, and planets ten, eleven, and twelve will be manifest?

They are manifest now, but they will be bigger at the fourth dimension. They will be much more visible, and the populations will be there and will welcome visitors. Of course, you will be able to travel in the solar system. You will be, for the most part, completely benevolent beings, so you will be welcome everywhere. Of course, there will also be visitors here because the planet will be beautiful. It is beautiful now, but I am saying "will be" because you are on your way there. It will be quite beautiful, and there will be lots and lots of visitors from other planets who are totally benevolent beings like you will be and as you really are in your soul and spirit selves.

That isn't something strange and foreign. In fact, it is exactly who you are with the personalities you have now but nothing that is associated with discomfort — as Zoosh calls it, and I like that term — so you will know other human beings very often at that dimension based on having known them before. You will recognize them on the basis of their personalities — not just the twinkle in their eyes, but who they are. But there will simply not be any discomforting qualities there. No one has to adapt or struggle or try to get over suffering. There won't be any suffering. There will be complete benevolence.

You won't have technology as you understand it today. The ships that will travel will not be ones that are made on Earth. But that's not unusual; it is very typical that other societies who have the means to create such vehicles share them. They will be shared with your people who wish to travel to other planets and star systems. The ships will be made available, and you will be able to travel without having to learn how to operate things and build things out of materials that don't wish to be turned into those things. The vehicles will not be made up of anything that is associated with Earth at all. They will be shared by other civilizations, and because everything is benevolent, the ships from other civilizations will be completely acceptable by Earth — meaning floating above the planet — and people will simply be able to get to them from the pod cities. The vehicle, for instance, might come and be able to enter the pod city, and people who wish to go someplace — maybe they want to go to the Pleiades, for example — will simply get on the ship, and away it will go for as long as people want to visit. Or they might want to visit Jupiter. Jupiter at that level will be well and thoroughly peopled. So the ships will not be made up of anything from fourth-dimensional Earth. They will come from other places and be available for transportation.

The Explorer Race and Contact with Other Beings

What about the whole Explorer Race idea? Over the course of all these books, we were told that we would go out to many of the other civilizations and star systems and that our lust for life and our curiosity and our energy would stimulate these other civilizations and planetary peoples into a growth that they hadn't taken advantage of previously.

Yes, that is still the case. It will be civilizations, however, that desire growth and cannot grow any more based on what they have now. And those who desire the growth will be welcoming of a minor degree, as has been said before, of discomfort. It has been said in the past that it would be 1 percent, maybe up to 2 percent, but that has changed. It is now going to be no more than 0.5 percent. It might, in time, for various civilizations on one or two planets, go up to 1 percent or even 1.5 percent, but there has been a change on the consensus level that 2 percent is too much, so 0.5 percent is most likely, and that will be perfectly acceptable. Some of the Explorer Race — not necessarily everybody on fourth-dimensional Earth, but the astronauts and the cosmonauts of the Explorer Race who will number at least 100,000 and maybe close to 150,000 — will be the ones who go out in ships provided by other cultures. And the cultures of the planets in the universe that will welcome that growth curve for whatever reason will welcome those beings. So that is still the case.

It has been said many times that the first beings who would contact us here — and I'm not sure at what point in the journey between the third and fourth dimensions that would be — would be the half-human, half-Zeta beings. But now some ETs have said that we will meet human beings from other planets who look exactly like us. Will they be Pleiadians? Has that been changed?

I cannot state for a fact that it will be beings from the Pleiades, but it has been suggested — and I think probably rightly so — that the first beings you will meet will all look like human beings and will represent the races that you have on Earth. You will see beings who look like they are from China or Japan. You will see beings who look like they are from Africa, and so on. So you will see these different shades of beings, and people will love it because they will get a chance to understand the root culture from which they appear. So it will be like that, but the first nonhuman beings you will meet will be some beings who look something like a cross between Zeta Reticulans and smaller human beings, meaning beings of about 4 feet tall — 4 foot 2 perhaps. So those will be the first not-strictly-human beings you will meet, so that is still there. But it was believed that it would be better to begin with beings who Earth human beings could recognize as similar to them. And of course you will still have all of the races that you know on Earth in the fourth dimension.

Root Civilizations on Other Planets

Various of you previously had said that a special prototype human being was created for us to embody on this planet that was more vulnerable and lived a shorter time than humans on other planets. But I didn't know that the various races we have on this planet were actually similar to races on other planets — all of the different colors and cultures. So they all have their roots in a different civilization on other planets?

Yes. And it will be very comforting, I feel, for this knowledge to come out. Of course, when people are at that fourth-dimensional aspect of themselves, it will seem natural. It won't be something in which they are comforted and then they will feel better because they would not have been feeling bad. The better feeling takes place now so that people will know you will in fact be meeting these beings who will tell you a great deal about themselves, and you will recognize in yourself and in your children and other beings certain qualities that are associated with these other planetary cultures. I am not going to go into that because I don't want to spoil the surprise, but the main thing is that I can assure you that you will be reassured. Now, the reassurance doesn't wait until you get to 4.0. The reassurance starts to happen when you are at about 3.73, because at this point you will be so close to 4.0 that you will be almost completely benevolent. There will still be some traces — maybe up to 3 percent — of discomfort, but that won't be enough to prevent contact from taking place. So I just want you to know that you don't have to wait to get to fourth-dimensional Earth. You will be in mid-gear, so to speak, and at that point, you will experience something that is akin to fourth-dimensional Earth.

You understand, you are not going to suddenly disappear and reappear at fourth-dimensional Earth. You will go through a stage where the planet will get bigger, but then everything will get bigger relatively. After a while, you will go through a stage, and that is the stage you are in now. Once you get to about the 3.73, you won't get any bigger, but the planet will get bigger. And the planet will be changing, so there will be a transitional state before you reach 4.0. It is in that transitional state that a lot of the contacts will be made, and people will feel wonderful. Oh, they will meet the people who were the root races of the African races, and so on. It will be a wondrous time. And that is what I am talking about: People will be reassured and thrilled and happy, and they will enjoy the experience. So parents, know that your children and their children's children are going to have this experience, and it is going to be wonderful.

We have talked to some of them. Last year those who had seeded the Mongolian race and culture talked through Robert from a craft, and others had talked in the past.

It may be possible in the future to talk to others.

Recently an ET linguist said he had found traces on Earth of over 300 languages that he could source to ET cultures and civilizations. That is an incredible number.

Well, that is because there are a great many races that existed on Earth going back in time — the Earth that you are on now — that do not exist now because, as is typical with a planet when the population gets bigger and bigger, people fall in love with people who look a little different, and races gradually evolve into fewer groups that are classifiable. But that doesn't mean that those races are not still present; they're just present within their genetic codes.

And some of the languages hang in there as dialects.

Yes, dialects in some cases, and in others, languages just merge based on whatever the predominant culture is at the time, depending on where you are living. So some languages are lost, but they are not lost completely. When you begin to have contact with these beings from other planets, they will expose you to their languages as they speak them. But there will be very great ease in communication, and there won't be a problem of trying to understand beings from other planets in their language and vice versa. So there will be ease in communication, but you will also be exposed to their language so that you can hear what I would like to call the music of the languages. Some languages have a sort of high and low register, and they go down and come up. There will be things like that. And there will also be different sounds. To some extent, one has heard, even in recent years, sounds in languages — clicking sounds, even whistling sounds, and so on. That is not unusual in some other planetary cultures.

Current Discomfort Levels on Earth

Overall, what is the percentage of discomfort on the planet now?

Well, I have to average it out. I recognize that you are asking for an average. On an average for this exact moment, it is 38 percent. It has gone up to as much as 46 percent, but it is not there at the moment — 38 percent as of this exact moment [**Publisher's Note:** 7:11PM on July 27, 2012, Arizona time].

Well, that is awesome! The last time I asked, it was like 65 percent.

Yes, it goes up and down. I don't think it will go up to 65 percent again — that was an extreme situation. A great deal of work has been done since then.

What number would you put on where we are right now — three-point what?

I will put it on the 7:11AM time above — I will coordinate it to that: 3.54. You can see that if you have 38 percent discomfort at 3.54. By the time you get to 3.73 it will be unusual, but the percentage of discomfort might bounce up as high as 3 percent. Yes, that is why you have to go very slowly, ploddingly slow, to move forward — because we don't want something to snap you back. So everyone has to come along slowly but surely. It may not seem possible now with violence and extremes and strangeness and so on going on, but some of that is purely accidental. Meaning there are ... I will give you an example. Sometimes people in your day and age take drugs for medical reasons; sometimes people take drugs just for simple medical reasons, like for a headache you take an aspirin or something similar; and sometimes people take drugs for fun, meaning recreational drugs. And sometimes this fun turns into an addiction because the drug is not really meant for fun. It is meant for somebody's profit, and that is unfortunate because lives are ruined that way, but you understand that.

Now there are microwaves, radio waves, and so on. There are broadcast frequencies for various communication efforts for some people — in rare cases, but it's true for less than 1 percent — a combination of certain drugs and certain frequencies of communication energies, microwaves, or even exposures to combined microwave frequencies. You get the idea. I don't want you to blame anybody. The circumstance has to do with the brain wave of the individual who might be utilizing some illegal drug, might have been exposed to an illegal drug unknown to him or her, or is in some extreme situation. It depends. It could also be in a war zone, and the individual's brain wave is out of sync with what it would normally be if he or she were not in that war zone, meaning before the war or many years after the war and the individual recovered somewhat. In short, there are many variables involved.

This isn't happening purposely, but because of all the technology involved and people's brain waves being very susceptible to some technologies — albeit temporarily — with a combination of some drugs, this can make people do things that are extremely violent. And they would never have done it otherwise. Sometimes these people remain in those states for years, and sometimes people remain in those states permanently. Certain drugs that people say are mind altering these days are particularly hazardous. These drugs are known, even without being exposed to any other extremes, to cause psychotic states. So if people who are on those drugs happen to be exposed to these various microwave resonances, or even just radio waves — how can we say? — in the wrong place at the wrong time, it can create temporary or permanent insanity that either makes them extremely susceptible to very violent states or potentially takes them over the edge, and they become extremely violent.

They could easily become extremely violent toward people they might otherwise love. And this is why people sometimes wipe out their whole families and afterward realize what they have done and are totally aghast and upset and distraught and immediately kill themselves. So this can be a temporary situation. It doesn't have anything to do with spirituality; it has mostly to do with technology. And ice [crystal meth] is a surefire drug to create psychosis. It also permanently alters the brain waves of those who take it.

Transitioning into the Fourth Dimension

We published information a few years ago on the First, Second, and Third Alignments. Would you say we are beginning to move into the Second Alignment at this time? [See Shining the Light, Volume 7, Light Technology Publishing, 2005.]

Yes, you have started moving into the Second Alignment. That is where you get a lot of the spiritual integration and people suddenly discover that they can do things they didn't know they could do. That is why this channel had put up videos on YouTube about this — so people won't be alarmed when they suddenly discover that they can see beings from another dimension and so on.

Are there beings on that fourth-dimensional Earth now?

Yes, there are, but not Earth humans. There are beings, some of whom you will recognize. You understand that many of the animals that can live in third-dimensional Earth could also live in fourth-dimensional Earth but could not make the trip with you from third to fourth because they are one or the other, and so some of them have come as far as they can. But for quite a while now, building up to the midway point that you are at now, there have been vast numbers — hundreds of thousands of animals have suddenly stopped existing, meaning that they suddenly died, that their spirits moved on. Many of those are water beings, and they have just moved on to fourth-dimensional Earth. So there will be what you now know as fish, but you won't eat them; they are beings you will communicate with.

Food will be quite different in fourth-dimensional Earth. It will be entirely that which is grown on trees — you would say fruits and vegetables — but there will be protein in there. You will all have what you need. You won't need as much protein as you do now, because you won't have to struggle to live life. So the need for protein will be greatly diminished, physically speaking. Nevertheless, what grows on trees and plants —

corn, string beans, and so on — all of these things will still be available. You will still have apples and strawberries and things like that. But these foods will have a broader spectrum of nutrients.

So as I say, there will be fish and birds and something that reminds you of an elk and deer combination, many beings like that, but they are not there for you to consume — strictly to communicate with. And a lot of them are there now. You will be able to communicate in ways in which you completely understand each other. It will be like having a conversation with another person right now. You will love it. Good night and good life.

Thank you very much. Good life.

CHAPTER TWENTY-THREE

The Soul and Spirit Are One

Isis

August 3, 2012

There is so much talk about getting us to the fourth dimension, but that is not the destination — that is just another point on the spectrum. We are not going to stay there that long, are we?

It depends who "we" is. If you are talking about Earth and the people of Earth, they will stay there for a while, as long as they want to accomplish something there. So the souls who create themselves there will be there for as long as they wish in order to accomplish their intention, and, you understand, there is more than one intention. It depends on the individual soul — just as all souls have intentions when they come here.

You are asking about the Explorer Race, yes? The overall intention? The overall intention is to move slowly so everyone can move at once and establish workable synchronization. It's quite obvious on the planet that now there are times of workable synchronization — teamwork, you might say — people striving for a common goal or common purpose, each doing "this" or doing "that." It is good training for spirituality as well.

When the Explorer Race manifests in 4.0, it will be a continuation of that effort. A lot of beings will simply want to stay there because it will be a nice place. It is not a rush to get someplace. I understand rushing is a desire when you have polarities and suffering — then rushing is something that is completely understandable — but when you have comfort and benevolence, there is no rush anymore. Stages of technology no longer require friction, so there is no suffering by anyone or anything. As a result, there is what you would call in this now time — "you" meaning those familiar with the Explorer Race idea — a vast slowdown in what you consider to be a pretty speedy process. It will take as long as it takes. It is very possible that many members of the Explorer Race will just stay there. But if you are talking about moving on, becoming a creator, and doing all of that, that will be *some* beings, not every being.

How many beings?

This is going to sound trite, but as many as it takes. Right now you have, considering those who are essentially waiting — doing other things but waiting, as we have mentioned before — you have, in terms of a percentage, about 98 percent — not the 99 you need to do the creator thing. So it won't take that many more individual souls to sign on to create what you wish to create. Also the whole idea of being a creator does not mean it is forever. There will be a certain amount of turnover, you might say, and some beings will choose to do this for a time and then they will say, "Okay, that's enough. Now I would like to participate on an individual basis." The idea of individuality will be something appealing, so there will be some turnover. I recommend that you consider the idea that it won't take much longer than at a maximum — believe it or not, I am going to give you years — of 100 years, and probably less than that, to have the 100 percent you need to produce a viable creator to continue the process that has been discussed in the past.

Your Soul and the Fourth Dimension

In the Explorer Race (Book 1): The Explorer Race *(Light Technology Publishing, 1996), Zoosh says that our souls have a judgment about negativity, and they won't join us — join the human physical — until we get out of negativity, or we would have been gone from this dimension a long time ago. Can you talk about that?*

They still have this. Instead of a judgment, though, I consider it, from my point of view, bias. Their bias, the soul's bias, is 100 percent benevolent, and they just aren't prepared to make a commitment to be entirely within most people all the time, ruling out when the body sleeps and the soul travels. So when you look at most people's auric field, there is a tendency to see the soul sort of bobbing in and out. If you could see the auric field, you would see it flare up at times — above a shoulder, above the head, something like that. This might happen more often if the physical person is involved in some memory or some experience of extreme negativity, meaning recalling suffering, recalling some trespass against the self or loved one, or experiencing hate or anger. Now, the soul won't try to leave but will actually become much more compassionately involved if there is pain, suffering, disease, or injury. Then the soul will engage entirely. So the soul is not trying to harm; it is not trying to escape pain. It's been prepared by Creator to have a bias to desire that move toward that 100 percent benevolence, which is actually the inner move and desire that is moving all people on the planet now and really functioning as the engine toward moving through the dimensional change from the third to fourth dimension, like the pedals and crank on a bicycle. So it is an intentional bias that Creator has placed in the soul.

The Explorer Race *says our souls reside now on the fourth dimension, and those souls are pulling us toward them.*

It may have been true then — in 1989 — but they are no longer there. They are anchored there. There is a difference, you see — they are anchored there, but they are with you. By "anchored" — picture it as an anchor with cords to your present placement in the passage from the third to the fourth dimension. This doesn't mean they are not corded to other places, teachers, guides, and so on, but they are anchored in that fourth-dimensional version of Earth so that it can also act as something that pulls you. But within each of your bodies, it also is creating that engine of attraction, kind of like a magnet's pulling and pushing, you might say.

This implies that the soul is a distinct and separate thing from our physical body but connected to it.

It is. The soul is a direct portion of your overall spirit. The physical body is, after all, loaned to you by Mother Earth, and the soul is really associated with your immortal personality and your overall spirit, meaning the total you. But the physical matter that makes up your body is Mother Earth's, and it is not going with you when you go between lives. You're not going to ascend physically. So the creation of selves is involved with the soul and the matter inside the mother coming together from Earth to form the baby and so on. But the soul is your true self as an individual — you on Earth, that immortal part of you. But the physical part of you returns to Earth and is meant to.

We are going to be on a different dimension of Earth, which I assume has different particles and stuff from which to make bodies. On Terra, are we in the soul body, or do we have physical bodies made up from that level of Earth?

Exactly — you have physical bodies made up from fourth-dimensional Earth. You do not have physical bodies made up from 3D or 3.5D Earth.

How does time work in the fourth dimension?

It is more vertical in the sense that you know what you need to know when you need to know it, meaning you still have day and night, the Sun and the Moon, but you are no longer on the clock, so to speak. You no longer work for eight hours or go to school for eight hours. The cultures and civilizations still have a lot of variety, which is something Creator is very fond of, but time is not the boss. I do not know how else to explain it because you will still experience time, but nobody will be wearing any watches.

You said there would be a lot of travel. How do we know when to meet the vehicle to the Pleiades if we don't know what time it is?

You don't need to have a bus token. If there are people who are interested in traveling "here" or "there," and a Pleiadian ship is passing by and can pick a few folks up, they will know. They will be able to feel your needs just as you will be able to feel their needs. Granted, they will still have to use a very small portion of their filter to protect themselves from the tiny amount of your so-called negativity — at that level, it will be called mild discomfort — but it is not so much of a filter that they will not be able to respond to your needs. You won't have to call them as people, and they won't have to ring a bell saying that they are here. So it will be a response based on easily shared feelings. It's like saying they will know not because they are any more evolved than they are now — they are just as evolved and no less — but because it will be safe for them to know. They won't have to deal with all of these extreme feelings you have now. And thus having to deal with that, they need a filter that protects them so much they can barely know what you are feeling at any given moment — with the exception, of course, of the very young or the very old who are in transition.

So the body that is made up of the physical fourth-dimensional Terra and the soul body, which has some mass, right?

Not a lot.

On that level, will the two be totally joined? Is that the way it works?

Well, they are totally, absolutely joined now, but if you are saying they will be joined better or more than they are now, my answer to that question can only be noooooooooo. Well, okay, but it has to include all of that sound because ... you're going to have to change that question.

You just said that the soul doesn't want to join the 3D or 3.5D human because there is negativity on this dimension, so how does this joining work on the fourth dimension? Does the soul stay in the body more?

Yes. You understand. With fourth-dimensional Earth and the Explorer Race there, at any given moment there will be no more than probably 1 percent to 1.25 percent discomfort. You notice that there is a change there.

Yes, always previously you have said we would have 2 percent discomfort.

But that has changed. So that raises a question: Why are so many people going to stay there? Well, the reason so many people are going to stay there is that it will feel really good — better than beings expect — because the 2 percent discomfort was expected. But it is not going to be that, so people will stay there.

The Physical Body and Spirit

Is there any level in which we actually live as the soul in the soul body without physical matter? Is there some level ahead of us that ...

Not ahead of you — it is not something that you are evolving toward from point A to finally achieve point B. It's always point A, or point Z, or whatever it is you want to say. Time is not a process of evolution. What would Zoosh say?

"Never forget that."

Right. Time is simply an avenue by which to express your personality's characteristics to the degree you wish to express any given part. But it is not a route from one place to another.

Well, let me rephrase that. We have talked to ninth-dimensional Zetas who live in a plasma body. Is a plasma body the soul body, or is it still some type of physical matter?

In the Zeta's plasma body, at that ninth-dimensional level, there is some physical matter. You would say it sort of — if you have the electric energy with the magnetic energy — is predominately electrical, but there is, recognizing that magnetics are part of electricity, enough extra magnetics to make it sufficiently soft, you might say, so one could express oneself in the feminine more than in the masculine, regardless of gender.

Is the soul made up of magnetic energy?

The soul is largely magnetic, but it can adapt to electricity in worlds that require more physical action. Let me put it this way: A sunrise is magnetic — this is a simile — whereas a fulcrum is electrical. Don't take that literally; it is just meant to help you understand the difference between a natural phenomenon, part of the nature of all life, and a mechanical function of a movable machine part or physical body. So to get back to your original question, there are many levels of experience and life that a soul might experience without a physical body at all. So yes, this is something that might very well have happened in the past, in the present at other dimensions or to other portions of you, or in the future. You know when the body really is at its deep sleep level, the soul functions as itself, going off here and there. It doesn't hang around, but it is corded to the body so that the body doesn't get frightened or start to return to Earth.

There must be a lot of cords floating around up there.

Yes, but the network is very finely tuned.

At some point, the soul, being part of the spirit, is subsumed up into spirit and there is only spirit. Is that right?

Before there was soul, there was spirit. So spirit is a portion of the soul, but it is not a linear connection. It is a constant. So the soul is spirit, and spirit is the soul, but to experience individuality without the very powerful presence of your entire spirit, it is helpful to have soul so that the body is not overwhelmed by that entire spirit.

So it is a connection, where we are, between the physical body and the spirit?

The soul and spirit are one — it is not a connection. The soul and spirit are one, so the soul literally is all of what the spirit is but not with the same amplitude. If you had your entire spirit in your body, there would be no way that you would not be your total being, and that would simply derail the purpose of the Explorer Race. You couldn't possibly forget anything if your total spirit was in your body, but as a soul, you are able to do that because the totality of you is essentially elsewhere. It depends how you look at it. Not in some other part of the universe — you know we are talking about time and space here, but simultaneously we are taking about something that is within something else. You can't describe it in a linear fashion is what I'm saying.

Could you say that the soul is a transduced-down version of the spirit?

No, the soul is the simultaneous version of the spirit. It is not down. There is no down.

Well then why is the soul so afraid of negativity when spirits aren't? Immortal personalities aren't.

Spirit is not compatible with negativity.

Well, it is not compatible, but it doesn't have that bias toward ...

What is the difference between bias and incompatibility? You are the one who is making the difference — I didn't say that.

Speeding Up

I read in Explorer Race *that our atoms are speeding up, and I assume that as they speed up, they expand. So at a certain point, is that rate of speeding up in frequency what puts us in the fourth dimension?*

Well, you understand speeding up doesn't mean moving from point to point — it means more that the atoms are in an excited state, speaking in terms of physics (not speaking as in looking forward to the circus), so in an excited state they are just ready — you might say more ready — to do something. So that's what is being sped up.

So in 1989, it was said that as we speed up, there will be a breaking point as we pass from fission to fusion because what happens in that moment is that all of the unresolvable karma will be resolved. And then it says that the planets that were blown up will implode and fuse. Is that how we get into the fourth dimension?

What is your question? That was a long quote. I can think of five or six questions there easily. What's your question? Don't assume. Things have changed. You cannot make an assumption in today's world based on that book. That book was for those times, just like the Blavatsky books were totally and completely relevant for those times. That doesn't mean *The Explorer Race* is no longer useful — it just means that certain things have changed. You want that change, I think, because this means progress.

You are thinking, if you don't mind my saying, that the marker of, say, 3.47, 3.52, or 3.56 involves progress from the third to the fourth dimension, but that is not true. Those markers are given to you so that you can understand the level of excitement of the neutrons and protons and all that business. But at any given moment, if everybody was ready to move on a personal basis at the same moment, you are not going to have to go to 3.75; you will just go from wherever you are straight to 4.0. The reason these numbers are given to you is not because *we* are attached to them; it is because *you* are attached to them because you are in a linear world and you are, of course, speaking for human beings. It doesn't mean this is a personal attachment. So understand that the change now has to do only with waiting for everybody — every last human being on Earth — to say, "Okay, let's do this." But not as a thought; it doesn't matter what you think. The feeling has to be present. If the feeling was present on an ongoing basis for everybody saying, "Okay" — interpreting a feeling as a thought — "let's do this," but not as a thought as a feeling — then *bing!* straight into the fourth dimension. It is not a linear migration.

So what has changed since that book was published? What is different now from then?

Beings have changed. Keep in mind some people have moved on, eh? Not everybody on the planet in 1989 is still here. That doesn't mean they are bad; it just means they've moved on and they are doing other things. But what's been added?

We decided that we were going to do it right this time.

It is much simpler than that. Some souls have moved on. Has anybody been born since 1989?

Oh, the newborns have souls that already move faster — their frequency moves faster when they are born.

The saturation of the new beings now — the children, some of whom who are no longer children — is enough of a saturation that that is what has changed.

Is there still the breaking point when Zoosh said we go from fission to fusion when we resolve this (formerly) unresolvable karma? Is that still ahead of us?

No. That has mostly been resolved, even within the context of thought. Certainly so-called unresolvable karma is resolving even as we speak because of the much greater ease in worldwide communication. There needs to be considerable improvement, but there is much greater ease, and people are able to communicate and discover how alike they are, and that is really a vital aspect. And who is doing that the most? The very young. Who are they?

These new souls who have a faster vibration.

There you are.

Transforming into the Fourth Dimension

There has to be a point where the third-dimensional physical body actually falls away because Earth's third-dimensional physical matter has to stay on third-dimensional Earth. Do we zap into the fourth dimension as adults?

I am going to try to paint a picture with words, but it is very difficult. I will do what I can. Imagine a video in which there is the baby, then there is the child, then there is the young adult, then there is the adult, and so on like that — but imagine that sped up. Generally speaking, you are all going to arrive there at different ages, ages that you find the most appealing — meaning not necessarily ages, but the level of physical maturity you find the most appealing. So for those who choose to go there, it will feel very much like you are moving through at a high speed — that's the best way I can describe it. And this is probably an esoteric description, but some of you may have seen this portrayed in one way or another, such as people who experience their whole lives flashing before their eyes. This happens sometimes to people who have had near-death experiences or something like that, and many of you have studied or read about these. So it happens very rapidly, and it is something that is felt. It will feel very comfortable. It happens in considerably less than 0.0001 second, but you feel it happening much slower than that, meaning your feelings experience it because it is a wondrous thing. It is like birth and painless death and birth again — painless in all parts, for some — but there is not necessarily birth involved at all. It is hard to describe because I tried to give you the image of the sped-up video — if you were standing off to the side and watching it, that's what you would see.

The way they film a flower blooming in time-lapse photography to show the petals opening?

Yes.

So we arrive there with our memories of who we are or ... ?

You will arrive with a sense of being well. You will have your personalities. You don't bring along any painful memories. How would that work there? It wouldn't.

There are seven billion people on Earth. How many beings will choose to go there, everyone?

That decision hasn't been made yet, because it requires everybody to make a personal decision, and it is not my job to make that decision for you. Keep in mind the greater size of the planet: If everybody decides to go, there will be plenty of room, but I don't think everybody will.

So who decides? What level of the total being decides to go there or some place else?

Just before the big move, the blur of motion, each person will decide. By that point, during the blur, as I am describing it, referring back to what I said, every human being will decide right in that moment whether he or she wants to be on that fourth-dimensional level of Earth, and he or she will be able to feel it. It will feel wonderful. The person will decide whether he or she wants to be on that level of Earth or some place else, whether to be involved in the group creator thing or to go somewhere else and do something else. There is total freedom. It's not something separate from you — it will be you.

Thank you for telling us how that works. Now the subatomic particles in all of the neutrinos and quarks and all those bits that make up our cells go faster and faster — and they expand, right? Does the speed correlate to the expansion?

The rate of excitement correlates to the expansion.

So the excitement is caused by our becoming more benevolent, by these new beings being born who already have that level of excitement ...

A moment. It becomes more excited on the basis of the feeling of Home. Fourth-dimensional Earth will be, physically speaking, something that feels very much like Home — and, of course, with the new beings who have arrived since '89.

But are there other elements that figure into this, like the particles from the Sun, cosmic rays, or the fact that we are moving in space to a place that has a different frequency? Does any of that figure into this as a cause?

Certainly, because cosmic rays do represent particles, and ultimately your physical body is made up of particles. I can't say that your spirit is made up of particles, because one particle, ten billion particles — it just doesn't factor in. But at the very least, your physical self is made up of particles, so certainly. The Sun is not excluded.

I mean do the cosmic rays and the rays from the Sun stimulate our excitement?

No. That is not what stimulates it. It feeds it, but it does not stimulate it. It means being energized — it's not exactly photosynthesis, but you're energized by the Sun. You know this. [**Editor's Note:** When you feel tired and need energy, go outside or by a window and face the Sun with closed eyes. Take several deep breaths, focusing on bringing the Sun's energy into your body.]

I am still curious. I have this image of the Terminator flashing into Earth from the future, or the ET in Starman *who cloned a body to use until his ship came to get him. When we arrive there, do we have clothes on?*

[Laughs.] If you want to. Again, it is a personal choice for each individual. Most likely you will have garments of some sort. But you know, if you would rather do otherwise, no one will call the police.

Let me give you an example. Say you are married and have a couple of children. When you get there, you will still be married and have a couple of children. And the chances are you will be more in love with your mate and get along great with your children, and they will get along well with you. Remember, discomfort will not be a part of that experience — with the exception of the tiniest amount, 1.25 percent discomfort — so everyone will get along much better. No more sibling rivalries.

This is amazing.

Yes, it is a wonderful thing.

You're saying this has never been done before — ever — in this entire creation?

Not according to what I know. I am not aware of it being done in this creation any time before. You have to keep in mind that there is a big thing going on here. Many beings of the Explorer Race want to get together and see whether they can run the universe. Creator will stick around for a while, so you will be kind of assistant managers, and then Creator will say, "Okay, it looks like you can handle it pretty well," and you'll take over and see how you do in the universe. You will probably make a few changes, but that's only natural. Still, you are made up and largely influenced by this Creator, so they won't be radical changes.

Well, we won't go into it now, but we're not truly made up of this Creator because we come from somewhere else, don't we?

Yes, but you've been here long enough.

We're influenced heavily.

Yes, indeed, and you wouldn't have stuck around this long if you didn't like what's going on here a whole lot. And I am talking about the entire universe, not simply this current passage through the school of the Explorer Race.

So we are in the fourth dimension. Then what? During the time we are there, this rate of excitation keeps going as a natural process toward —

No, it slows down — way, way down — because there is no longer the compelling desire to get on to something more benevolent, more like Home. No, it slows down quite a bit.

So will the span of life be longer, then?

Yes. On that fourth-dimensional Earth, it will be typical to have lifetimes of, say, 700 to 750 years — maybe longer, like something described in the Old Testament.

I think you said that we, the humans on this planet, were 6 percent of the Explorer Race. At what point do we connect with the other 94 percent?

You are doing that now. You are never totally disconnected from them. You can't be totally disconnected from your total being. Now, I understand that I said your spirit is your total being, but that is only within the context of your personality. The total being of the Explorer Race is associated with all of you — the beings who are committed to being the Explorer Race. We will stop here. Good night and good life.

Thank you. Good life.

CHAPTER TWENTY-FOUR

Human and Andromedan Minds

Isis

August 13, 2012

In the third dimension, we have all of these levels of the mind. Many of you beings have said through Robert in these books we have published that the mind is foreign to us, that we are using it in service of the Andromedans so that eventually they can merge their linear minds with their feelings. Would you say a little about the Andromedan mind for those not familiar with the Explorer Race books?

I'm going to get there, but you have given almost all of that back to the Andromedans. And that is another contribution toward being unable to remember things because the Andromedan mind has to do with the past and the present. It doesn't have very much to do with the future, so that is part of the reason the Andromedans often consider themselves to be historians: They are very interested and attached to the past. And while that is all right in a civilization that is totally benevolent, when a civilization has considered and has flirted with the 1 percent of discomfort, which the Andromedan civilization has done in its past, then you find — remember we said that this experiment was tried a few times — that they remember the experiment, the discomfort, as being jarring. So they don't think much of it. And that is because their society is very masculine and the discomfort was felt by them in a masculine fashion — not by all beings in Andromeda, but the ones who tried the 1 percent discomfort. So the Andromedan mind is something that is not fixed or attached to the past, but it is fascinated and loves the past and is also interested in the present. Generally, lines from the past merge with the present for them, and the present merges with the past. That is why, for the past few thousand years, the people on Earth were volunteered to take on the Andromedan mind — not only to have a means to be more conscious of the stages of existence, meaning thought, but also to have the capacity to create resolution, which is one of the primary reasons for the Explorer Race on Earth. This, of course, has all been covered in previous books.

So the mind of the Andromedans — what they loaned you without losing any of their own — has really been given back. There is only about 7 percent of it residual in Earth society, and that's part of the reason people have a hard time remembering the past. It is in your nature to be in the present moment, and all this talk and channeling and all these people saying in various therapeutic ways that you have to be in the present — not necessarily "here's why" but "here's how to do it" — is entirely about something that is completely natural for you. The idea of being in the past or being caught up in the past or attached to the past is totally unnatural and immediately felt by the people of Earth as uncomfortable. Unfortunately, that is one of the things that has expanded the level of discomfort.

We are told there are levels of the mind: the subconscious, the conscious, and the part that used to be called the superconscious. The subconscious was the connection — it was like a buffer between the conscious mind and the soul, wasn't it?

No, it is between the conscious mind and the body.

Okay. So in the fourth dimension then, you or another of the beings who channel through Robby have said we won't have a subconscious mind.

No, because you won't need that. You will be in the moment, and you will be totally aware of your physical bodies — you won't need to have anything insulating you. In the so-called higher consciousness realms, you might say that the soul doesn't need insulation, so the conscious mind is utilized not to generate inspiration but to receive it. The subconscious brings up some word or two of inspiration from the physical body or perhaps from guides or teachers — mostly from the physical body, because the physical body is a portion of that. But for you on Earth now, you understand, it is the conscious mind that has to receive it so that the word is understood in your own language. And therefore the process of the subconscious will not be needed, because at that higher level — at just the fourth-dimensional level — you are not going to need that stage. Your conscious mind will be totally in the present, you see.

And as a result, you won't be thinking about the past; you will be entirely focused on the present, and you will know what you need to know when you need to know it. But the root orientation of the subconscious mind will be unnecessary because you will honor your physical body as your immediate teacher, and it is that portion of you that is always in the present moment. So in the fourth dimension, you will have the conscious mind, and you will have a different definition of the superconscious. There, the superconscious will be that portion of you that is always consciously connected to guides, teachers, and inspiration — not just a word here and there but always available. You won't just sit down and totally be in that all of the time, but it is always there and readily accessible in phrases, not just words, in whatever language you may be using.

Education, Science, Art, and Medicine in 4D

All right, we will be in the present, and we will be in contact with our bodies and our guides and teachers. But we won't use the mind, thought, or the structured mind, right? We will be more flowing, more ...

Yes.

So how does that relate to what we know as culture now? Will there be no formal education?

There won't be formal education as you know it, but of course parents will be inclined to teach children not only what is helpful and fun — "this is what your brothers did," "this is what your uncles used to do," that kind of stuff — but there will be an educational process just to learn. Really, you know, it is essentially parents, siblings, family, and friends who teach children to learn how to speak, so there will be things like that. But there won't be schools. You are not going to have to leave the house and go to school to experience education and all the other stuff that goes on in the school that tends to disrupt, corrupt, harm, and injure not only the physical body at times but also the orientation toward spirituality. In your now time, children can be taught all about good and evil and so on. They can be taught to be good; they can be taught that "this" behavior is good and "that" behavior is bad. They go to school, and the example of other things is all around them, so then they have to confront the evidence of their eyes and experience. School will not be like that in the fourth dimension. School will be in the home, but children won't have to learn algebra. Not that algebra isn't a significant contribution in your now planet, but you won't have to learn that in the fourth dimension because you won't be building bridges and you won't be constructing vast buildings. You will live in a totally benevolent society on a totally benevolent world. The only structures, if you want to call them that, that will be built will be those created by stones that want to come together. So some of that will be because people are taught how to interact lovingly with stones that wish to come together, or the stones themselves will wish to come together and people will sometimes notice it and it will be fun. Stones will celebrate life as much as all beings. One of the things you do when you celebrate life is humor, so the stones might be funny.

So there won't be science and technology?

Not as you know it now; it won't be a separate pursuit. It won't be needed because one of the vast reasons for science and technology is to help resolve something. That is it at the core — it is "How can we fix this?" But there won't be anything broken.

What about art?

Oh, lots of art. But it won't be with chalks and paints that didn't volunteer to do that. It will be by other means — by dance, of course, which will be very much demonstrated. But if you are talking about paintings, not really. It will have to do with — say you might have a picture in your mind's eye of some place you've been, or visitors will come and say, "Oh, you can see this." They will probably use something like liquid light so you can see something. You will learn how to do that. So art could be recalled, meaning you would think of something and then it could be seen by others, and then it wouldn't be available. But then the moment it is desired again, it would be present. In other words, it won't be a fixed piece of canvas on which oils have been spread in a masterly fashion or otherwise. There won't be a frame made out of a tree that didn't volunteer to do that. I am not trying to indict you; I am saying this is how it will be there, because there all of you will remember who you are and who everybody else is. So you wouldn't think of cutting down a tree — not even for a moment.

You said there would be families. Will the method of birth be similar to now but painless?

Yes, and there will be ETs who will come and explain cloning, but you won't be interested in that. It will fall on deaf ears, you might say. It will be the method you have now, only there will be no pain whatsoever — no wounding, no injury, no pain, none. Of course, one of the reasons is that babies will be smaller.

What about doctors and nurses?

They won't be necessary. A mother will be able to receive her baby as it comes out, and it will be a sacred thing. There might be midwives, but doctors and nurses will not be needed because there are no diseases. Birth will not be treated as a medical crisis, though it is sometimes in some cases for you now in your society. It will be different: It will be totally benevolent. There won't be some huge thing a woman has to get out of her body through a small opening. It will be a nice, small, complete thing that the woman will be able to get out of her body easily and gently and receive with love into her hands. It will be a beautiful thing, and the baby will be stable. You might put the baby in some environment, but it will be stable. The baby will not suddenly grow. Childhood will not be lost. Childhood is still a wonderful thing, and the baby will live through childhood. You have to remember also that people will live longer in bodies that don't have disease or anything like that. So childhood will take place.

A life needs an interest, a purpose, something to focus on. How will these interests come into being in the child and the adult if there isn't anything to do?

Oh, you are mistaken, completely. But it is understandable that you're asking the question, and certainly a lot of people would ask the same question. All souls now on your planet come in with interests and things that they want to do, and that is what they will do — just a variety of things. No soul comes in with a desire to make stuff out of other stuff. That has never happened. That kind of interest evolves in the society if that is what the society does. Souls come in because they want to pursue something — art, music, communication, and all kinds of beautiful things, loving things.

The Art of Communication

How would they pursue communication?

Well, they might be interested in the subtle communications that nonhumans have with humans, for instance. And they might become experts on such communications, and it might become their specialty — the communication between humans and, say, trees. And that might be something they would choose to pursue if they are interested, perhaps even visiting other planets when visitors come. The visitors might say, "Oh, if you like to do that, we know this place that has all these things, and we can go there for a time, and then we will come back. And some people will want to do it. Most people would want to stay on the planet, but the offer will be made.

ETs have science and technology and build spacecraft. What dimensions do they live in?

You are saying that as if they all do. No, only a minority of ETs have that. The only reason you have tended to interact in the past with ETs who have science and technology is that this is what you are interested in and — as you know quite well — what other people on the planet are primarily interested in now. But I would say of all the worlds that are peopled — not just with humans but humanoids in general — the places that have science and technology and all of that would be about 0.5 percent. Of course, that is still a large number.

What about all those people with curiosity and lust for life and an expanding mind — what do they do?

They don't have to expand their minds anymore, because they will be totally in the present, and inspiration will be totally in the present. That doesn't mean they know everything — it just means they will develop. Say they come in with an interest in music: They will develop more and more in the application of their interest as they go along. They are not going to play a guitar like you have today because that is made of materials that didn't volunteer to be the guitar. But they will find a way to make music in the natural world they are living in and in the most obvious way — singing. So they will produce that, and they may discover along the way that singing is part of communication. Those people who are interested in communication might get together with people who are interested in the music of singing, because one of the ways that trees communicate with birds is through sound — the wind moving through the leaves and so on. Birds love that sound.

How will people on that dimension interact with ... will we call it Mother Earth or Terra? Will we interact with the fourth-dimensional planet with more awareness than we have now?

How will they interact with the planet? Like a member of the family. The planet will be considered a member of the family, to be loved and cherished. Not just a place you are living — there is no "just." "Just" doesn't exist there. The planet is a member of the family.

Will there be communion, interaction, communication, or ...

For those who are interested in communication, there might very well be. And perhaps the stone, the soil, and each tiny pebble will have something to say if there is someone there to interpret. And those who are interested in communication might learn that. Or those who are interested but not interested enough to pursue it themselves — those who just want to get the message from that stone — will know what they need to know when they need to know it. They will have it. But there will be those who want to help others communicate if they want that stone to do something. Nobody will throw a stone; they wouldn't even think of it, because the stone didn't ask for that. If the stone asks you to toss it somewhere, that is the only time that will happen.

What about what we call shamanism?

That means to understand the spiritual nature of Mother Earth and understand that you are a portion of it and so is everyone else.

So everyone will be a shaman in the fourth dimension?

In a sense, but it is just natural. Everyone will know these things, and they will be able to interact with all life benevolently.

Will there be people who focus on that?

Possibly, but most people will be able to do these things. You won't have to have ceremonies to purify things because they will be pure. I'm just using that as an example.

Physical Expansion to Expand Consciousness

It is my understanding that we are expanding — not just in consciousness, but physi-cally. What percentage larger are we now than we were at 3.0?

An interesting question, that! I'll see if I can answer it. You're one-third larger. Of course, everything else is also, so you can't tell.

If now, halfway, we are one-third larger than we were at 3.0, what percentage larger will we be at 4.0?

No, it doesn't relate. This process of becoming larger is a partway thing. You have to expand your consciousness, so you have to get big-ger. But at some point when you are around three-quarters of the way through, you won't have to expand your consciousness anymore, so that will fall away. Right now you are sort of using the volume system to expand your consciousness, but that will not be needed by the time you are at 3.74. That will just fall away, but you won't notice any difference. And if anybody does, they will say, "Oh, what was that? Oh well." It will be something like a light phenomenon.

So we will shrink back then?

You won't notice it. Everything will be relative, but you won't need to expand any more.

Physical expansion to expand consciousness. Wow! Who set this up? Is there somebody out there doing this experiment?

Who else could have possibly set this up but one who loves variety?

Creator, okay. You talked about the particles having more space between them because they were excited. So is that part of this process of getting larger, that ...

Yes, excited in the scientific sense, not excited with happiness.

But moving faster. So you said we will only be four feet tall at 4.0, so ...

You will be taller than that — almost five feet tall, or maybe four feet, eight inches, something like that. So of course the planet will also seem bigger, but the planet is way bigger. But it is not so much bigger that you could have trillions of people living on it, because not everybody will want to do that.

So I understand that the vibration, or the excitation, is faster on the fourth dimension. There is more space between the particles or the atoms; there is a higher frequency. Yet we will do all that in a smaller physical body?

Wait, I have to correct that. There is more space, but light is also experienced differently. If you had more space between atoms, you still ought to be able to detect those atoms with an instrument at your level now — but that is not all it is. The experience of light is different; the phenomenon of light is different. Light will be experienced differently so that, essentially, the atomic weight of something is not as perceptible. If you could see the weight of something, the mass of something ... you can see the mass now through an electron microscope, but that is because of the way you experience light. In the fourth dimension, light is experienced differently. It is still light, but I cannot really say right now the difference because it would be too easy for you to stumble over it and create a problem. I will just say that life and light are different there — more benevolent, of course, but also different. So it is not just the spaces between the atoms.

If we looked at someone in the fourth dimension from where we are at this moment, would we see them, or would they be vibrating too fast for us to see?

The basic answer to your question is no. But if they wished to be seen, or if you were trained to see higher-dimensional beings, then you might get a quick view in those circumstances.

So there could be fourth-dimensional beings wandering over our planet right now and we wouldn't even see them? We would just walk right through them?

For that matter, there are eighth-dimensional beings wandering around. You can be in the same place at the same time; you just don't bump into each other because you're not occupying the same light refraction.

And that is why for years you kept trying to call it a focus, and I didn't understand "focus" and kept calling it a dimension?

That's why. Well done.

Okay. It is hard to ask questions about something I don't totally understand.

Of course it is. You are doing very well, considering.

So we will consider ourselves as planetary citizens, since obviously we can't have countries underground?

You will not even think of having separate countries — it just won't even occur to you. There might be different cultures based on the people's interests, but they won't all be in one place. You might visit somebody who has a similar culture just for fun, but no, there won't be countries. It would be like now, if someone came from another planet, they wouldn't consider you to be German or Italian or African — they would consider you an Earth citizen. They would never think of saying that — they might have some judgments, though. You wouldn't consider them judgments if you heard them, but it would be in their voice — sort of how they said it. It wouldn't be *what* they said. Now, you've noticed that before because sometimes you will say exactly the same word in different ways and it means different things — different tonal structure. For the most part they would say, "These are Earth people."

Can we come back and visit this dimension after we leave it?

Why would you want to? You could choose to be born back here on third-dimensional Earth if you wanted to. I don't think you'd like it. Once you are in a place of beauty and wonder and total love, why would you want to go to some place that isn't like that? Keep in mind that people will sometimes study ancient times and say, "Oh, wouldn't that be fantastic if I could live there!" But it comes as a complete package.

Yes, with bad plumbing and no hospitals, hot showers, phones, or takeout food.

Right. Now in closing, I will say that all souls agree on the soul level that moving to the fourth dimension — to a totally benevolent planet, a totally benevolent life — is something desired by all souls, and it will go as fast as it goes. Good night.

CHAPTER TWENTY-FIVE

Nuclear Radiation Is a Threat to Life on the Planet

Isis

December 3, 2012

This is Isis with a brief reminder. Right now in the seas of the world and spreading across many oceans, especially the Pacific, you are going to find a lot of jellyfish, especially the round ones with hanging tendrils sometimes called Portuguese man-of-war (but I don't think war is their intent). This is because not only are they committed to protecting the seas for all beings but they are also able to do something about nuclear radiation. As many, if not all, of you know, the radioactive materials are still coming out of that reactor — at least from one reactor, maybe two — in Japan and even other places. And the seas are gradually getting completely poisoned because of the means used to attempt to keep the radioactive pile, as you call it, cool. This is a little difficult to do when the containment vessel has holes in it, so the process of running the water used for cooling into the ocean is basically poisoning the ocean. It is important for you to know this because there may be something you can do.

First off, if you hear that these big jellyfish, the ones that people take pictures of sometimes because they are so beautiful, are in the water, please stay out. Don't disturb them. Keep away from them. If they are there, they are probably doing something to prevent radiation from coming your way or dealing with radiation in some way. They are able to do this.

I am also going to recommend that those of you who do living prayer or benevolent magic say the following living prayer. First say,

> "I am asking that all of the most benevolent energies that are available for me be all around me and all about me now."

Pause for about ten or fifteen seconds. Or, for those of you who feel energies, wait until they fade just a little bit — the fading "just a little bit" means that you have the go-ahead to say the other words for what you are asking. Then slowly say,

> *Living Prayer*
> "I am asking that all jellyfish and other beings of the sea, land, and sky who are able to reduce or transform the radioactivity in the waters, on the land, and in the sky now be supported in the most benevolent way and protected in the most benevolent way to do these good works."

What other land, sea, and sky beings are able to transform this radioactivity?

To an extent, deer are able to do this, sometimes antelope, and often reindeer — not elk so much, but they know about it; they are just not able to do much about it. Also earthworms are able to do something. In the sky, among other beings — I am not going to say all of them — orioles, ravens, and occasionally some crows can do this. There are a few other birds — generally speaking, the most colorful ones: some parrots, wild parrots, and also a bird called cardinal and a few other colorful birds — that are able to do something. But human beings must also be encouraged to do what they can, and many are doing a great deal.

Do the sea, land, and sky beings work with benevolent magic, or do they actually work with the energy of the radiation? What do they do?

I can only say that they work with the energy, because uranium in its natural form — in the ore pitchblende — is a natural substance, but after being used in an atomic reactor it is no longer natural. But to the degree that it still is natural, that is what they can work on.

What percentage of this can they transform?

Perhaps all of them working together — not counting human beings — perhaps 15 percent.

Figure 26.1. The Fukushima nuclear station after the tsunami. Image credit: AP. Permission requested.

If humans work together, how much can they transform?

I am not talking about humans working on transforming the radiation. At this time, I am talking about scientists and so on. Others — human beings from the scientific realm — at this time cannot transform any of it.

But shamanic human beings —

They may be able to help. The capacity to transform would be most efficiently done by human beings who feel energies. I am not saying you are excluded if you don't, but for those of you who feel energy — especially benevolent energies — at the top of your head, in your chest, or wherever you feel it, ask for the energy to come up. It may just come up automatically because your intent will be felt. And then say,

> *Living Prayer*
> "I am asking that all destructive radiation that is in the wild on Earth now be transformed in the most benevolent way for all beings."

Ah, in the wild — separating it from the uranium being used in atomic energy plants.

Yes, exactly. An awful lot of people are using atomic energy to light their homes and to power their factories and so on.

Okay. We hadn't received the words for the benevolent magic for the radiation before. So what has changed?

Nothing — just the urgency.

CHAPTER TWENTY-SIX

The Effects of Overlapping Planets

Grandfather

Transcription of YouTube video posted December 3, 2012

This is Grandfather. There is a temporary situation that has developed, though it has been coming on and getting more intense over the past few years, and recently it has begun showing evidence of that intensity. The situation is this: You are currently in a situation that could be called overlapping worlds. I know that there have been a lot of predictions about a collision between this planet and another planet, but this is not a physical phenomenon. It is, however, something that will impact you — especially many of you — in a completely unexpected way, on your emotional level and to some extent on your mental level.

This is how the impact will take place: It will feel as if you need to be doing two completely conflicting things in the same moment. And I am going to give you an example. How many of you have had the experience where you go to drink water and it goes down the wrong way? Either you were distracted or, unconsciously, you started to take a breath as you started drinking the water. That's a perfect example of a conflict that has a physical impact on you, but the cause is associated with two different impulses at the same time that don't coincide with each other.

This is the impact that is going on now. This is part of the reason there have been so many crazy and unexplainable events — and by crazy, I do not mean people who are out of touch, even temporarily, with their thought processes. I am talking about circumstances that happen in a moment but that are so overwhelming that they might cause a person to do something so completely out of character that others who knew them or loved them or even just saw them around would be completely baffled as to how this could have happened. Now, many of you have knowledge of such things, circumstances, or events — if not firsthand, then at least secondhand.

This is what is going on: There is a situation right now where you find yourself in overlapping worlds. One is a world — a physical world, a physical planet — but it is billions of miles from here, so there is no danger of physical impact. This other world in a completely different part of the universe has some parallels with you here. Many of you are experiencing other lives there within the context of reincarnation, and therefore those of you who are experiencing other lives in that world are the most susceptible to these strange conflicts. For the majority of you, this strange conflicting situation will happen in a dream, and you will wake up and be almost overwhelmed by the dream, feeling as if you are in this world that you are in now and simultaneously pulled by some other strange force that has no context in this world at all. This is another example.

Those of you living stressful lives and experiencing such things will have to be very careful. The first thing — and this is the most important — is if you're feeling overwhelmed by your life, you must make some effort to give yourself more time or stop doing certain things, whatever they are, so that you feel you have more time. This will require discipline on your part to take at least one day off; for those of you who are overwhelmed by responsibilities that you must serve, take at least six hours off while you are awake during the week sometime. It doesn't have to be on a weekend; it can be anytime. Get somebody to spell you, somebody to do what you need to do in that time. And if they need help, you do what they require so they can take six hours or half a day off — or a whole day would be better.

You must discipline yourself during that time to do no work whatsoever. You will feel an urgent sense to be doing "this," "that," and "the other" thing, but your physical emotional body — meaning the physical feelings in your body — requires complete relaxation. When you get good at this, you will find yourself sleeping, just napping, during that time and doings things that you miss doing, such as reading a book, just staring out the window, sitting in the backyard playing with your dog or petting your cat, or singing — doing something that is really relaxing and comforting to you in the most benevolent way. This is available for you.

So now I will give you a further explanation. These overlapping worlds are affecting each other. There is a tremendous similarity between the worlds, except in size. The other planet is three to four times the size of this planet, and thus, if you were on that world in your now bodies, the gravitational pull would be overwhelming. So that world also has another situation like you have. It has a sun, it has other planets in orbit around that sun, but in this case, there are thirteen planets, whereas here you have — and I am going to count Pluto as a planet — apparently nine planets. There are more planets here in this solar system; they are just not obvious at the moment. But some astronomers have been able to detect their presence on the basis of various gravitational anomalies and so on. And please pursue that — there is a tenth and even an eleventh and, depending on how you count, a twelfth planet here.

For the next three months, there are and will be these strange situations. You must discipline yourself to take time off. If you have time off and more time on your hands than you need, if you have friends or relatives, do things for them so that they can take time off — but not so much that you become overwhelmed also. You will be able to help each other through these times, and knowing that there is something going on will also be helpful.

There is one last important point, and that is the world is not going to come to an end. It is not even going to be more intense. It will seem just like any other day, but you will still be functioning within the essence of what I am talking about here. As I have said, it will be at its most intense for the next three months, and then it will fade rapidly. The world will continue on, so please don't worry about that. It is not time to do those things that you always wanted to do but didn't because of how risky they are.

For those of you who have weapons in the house, if you feel overwhelmed, put them under lock and key. And if you have other family members who seem to be overwhelmed and just acting out of the ordinary and you have weapons in the house, put the weapons under lock and key. It is okay to have them available for emergencies, but put some kind of situation in place where weapons are carefully kept from everybody.

For those of you operating in illegal situations, meaning breaking the law — and this is a large percentage of the population — this is particularly important for you, since you often have weapons. And even though you might think of yourself as rational, you may not be rational in various situations. So you might find yourself being totally explosive with people you work with or doing something that even afterward will cause your friends and associates to say, "What happened to him (or her)?" or "Why did he(or she) do that?" It is going to affect you as well, so I am addressing you. Pay attention — you are not immune to these things.

Now, for those in law enforcement, it is the same for you. You know how very often your lives are overwhelmed by too much to do and way too much overtime. So those of you who have assisting backup volunteers for law-enforcement duties, this is the time to ask them to help, especially over the next three months. This is particularly important for those of you who are running the departments, but sometimes there is someone advising the department or in a politically influential situation, so please make it clear to the chiefs that it is fine to have people come in and volunteer in positions where that is possible.

Take time off, even if it takes discipline. Relax, play with the dog, or play with the children. Do things that you remember you used to have time for, and do them in the most benevolent way. This situation will pass, but it is a time during which you will feel conflicted and pulled in ways that don't seem to be rational or real. But it is temporary and you will get through this. Help each other.

Also, one last thing: This is not a prediction — this is happening right now. You can get through it. Help each other, and help yourself. Good life.

CHAPTER TWENTY-SEVEN

How to Cope with the Harmonic Energy of Overlapping Planets

Isis

December 3, 2012

There is another world across the universe that is overlapping our world and causing us to do two conflicting things at once. What is the dynamic? Is it only humans who are having incarnational lives on that planet who are being affected?

The people who are most likely affected — and, generally speaking, not in ways that are out of control, so to speak — are people who have lives in some form on that planet. Right now that is equal to about 15 percent of Earth's population. That's a lot. Most people will have this experience as a dream, and while the dream is upsetting, you can say, "Okay, that's a dream, and now let me get on with my life." But I guarantee you the dream is upsetting. Sorry, that is just the reality.

However, some people who are leading highly stressed or way-too-busy lives, regardless of how normal and healthy they might be, could be tilted over the edge. That's why it was recommended, you see, that all weapons be locked up with a keylock. People have weapons in some circumstances, so somebody ought to be wearing the key around the neck or on a keychain, but it shouldn't be just readily handy all the time. You will know if you are one of the people who's affected if you have the dream. But once you have the dream, that's over for you — you are not going to be affected some other way.

The hazards are for people who are having, as I said, extremely busy and overwhelming lives. If you can get at least six hours off a week — a whole day would be better — then you probably won't be tipped over the edge to do something destructive to yourself or others. It's not necessarily going to make people crazy, but it could cause you to do something that is way, way out of balance for you on a temporary basis. The reason for this is that the other planet functions largely in a completely different realm than yours does. It is not just that it is a different dimension, but that world is completely different. It is not violent; it is just that what those people do and what you do are so diametrically opposed that they can create temporarily — for ten seconds here or fifteen seconds there, not for hours on end — an extreme conflict that will confuse people so much that it will be as if they briefly stepped into a different dimension.

Now, a long time ago it was stated through this channel that if people temporarily stepped into a different dimension and were able to find their way back, they would probably be crazy for the rest of their lives, because things like that cannot be done safely on Earth, as it is now without protection. If you are very carefully protected not only spiritually but also mentally and technologically, it may be possible, but not as a regular habit. I don't recommend it. So that's the big issue.

Diametrically Opposed Ways of Life

Is this planet in the paradoxical realm or something? Is that what you mean by "so diametrically opposite"?

No, it is just their way of life. It is very typical that beings on other planets are living lives that are completely different from yours. That is the norm. Living your life the way it is on Earth is totally and completely unusual. So the fact that other people live lives that are completely different, or even diametrically opposed, would be normal. So this is not an exception.

So only the 15 percent of humans on Earth who have lives on that other planet are affected, or everybody on Earth now is affected?

It could be anybody — it's just that those 15 percent are the *most likely* to be affected.

What's the dynamic with the people who don't have lives there? What's the connection?

You're on Earth — that's it. And it's a temporary, overlapping energetic situation that has been building for a while. And that is part of the reason there have been all these predictions about colliding planets from very well-intended people. However, the collision is not happening physically; it is happening energetically. This planet is billions and billions of miles away; it is on the other side of the universe.

How are we affecting them?

They are having a hard time, but because they do not have what you call negativity or polarity, it is easier for them. But there are a lot of beings there to give aid and comfort, and mostly what is working best for them is to be put into a deep sleep. So they will basically sleep for the next three to four months.

Was it known in advance that this would happen, or did it just happen and everyone was surprised?

It wasn't expected, but it happens because of the current resonance. It is not unusual for things to be extreme for your planet right now. How many times have we said that traversing while everyone is alive from one dimension to another has not been done before? So not to be confusing, but the unexpected should be expected.

You said the current resonance — is there something different about the next three months?

It's not just this three months; it has been happening for about three years. It's just that it has now built up to a crescendo.

But three months and it will be over? How many on that planet are affected?

They are all affected now. They have been affected for quite a while. Some of them have been asleep for a couple of years.

But then what happens to their society, their culture, their civilization?

If you have beings from other places who are not affected, they can keep things in a suspended state — everything just stops. Keep in mind there is no polarity there, no negativity.

Are these beings who are affected human beings or some other life form?

Another life form.

And what is the attraction for humans to want to have a life there now? Why so many of them in that one place now?

It's calm. A lot of human beings — especially if told that they could have a life, even temporarily, that was completely calm right now — I assure you that a lot of human beings would say, "Yes, yes, please."

But if these beings are sleeping, how then are we feeling this urge to do two different things at the same time if we are not connected with live, walking-around souls?

You're not connecting with *them* — it is the planets themselves.

Helping Out

The planets are overlapping. So what is the mechanism that makes us want to do some-thing different? Do we want to do something that is happening on that planet?

It is the harmonic. We have given this example before — when you can tap something and it creates a resonant tone, other things might res-onate also, even though you might not hear them. That's the thing. Nor-mally when a planet is moving — granted, this is very rare — but when a planet is moving between dimensions, every harmonic is completely in tune, and the planet does not have to take care of anything other than itself. Think about all of the life forms that are on the planet now. Should Earth have to take care of them too? That is too much. So there are times when she is just trying to survive and to care of as many as possible, but you have to help out.

How do we do that?

We already gave that: the six-hour rest — six hours or more per week. One of the other things you can do is sing more, even if you don't consider your singing voice particularly good. In times past when the churches were more filled or when people used to just gather and sing together around the piano or what have you, this used to be very fre-quent in families and communities. Even going back 100 to 150 years, people did that a lot. But now it is not typical. Even at sporting events in the past, people would sing their anthems, school songs, state songs, and the like. Now, it is not so common. Somebody sings and everybody else listens. Sing more — it will help. Sing whatever you want to sing. Singing will help a lot.

So what percentage of the 15 percent might feel so stressed that, as you said, they might tip over the edge?

I don't want to say, because if I say, that fixes it. It's been happen-ing, and it's not okay. Lately there seem to be people going off the deep end. They go someplace, they shoot a bunch of people, and then they shoot themselves. This is not typical. Granted, if a world is overpopu-lated, there is a tendency in a polarized world, such as you have here, for people to be more suicidal, and they don't always give evidence of that. It might not always be obvious, but generally speaking, that's why we advise taking time off — that will head a lot of it off. It might even be a discipline to take time off, but take the time off to completely relax. Don't take time off to catch up on your email — that's not relaxing. You need to alter your lives. Try to do some of the benevolent things that were done before.

Now, this is different from what you had said before about some people who, if they were on certain kinds of drugs, the drugs would interact with their brain waves and cause them to, as you say, "go over the edge." This is different from that, right?

Right.

All these things that are affecting us!

That's because it is really up to you to be doing things for yourselves right now as human beings. Granted, there are several spiritual people doing things, and actually many spiritual people doing things, but they can only do so much — they have to sleep, they have to eat, they have to rest. Other people will have to do things too.

So here is the issue: Your planets are not at odds; this is just a harmonic that is happening that wouldn't happen otherwise, but because you are shifting between dimensions, that is what's happening. In about three months or so, it will just rapidly fade, but it is important for you to know about this. Those of you who have been doing benevolent magic and living prayer for a while, make up something on your own. I recommend that you do a living prayer, because it will be for everyone and will include you. If you want to do something particular for yourself, do that too, but make it up on your own. Use the Mini-*Transformation Book: How to Change the World by Changing Yourself* or the *Benevolent Magic and Living Prayer* book (Light Technology Publishing, 2005) to follow as a guideline if you want, but I can't always give you the words. We expect you to do the words also. Good life.

Thank you. Good life.

CHAPTER TWENTY-EIGHT

The Dolphins Are Working Hard to Awaken Humanity

Dolphin Deva

February 20, 2013

Dolphin Deva.

Dolphin Deva — that's a new one. Welcome.

Migrating Dolphins Are Distributing Awakening Energy

There is curiosity about the migration patterns of many dolphins. Let me see what's going on. It does not seem sensible to people because, very often, a dolphin goes "this" way and then "that" way. But what is happening is dolphins are distributing energy. It's not so much that they are going somewhere, but I'm calling it a "migration pattern," because that's how it is being perceived, you see.

To contribute to speeding up your awakening to your natural state, the emanation of energy to support that is being broadcast in this fashion. You know that if you were to go out and run around the block, your energy would be going out. Some people do this just to feel better. But in the case of many dolphins doing this, a tremendous amount of energy goes out. They are very energetic beings. This goes well beyond the area where this latest video was taped [see http://laughingsquid.com/1000-dolphins-stampede-off-the-coast-of-dana-point-in-california/]. So it would spread, for example, not only through Southern California, but also northern Mexico. It would eventually migrate energetically to

Southern Arizona and, to a lesser degree, points north of the areas mentioned. However, there have been other emanations from dolphins — and sometimes whales, but whales are not in large enough number to do this anymore — further up the coast in the area of California. This is partly because many dolphins feel welcomed by people who live in California. And this extends into Baja, California, as well. Many people there like or love dolphins, so the area is considered relatively safe for dolphins to do this.

The effect of this, at least in those areas, will be that the people there

Figure 29.1. A pod of thousands of dolphins off the coast of Dana Point in California. Image credit: www.DolphinSafari.com.

will have an opportunity — if their souls agree, as well as their angels, guides, and teachers — to reclaim their natural spirit capabilities about one and a half times as fast as the rest of the world. There is hope that this seeding of energy will help to bring about normalization of the stress point associated with the need level for human beings to wake up spiritually. This need level is very, very high, but the process of transformation, while it is faster than it once was, is still very slow.

Human Resources Are Limited, but Some Animals Are Helping

There is a hazard here: There are only so many human teachers on the planet. Even with your improved communications these days, many of those things must be taught in person on a one-to-one basis so that the energy is compatible between teacher and student. It is not sufficient, most of the time, for this to happen in a video or in print, for example. It must be in person. So given that the teachers are few and far between to learn even basic things, there must be a means to amplify. Some of the human teachers are working now to amplify the energy that they are able to broadcast, and this is also helpful.

There are other species of beings on the planet who are also helping to amplify this energy, though they also have to deal with hazards, mostly having to do with humans not understanding who they are and that they are really supporting the human population in many ways. I will name a few of these species, but there are many more than I can name at this time: dandelions (you call them), ants (you call them — I'm giving words that you use), bear, and antelope. These are just a few of the more than 10,000 species that are involved in broadcasting this increased amplitude. I mention them because they are doing a great deal, and other species cannot do as much for various reasons. Some species, of course, are retiring from the planet. They will broadcast that amplitude, and then they will leave. Sometimes it will be portions of a species, greater or lesser. Other times, it will be the entire species, except for whatever matter is remaining in the soil or in the sea that might possibly be reconstituted or re-created by those who either have such techniques or will acquire them. The purpose of the dolphins' apparent migration is primarily to radiate, or emanate, this energy.

How many dolphins are left on the planet?

I cannot say. I will just say it's less than a million.

So 100,000 at one time is really phenomenal.

It requires a lot of — I'm going to make a joke — it requires a lot of planning. [Chuckles.] Such an appointment! There are usually a lot of dolphins in various areas, but to get everybody there for 100,000 or so requires a plan, so it took a few weeks to get that organized. Of course, it wasn't how you send out communications; the communications are sonic — felt and heard.

And helped by beings like you?

No, they can do it themselves. We don't have to help; that's not our job.

The Job of a Deva

What's your job?

Our job is to help them to live their lives better.

How many are there like you?

What do you mean?

You said you were a Dolphin Deva.

I am it.

You are it. Have you always been that?

In the case of Human Deva, it is the same.

There's only one?

One — you don't need more than one.

What does a deva do?

It's a spirit that helps to maintain the balance of energy so that the being can exist. It's not necessary on a benevolent planet, but for the polarized experience here on this planet, it is necessary so that dolphins can exist in sometimes hostile situations.

Have you always been with these dolphins on this planet?

Yes, always.

What did you do before you took on this job?

I have always and only been this. Generally on other planets and star systems, that would mean supporting individuals here and there, but nothing like constant support for all individuals here in great numbers. So you might say that in my previous job duties, I had more leisure time.

Helping Matter Become

Have you had emergencies here?

No, because it isn't like that, all right? It's for me to help you to understand what it is. Imagine matter, all right? And imagine that matter is formed into a dolphin inside a mother dolphin. In order for that matter to be able to become a dolphin — that's what I do.

So you're connected to the soul of the baby dolphin?

No, no. I knew you were going to say that. It has to do with matter becoming. Period.

Before the soul even gets involved?

Period. Not before, not after — matter becoming. That means "in the moment," "present," "matter becoming and being stabilized to be that." Beings such as myself exist for all forms of life on this planet and beyond, I'm sure. I do not know how to explain it any better.

So it's like the particles are called to form that baby, and you work with those particles to become flesh?

No. I don't know how to explain it. It's much simpler than that. I understand that you're living in a world of beings, plus science has that perception as well, but what I do is a whole thing — not individual — so it's hard for me to explain using individual things like I did with the baby dolphin, because it's ... I don't know how to explain it. You will have to trust me that it is what I say it is, and you may not be able to understand it.

But love is supposed to hold everything together, so I'm assuming you use a lot of love.

I am love.

Was it easier in the past? Did it get more difficult as the negativity rose?

It got more difficult as the human population rose because the human population, as you understand yourselves at this time, you are the Explorer Race. You are trying to accomplish something for others, but you became more and more polarized. Then it got harder for everybody. The polarization is the problem.

The Negativity and Violence on Earth
Are Not Native to Human Nature

In your nature, who you are, you are not violent — none of that. You are not negative, as you say — none of that. You are totally positive, benevolent, loving beings. That is your nature. You are completely out of touch with that — many of you. Babies are like that; sometimes very old people are like that,once again. And there are moments in your life that you are like that, but life here does not support and sustain your natural way of being, so it has to go inside and other places and sort of hide, you see? But the point is to attempt to free it up for you — the discomfort, as it's called by others.

But the violence and the harm and the hurt are not your natural state. It is completely foreign to you as human beings. And when you come here as souls ... very often babies cry for no obvious reason. And when babies cry, usually they are crying because of the violence that existed somewhere. Maybe it was in the house, a shouting argument. Maybe somebody next door got slapped. Maybe somebody got hit fifty miles away. The baby would feel all of that.

When babies arrive, they are their natural spirit selves. They feel things happening on the other side of the planet. And this is why sometimes babies cry, human babies, for no apparent reason. There's nothing wrong with them physically, but they are hurting spiritually. And when they cry, to a degree, that cry transforms the pain they are feeling from somewhere else. So they — and all babies everywhere who are crying in that moment – are transforming that pain as best they can. Crying is a way to do that.

It works for the individual as well. When people cry ... when they have grief or something, they cry. Sometimes they feel better. They don't feel better when they're crying. Right after they stop crying, they don't necessarily feel better, but it does release a lot. Eventually, they feel better because of the crying, so maybe more crying would be better.

Supporting the Form of Dolphins

So in addition to the work that you stated, are there other things you do? Or is that the focus?

I support the constitution, the capability of matter to become dolphin. And I continue; it doesn't start when they're born and proceed through their lifetimes. It's not linear. I support, as you might understand it, the shape of the dolphin. I support the dolphin as a being, the way it looks, its matter. Like you, dolphins eat, they release, and the body/form/cellular structure transfers, changes over, just like your structure does. I support their forms so that the dolphins can exist. Don't try to say it any other way. So don't try to say, "The work that you do," and then give an example. I know you're doing that for clarity. Just say, "The work that I do," and leave it at that. This is what I recommend if you're going to ask me such a question.

I didn't understand. That's millions and millions of dolphins.

If it were only one, it would make no difference. The energy that I broadcast to support this is no different for one than it is for as high as you can count. It's exactly the same. You understand that, because in that is a clue. That's a clue to explain all mysteries on your planet about everything. I do not expect you to have a question about that. I am speaking to the reader, to the scientists who look at these things. There are those. It's important for them to understand the simplicity, and it's much, much less important to understand the complexity.

The Difference between Waking Up and Remembering

Is there a time frame — like a hundred years or five years or a thousand years — when all the dolphins will be gone? Roughly.

Yes, but it is not based on years. And now we come full circle to why the dolphins are emanating this energy. It's because the energy is meant for you human beings to wake up and remember who you are — not who you've had to become to live on this planet, but who you are when you arrived physically from your mother on this planet. You were completely pure. You were yourself totally. All of the things that you could do as spirit, you could do as a baby for at least the first three days of your life, even if you didn't live any longer, which happens sometimes.

After that, there's a very slow tapering off, so by the time you're six months old, you're more immersed in who you're not, because you've had to adapt to live on Earth the way it is and in cultures the way they are, as opposed to your natural state. But I bring that up not to blame anybody. Of course you have to do that. I'm simply saying that the waking-up procedure isn't associated with who you are as spirit. I know that's been stated, and I might even have said that myself, but in fact, the waking-up process has to do with who you were in those first few hours when you were a physical being on the planet.

From that point, you gradually went to sleep in spirit. Spirit goes to sleep except when you're at the deep levels of your sleep and at various times throughout your lifetime, all right? But the waking up is associated with who you have already been physically on this planet. That is not as difficult as waking up from spirit. That is why babies are such amazing beings. And you see it sometimes when you look at them. If they're fully present in their eyes, it's like you're looking into pools of wisdom and love. But you have to have at least love in your eyes to see that. So that's a very important thing to know.

There's a big difference between waking up ... if you had to wake up to who you are in spirit only as human beings, it would take you 1,000 years. But if you can wake up to who you are and who you have actually been physically on the planet, there's hope that that would take as short a time as possible. Meaning, I can't say five years, I can't say three years, and I can't say ten years. It'll take as long as it takes. But the advantage is you've already done it. You've already been it. So it doesn't have to take long. Or it will take as long as it takes. It won't take as long as 1,000 years.

So the time of the dolphins leaving is based on our waking up to our once-physical selves?

What they're doing, yes. And what other species are doing also. Dolphins are able to swim very far and very fast. In the case of ants, they don't travel, but there are a great many of them all over the world. And they have taken on this project as well. That's why sometimes they'll walk around in your midst even though they have no place to go and nothing to do for themselves or their families. They are just broadcasting that energy to help you to wake up. So try to watch where you put your feet, okay? They might be helping. If there's a stream of them going somewhere, then they're doing something for themselves and their families, but if you see just an ant walking around, one or two ants walking around, they're undoubtedly doing that. They're willing to take that chance. They're willing to die to help you, because that's what it is — walking around a place where people walk from one place to another and don't watch where they put their feet. That's pretty special.

Vulnerability and Benevolent Magic

What would you recommend humans do to help facilitate the process of this waking up?

Ask for it. Pray for it. Ask something like this — and you're using that technique. I think I'll put it in the form of that technique. You could say ... [pause]. I need a shaman to say this, but I'll do the best I can. You could say: "I ask ..." I'm going to give you the basics, and then you ask for somebody afterward to put it in the proper way, okay? "Asking to be the full spirit being of my babyhood as myself now" — all those words, but put in the proper format.

Okay, I will. When we're through, I'll ask somebody to restate your words as benevolent magic.

See, it has to be that you want your full spirit being, but you also want to be yourself. You don't simply want to return to being a fifty-six-year-old baby — that's not good. You want to be yourself, but you want to also be your spirit self. But the thing of it is you're going to have to request for it to happen in a kind way, a good … what's your phrase?

In a benevolent way.

You have to request it in a benevolent way so that it happens at the right time, because you're living in a hostile society. It's not always hostile, but very often, and it's more hostile than you realize. Sometimes people just say things that are uncomfortable, but as a baby or as a child, it's not just uncomfortable; it's painful. As an adult, you've become used to it, and you've built a shield. The shield protects you from feeling the full pain, but it also protects you from waking up. The shield could fall away, you see, so you have to ask for it to happen in the most benevolent way, as you said — so that it will happen in the most benevolent way. Otherwise, you might feel very vulnerable indeed. Of course, you will be highly sensitive, and you will be able to do many things that you can't imagine doing as a human being. You will be highly sensitive, and little things will have an effect on you. You might say now, "Oh, that's a little thing — don't think anything of it." But that's your shield working for you. If the shield falls away, the little thing will be a big thing.

And we will be very vulnerable, right?

Yes. This is why most people who have been trained to do these things and are very sensitive live in protected environments. There are places like that — not as many as there used to be, I think, but there are still some places.

Not Just Another Beautiful Mystery

This is marvelous! What other advice can you give us?

Well, I'm not here to advise you. I'm here to do what I did — to say that's what this gathering of the 100,000 dolphins is about so that it doesn't just fall under the heading of being another beautiful mystery. It's important for you to know that it has purpose, and the purpose is to help you. And that's why it's important for various types of beings to be on the planet. Some of them have withstood a great deal of suffering for their species to be on the planet and do what they're doing right now.

To help us, yes.

To help you, yes, yes. Not the least of which are ants. Bears are almost eliminated, and I'm not saying that they could be among you, but of course if you were your full spirit self as your day-to-day self, bears would not be violent; they would be friends. You would walk down the forest path with your bear friend — like that. There would be no discomfort at all. If there were bees around, they would never sting you. They wouldn't even need stingers anymore.

Is there anything that we can do to draw some of this energy to those of us who don't live in the area where the dolphins are radiating this energy?

Yes. It would be useful to imagine dolphins. Imagine being in the water swimming with dolphins. This works much better than looking at pictures, but if you need a picture — or a video, as you say — then look at that first. Then imagine being in the water with dolphins. That will help a lot. Use your imagination. Some of you are out of touch with your imaginations. If so, look at pictures and such things and say the words of benevolent magic I gave. When you say the thing I gave, when you get it right, it is to be said only once. I understand that some of you do regular prayers and rituals, which is fine, but these kind of things for such a specific request are to be said only once. And you say it only for yourself. If you want to share it with others, you can write it down or tell them how it's said, but you only say it for yourself once.

Good life to you, and thank you. Maybe we'll talk again when you figure out what you're going to do in your next job.

Maybe I'll see you there.

[Laughs.] Okay! Thank you!

Tap In to Your Natural Capabilities

Shamanic Teacher

Shamanic Teacher.

Welcome!

You have something for me to interpret?

Should I read the words that the Dolphin Deva said?

Yes. Slowly.

Okay. "Asking to be the full spirit being of my baby — "

I'll take it in parts. "I request to be the full spirit being ..." Go ahead.

"Of my babyhood ..."

All right. [Long pause.] " … of my first day as baby." Go ahead.

"… as myself now."

All right. A moment. [Long pause.] "… as my overall being now …"
Go ahead.

I don't know what the Dolphin Deva said next. I wrote down "in the most benevolent way."

I'll be just a moment. [Long pause.] "… in the most benevolent way
now for me, resulting in the most benevolent outcome." That's it.

> *Benevolent Magic*
> "I request to be the full spirit being of my first day as baby as
> my overall being now in the most benevolent way now for me,
> resulting in the most benevolent outcome."

Marvelous. Is there anything else you want to say about this whole dolphin emanation?

I feel it was very timely, Dolphin Deva explaining. Dolphin Deva
understands things in simple concepts. This does not mean that being is
not brilliant; Dolphins Deva strongly believes that the simpler, the better.

Feeling Out in the World like a Baby

It is very important for you to know that waking up as your spirit being
is something you've already been on this planet. This is essential, because
then it is much easier to know and understand, especially parents who
have been around beloved children for the first day or two. The soul
and the spirit of the human baby are very often right there on the surface. That's why a baby is so sensitive physically, spiritually, emotionally,
instinctively — everything. A baby is profoundly spiritual.

You could approach a baby and touch the auric field, even ten feet
away, and the baby would feel it. You don't have to walk over and touch
the baby; the baby would feel that contact — maybe even much farther
away, depending on how far the baby has been feeling out. The baby feels
out into the world — it does not have to make physical contact (as you
would understand it, "touch") — but for the baby, it feels just as physical
to touch something, even a tree 100,000 miles away, the Moon, or Mars.
It feels just as physical as touching somebody else, touching something,
touching a book or a page. The physical contact feels the same. You all
had that once.

So, knowing this, you had that not just in spirit — you were born with that capability, and you all did it. That's one of the first things babies do when they're on the planet for the first few hours. Of course, if they're born in hospitals, it's a little harder because they are traumatized there, but if they're born more gently, maybe at home with a loving midwife or others in a more gentle environment, then the baby immediately reaches out. It's natural for your spirit to be your physical form, then. It's that way. Your spirit is your physical form when you are a baby for the first couple days, see? And after that, as you begin to adapt, you sometimes cry as a baby because you feel your spirit moving off. You don't have the awareness of your soul.

The soul is a portion of your spirit, but the soul is the portion of your spirit that is able to adapt to live in whatever environment you have to live in as a human being on Earth. The soul is that adaptive portion, and essentially it stays connected to your overall spirit, but it can be with you in the hard times and in the good times, of course. The soul also acts as a bridge to keep you connected to your spirit self so that when you are sleeping or in times of great need, as they happen — emergencies, perhaps something else — you are able to connect not only to your spirit self, but maybe you know how to do something that you didn't think you could do. You've heard of people lifting cars off other people — that is a direct connection to the spirit self. If your spirit self became your day-to-day self, should it ever become necessary, you could lift a car because your body does not know it can't. That's the simple explanation. As a baby, you know you can, and that's why the explanation from Dolphin Deva was so important — it lets you know you have been this on Earth already.

Yes, you're not asking us to be something new; we've already done it.

You're not trying to do something impossible; you're trying to do something possible, as you've already done it.

Wow, that's marvelous. Have we talked to you before?

You have not talked to me before.

Do you want to talk in the future about anything else?

If you have a question, you have a name you can use now.

Do you usually work with people on Earth?

I can be wherever I am needed; you are the same way. This is why human beings die when they do. Sometimes it seems to be this. For example, everybody died at once in an area because of some tragedy. But every one of those beings who died was needed somewhere else. So when you're needed somewhere else — in some cases, you're needed urgently — then the transition from one life form to another is often much more direct. It is not immediate of course, but it is much more direct. Whereas if there is no immediate urgency for your presence elsewhere, then you might have some experience between lives, do what you wish, explore. Beings do different things.

Bodies Like to Be Touched Gently, Lovingly

Do you have any advice for people who would like to live a long time in their present bodies?

Yes. Tell your body in a nice, gentle way, with smooth strokes going down from the nape of your neck, down your chest, and down your arms and all that, as you would pet your cat. Pet gently, yes? No thumping the cat; cats don't like that. So go very gentle on your body. All bodies are the same — they like to be touched gently, even though human being personalities in bodies might be different. But bodies themselves like to be touched gently, lovingly. So strokes downward, all right? This is one of those things you can say more than once: "I know you can do for yourself ..." No, I want to give you the words you can say many times. [Pause.] "Be yourself." When you talk to your body, you can't just talk to your head. This isn't something you're saying to your mind. Your mind is not involved. You say to your body, gently, lovingly, "Be yourself." That's all — because your body knows no limits. If your body is itself, it will not be strapped by limits, and you might live longer. Or you might live better. Or both.

Good life.

Good life. Thank you.

CHAPTER TWENTY-NINE

This Is Your Last Life on Earth, So Stay Alive and Do the Best You Can

A Guide
September 2, 2013

I do not wish to alarm those of you who are reading this, but this is a time of tumultuous transition, and many of you are confused about whether to maintain your commitment to life. Some of you are in danger zones where there are wars and battles and a general sense of strife and anxiety, so it is understandable that you may not have such a commitment to life at all, including your own. But I would like to encourage you to stay with your lives as long as you can do so. That is why so much has been given through this channel on how to improve the quality of your life and the lives of those around you — not only so that you can be more comfortable, but also so that you can survive and even thrive in difficult times.

You Receive Gentle Guidance during Sleep

My job is very simple. I am one of the guides who escorts souls who leave their bodies and continue on in their immortal life cycles. I do this all the time, so I have had lots of experience. It is what I have always done. We are often called angels and other names, but I am just going to refer to myself as a guide. There will be no name given because I don't want you to think of me as anything other than someone you will meet someday — if not me, it will be someone like me who will escort you on the pathway that leads from your physical life to your immortal life.

Though it is not necessary to guide you too much, it is not an unusual thing for us to be present at the deep levels of your sleep. We guide you gently so that you can reach your teachers and other guides who will explain your life to you. They will remind you why you chose what you chose, and what you as a soul are attempting to learn in your physical life. There will be discussions. These discussions do not happen in words in your understanding. As your natural self, communication is largely felt. There is a knowingness, and the knowingness is exchanged.

If you were there — present — it would seem as if it were all over before it started. But there are deep and profound exchanges, and your soul — which very often has a hard time staying in your physical body because life is so difficult compared to all the other lives that you have lived on other planets and in other forms — often wants to leave before its time. That is why at the deep levels of your sleep, every one of you goes to visit guides and teachers who support and sustain your commitment to your physical life.

Oh, it is true that sometimes they will try to nudge you onto a more benevolent path or to help you to see beyond what you have been able to see and understand, so some teaching goes on, but they are reminders — not so much things you are learning, but things that you have forgotten, even in that extended soul version of yourself that is corded to your physical body. So that goes on regularly for all of you. This passage that you call death is actually a simple return of your physical body to Earth, and your soul (also called your immortal personality) continues on.

Live Out Your Life on Earth

Now, some of you will say, "Gosh, this is old stuff. I've known this for a long time." But it is important to speak of these matters again because in tumultuous times, as you have now, you will find that the unexpected is a daily occurrence. Sometimes the unexpected is a fun thing, a happy thing. Sometimes it is meeting old friends or hearing from friends you had lost and couldn't find again, even relatives and certainly loved ones. However, it is also a time when the unexpected can be tragic, and at those times, some of you are of the opinion that you cannot go on, that you must stop your life.

The reason I am here today is that this is becoming more frequent, and I want to encourage you, especially those of you who are spiritual, and urge you to make that commitment to stay on the planet physically as long as you can. I am not trying to suggest that you sacrifice beyond what you are able to do. If you are elderly or if you are not well, then of course you have to let go. If you are injured and you know you cannot go on, of course you have to let go. You will know that is the case — to let go — because you will see, feel, hear, or sense your guides or angelics. You will know it. You will see them. You may sense them. You might look in that direction; if loved ones or others are with you, they will wonder what you are looking at. This has happened so many times — numbers do not count that high — so for those of you who have had that experience with loved ones passing over, they are looking at their guide or an angelic.

Sometimes if they are not used to that, they might be surprised. Other times the being is quickly recognized because of the emanated love. If you are a spiritual person or are having a close moment with your loved one who is passing over, you might have felt that love. Of course, some of it comes from your loved one, but some of it also comes from that angelic who is present.

It is good to know about these things, so please make the commitment to finish your life if you can, and don't stop it on your own or make some gesture or action that will force others to stop your life. It is for you to know that there will be benevolent things you can do — good things, kind things, simple things, and uncomplicated things — that may mean very little to you in the moment but might mean a world of difference to someone else. You can tell I am trying to talk people out of committing suicide. But there are other ways of committing suicide than doing something overt. Sometimes it is just putting yourself in harm's way and not getting out of the way, sort of letting other people help you commit suicide, even if they don't want to. So I am going to ask that you don't involve other people in helping you commit suicide. Those of you who have had these thoughts know what I am speaking about.

You Will Know Why

I do not wish to sound gloom and doom, for it is not that. I wish to take you on a journey that will help you to understand what it is like for those of you who pass over, and you will all do that someday when it is your time. So when it is your time, I or someone else will be there. You will recognize us because we will be white light and gold light, and we will look like human beings. We are not going to be scary, and we are not going to frighten you. You will feel a familiarity. You will think in those last thoughts, "How is it possible?" Yet it will feel like an old friend is there.

For many of you, it is true that there would have been an encounter with us before, because every time your life ends — most of you have lived thousands of lives, counting where you have been on other planets, other universes, everywhere — the being who leads you is always the same being, the same angelic, the same guide. That is why there is the sense of familiarity. So there will be that sense, you see, and then you will simply step out of your body.

If you were a witness to that and could see it, you would see a version of the person you know and love or that person you are with as an observer. You would see a version of the person just step out of the body while the body remains where it was. And you would see a light (gold or white or both), and there would be a joining for a moment. You might see the person stepping away a few steps, and then the person would be gone. You might see the person go up, or you might see the person go in another direction, but the person would never go down. The person would always go to the left, to the right, or up, but the person most often would go up. This is how it goes.

Some of you will feel as if you are going through a tube, but most of you will feel as if you are just emerging from one place to another. Generally speaking, the tube experience happens to people who are potentially going to return to Earth, meaning you have perhaps read about or heard about people who literally die, but then they come back to life: the near-death experience. People like this will almost always have the tube experience, but generally speaking, you will not have that experience. You will be with your guide, and together we will very gently ease into another place. You will very often see friends and family. You will see people you know and love, and you will be overwhelmed by a loving feeling for you, for who you are. There are no judgments, ever.

You will move along this path with your guide, feeling initially like you are hand in hand. Eventually, you will feel closer to your guide, feeling almost partly merged with your guide or your angelic, and you will move on to a place where often there is an opportunity to look at your life and many of the deep-level experiences you have had when you were asleep. You will experience all of that in just a moment, and you will completely understand your physical life — why it was, why it happened, what it meant, what you have gained from it as a soul, and what must be discarded and left on Earth. You will have already discarded that and left it on Earth, but the reason it is explained to you is that at that time, you will still be thinking in the way you understand thought, meaning in that sort of linear way. But shortly after that, there will be no more linear thought. There will be only knowing, sometimes called vertical wisdom, meaning in every moment in which you exist, you will know what you need to know when you need to know it.

From that point on, you will go to a place that is entirely light and love. Many of you will want to stay there. You might have moments there for which you will not be able to tell whether you were there for years or seconds, but you will be completely purified there, and every last shred of anything unhappy or uncomfortable that happened in your physical life will fall away. You will also have a complete understanding of why those things happened. From that point on, you will move to a place where you have choices, where you decide where you are going to live.

The one choice you probably will not have at these times is to return to Earth and have a physical life on the Earth that you left. As you know, those opportunities for those of you passing over soon have come to a close. That Earth upon which you are all now living will no longer be open for you to return to it. It will be closed, but that is all right. Other versions of Earth will be available — higher versions, you sometimes say — where life can be and is wonderful. You might have the opportunity to see loved ones you knew in this life or other lives, but almost all of you will choose to have lives on other planets where everything is benevolent. This happens — how can I say? — beyond time as you know it.

If you were to live it in linear time, it would seem to take a long time during which you were bathed in totally unconditional love. But if you were in now time, or vertical time, it would be happening in an instant, and then you would go on. At that point, you go on and have a life that would be somewhere benevolent, for no one will have the opportunity to return to Earth where you now have a polarized world with discomfort and comfort, or you sometimes say positivity and negativity. You will not have that opportunity. You also will not have the opportunity to go anywhere that ever had that kind of discomfort, for that would be in the distant past, and there are only a few other places like that in this universe and none in any other universe. So you will have a benevolent life, and you will see me once again only when that life is over and when every other life is over — if not me personally, then someone like me, an angelic, a guide, as we say. We will meet again.

You Are Living on a Personal Planet

A moment. Water. [Noises, then laughter.]

What was so funny?

I have never turned a bottle cap to a bottle. Tricky, that.

What I am really hearing is that since no one living on Earth can come back, it is a time to really invest everything we have in doing the best we can for ourselves and for everyone while we are still here.

Well said.

Yes, last chance. What particularly is this tumultuous transition that you are talking about?

It is a time of commitment — not only to your own lives, as I have said, but also on a more universal level — to the transition from one dimension to another. It is sort of like a buffeting, you would say, so that is why things seem to be so out of sorts at times. You have times during the week or even during a day when you just feel overwhelmed, and then it passes. This is because of what Earth is going through and because your bodies are made of Earth; you feel it personally because it is personal. Everything with Earth on the physical plane — everything — is personal. There is nothing impersonal about it, and that is why you note that Earth's personality is quite volatile at times: volcanoes, whirling storms, and lightning. It is all quite extraordinary. It is not what you would call a calm day in the garden. So as a result, your bodies have this in them as well.

Sometimes some of you want to have excitement. When Mother Earth wants to have excitement, her winds will pick up and blow strong, and then after a while, she will just relax, and the wind will be calm again. Most of the time, you will feel that as a 10, 20, or 30 mph breeze, but sometimes she needs to disburse energies that are a bit overwhelming to her. Then she will do the tornadic action, a strong cyclonic wind that will not only stir things around but will hurl things out. It is not meant to cause harm to human beings or others; it is what she must do to maintain her own physical well-being, and it is all personal.

It is pretty important to think about that. If Mother Earth does things that are personal, then maybe that is why you sometimes have to do things that seem to be out of character for you. Sometimes you suddenly feel something; maybe you are driving in the car and suddenly burst into song, or maybe you yell when something happens. Perhaps you are in a traffic jam and say words you don't normally say or that your children would be shocked to hear you say. Sometimes this is for you like a 20 or 30 mph wind; it is personal. Understand that you are living on a planet that is completely personal; therefore, that's why things feel personal to you when others might say things or do things even on the other side of the world. It might feel personal to you because you are made up of a planet to whom everything is personal.

You Are Feeling What Earth Is Feeling

As we are moving between dimensions, is that affecting Earth and then us?

It is a lot to ask of a planet, to go between dimensions in this fashion. Planets don't do that; planets just automatically, instantaneously choose to have other dimensions of themselves or they don't. In order to learn what you came here to learn as a group you call the Explorer Race, you're asking the planet to be your vehicle so that you can very slowly migrate from one dimension to another to test your commitment to resolve the unresolvable. Keep in mind that for the Explorer Race to resolve the unresolvable, you must go through things that are not typical in other places. And by not typical, I mean unless people have lived during these times on Earth, referring to individuals all over the universe as people, you wouldn't have gone through it anywhere else.

So if you are going to resolve the unresolvable, you have to have a vehicle. You can't float through space as a group called the Explorer Race and expect to survive. You have to be traveling on some type of body — like a planet. So you are asking Earth to do something that is unnatural for her. (I am going to say "her" since people say that.) So that means that Earth has to do something that is unnatural, and that is why so many of you right now — going through this passage — feel the energy of being put upon.

Sometimes you will actually feel that people are expecting and demanding things of you even though they are not expecting or demanding anything more than they ordinarily do. Sometimes they are even doing things for you, and they will just seem like they want you to do something for them. In short, you will be confused. And that is because when you go through such transitions (and you understand it is Earth going through the transition, but you are made up of that, physically), you will feel all that Earth is going through as an emotional being. Earth is a feeling being, an emotional being, and you must carry some of the weight of that because she will need every last portion of herself to process this.

Therefore, as your bodies are made up of Mother Earth, she will need to utilize your bodies so that you feel what she feels. That is why I say that it is personal. So for many of you, when you have these unexplained feelings, it may not be you personally. It might not be your personal life. It may not be the life of those around you, your friends and loved ones or coworkers — something like that, whatever. Or it might just be people on the street or people in the country working. It might not be that at all. It might be something Mother Earth is going through, and it is about this: your personal relationship with Mother Earth.

When we go out physically from Earth to the Moon or to Mars or wherever, there is a point between the two where the Earth energy ends and, let's say, the Moon's energy starts. Is there a point like that between dimensions?

It is a nice analogy, and I would like to say yes, but it isn't exactly like that. Because with dimensions, it is not linear. You are using a linear example. With dimensions, it is all in the same bowl, so to speak. But in that bowl, there are a multiplicity of different vibrations. You understand vibrations in a musical sense, and a certain vibration will create a certain tone that tells you that that vibration and that tone are completely synchronized. They are one and the same, expressions of the same thing. You can all be in the same bowl, dimensionally speaking, but you will have your expression of who you are as the same thing, who you are as a soul, and who you are in the vibration you are compatible with. As a result, that is how it is. It is not linear.

Is there a point past that to which Earth cannot go and still be able to return this level of herself in the third dimension to clean it up?

She is remaining in the third dimension. She is remaining in the fourth dimension. She is bilocating. She has to bilocate, so she is still in the third dimension; she doesn't have to return. She will be in more than one place at once.

I see. No one ever explained that before. All right, back to humans. Is there a time or a duration when we are going through this tumultuousness? If we get through it, is there a calm place for a while?

There will be various calm places, so from time to time, everything will calm down. This will happen from time to time for a while yet. That is part of the reason the younger generation — though it always seems this way to the older generation — is so caught up in the idea of excitement. They are prepared for sudden and unexpected transformations. However, they are not always prepared for relaxation, so that is why your bodies are set up to have to sleep. Sometimes it is that basic. So I will say that it will go on for a while.

It is a time of transformation, yes. It is a time of moving through the unexpected for all of you. It is also a time of opportunity. One of the big opportunities you will have is to make new friends, to resolve friendships, meaning if you have had a falling out with a friend or a misunderstanding, it is a good time to get that sorted out in a way that feels reasonably good. Strive for that. It is not that I am urging you to finish things up and package things nicely because you are all going to transition, no. You will all transition when the time is right for you. It is a time of many personal opportunities, not just to achieve a higher level on the corporate ladder. The opportunities are all personal and individual. Do what you can to keep those opportunities benevolent for yourself and benevolent for others in the most kind and loving way you can accommodate. Good night and good life.

Thank you.

ABOUT THE AUTHOR

ROBERT SHAPIRO is largely known as a professional trance channel who has channeled several series of published books. As he is now, he is a mystical man with shamanic capabilities that are well and thoroughly infused into him. He also has many unusual skills that he teaches through blogs, the *Sedona Journal of Emergence*, and books. It is his intention to bring about the most benevolent change available on the planet through sharing his personal inspirations as well as his channeling. Learn more about Robert and his work at google.com/+BenevolentMagic.

His great contributions to a better understanding of the history, purpose, and future of humanity on Earth are his epochal works:

- The Explorer Race Series
- The Shining the Light Series
- The Shamanic Secrets Series
- The Ultimate UFO Series
    All are available as print books and ebooks.

🜟 *Light Technology* PUBLISHING *Presents*

THE EXPLORER RACE SERIES

ZOOSH AND OTHERS THROUGH ROBERT SHAPIRO

Superchannel Robert Shapiro can communicate with any personality anywhere and any-when. He has been a professional channel for over thirty-five years and channels with an exceptionally clear and profound connection.

The Origin, the Purpose, and the Future of Humanity

If you have ever questioned **who you really are, why you are here** as part of humanity on this miraculous planet, and **what it all means**, these books in the Explorer Race series can begin to supply the answers to these and other questions about the mystery and enigma of physical life on Earth.

These answers come from beings who speak through superchannel Robert Shapiro, beings who range from particle personalities to the Mother of All Beings and the thirteen Ssjoooo, from advisors to the Creator of our universe to the generators of precreation energies. **The scope, the immensity, and the mind-boggling infinitude of these chronicles by beings who live in realms beyond our imagination will hold you enthralled.** Nothing even close to the magnitude of the depth and power of this all-encompassing, expanded picture of reality has ever been published.

This amazing story of the greatest adventure of all time and creation is the story of the Explorer Race, all of humanity on Earth and those who came before us who are waiting for us. The Explorer Race is a group of souls whose journeys resulted in incarnations in this loop of time on planet Earth, where, bereft of any memory of their immortal selves and most of their heart energy, they came to learn compassion, to take responsibility for the consequences of their actions, and to solve creation's previously unsolvable dilemma of negativity. We humans have found a use for negativity: We use it for lust for life and adventure, curiosity and creativity, and doing the undoable. And in a few years, we will go out to the stars with our insatiable drive and ability to respond to change and begin to inspire the benign but stagnant civilizations out there to expand and change and grow, which will eventually result in the change and expansion of all creation.

Once you understand the saga of the Explorer Race and what the success of the Explorer Race experiment means to the totality of creation, **you will be proud to be a human and to know that you are a vital component of the greatest story ever told** — a continuing drama whose adventure continues far into the future. 🜟

TO ORDER PRINT BOOKS
Visit LightTechnology.com, Call 928-526-1345 or 1-800-450-0985,
or Check Amazon.com or Your Favorite Bookstore

THROUGH ROBERT SHAPIRO

Steps to the Path of Transformation
Volume 2 • Book 24

STEPS ON THE PATH OF
transformation
Volume 2

channeled through Robert Shapiro

A s you read this material, this is what to keep in mind: Your path might be completely different from what this book attempts to show you. So when you read this material, don't think, "I can't possibly do that." Rather, think about what is familiar to you.

You will experience times when you have read a page or two and something feels as if it resonates within you. It might not be a sequence of words that you find in a paragraph. It could be words that came together from different paragraphs, creating in you a sense of familiarity. This tells you that these books are not just about thoughts or ideas. The books are about transformation.

Even if you have difficulty reading the books in the language they are in, go through them and put your hands on some of the pages, or touch the pages to your arms or other parts of your body to see whether the books — with all the words, letters, symbols, and numbers — can in some way trigger a dream, a vision, or a moment of inspiration in you that helps to bring about a better life for you and those around you.

Good luck, and good life in this pursuit.

— Isis

$19.95 • Softcover • 306 PP.
978-1-62233-055-3

Chapters Include
- Be Aware of Emerging Sense Communications
- Silent Communication Becomes Apparent as You Wake Up
- You Need to Hurdle Two Obstacles to Achieve More Benevolence
- A Doorway Opened to a Benevolent Future Timeline
- How to Know When You Are Waking Up
- It Is Time to Shift into Your Natural State of Being
- Every Human Can Now Manifest Easily
- You Came to Earth to Learn How to Feel Physical
- The End of the Loop of Time

THROUGH ROBERT SHAPIRO

ETs on Earth
Volume 3 • Book 22

channeled through
Robert Shapiro

$16.95 • Softcover • 352 PP.
978-1-62233-044-7

Many of you are ready to welcome ETs — if not in your personal lives, at least interchanging with government bodies in large groups. Some of you are prepared to shake hands. Even a few want hugs. But it may not be that personal.

There are circumstances coming up in your now evolution toward your natural selves that make it almost imperative to have contact of a benevolent nature between Earth people and extraterrestrials. For now, many ETs are shy about coming here. They will, at some risk to themselves from time to time, show you images of themselves literally (in the skies you will see them defined by clouds), or you will see something that reminds you of ships. I'm not just referring to lenticular clouds. It will be a cloud form, often all by itself in the sky, that reminds you of a ship and has details that could be nothing but. So look for that all over the planet, and don't be afraid.

As your cousins, which is the way they see themselves (the ones you are most likely to meet), ETs recognize that you are a version of their extended family. So read this book. You will find many reminders of who you might have been or who you might be in other lives or who your extended family is now.

Chapters Include
- Beings Who Communicate through Mathematical Expression
- Hope Benefits the Pleiades
- The Road to Compassion Is Paved with Growth
- Change Represents Growth for You *and* Other Beings
- From a Light in the Sky to the Solution of a Great Mystery
- Sound Feeds Life
- Be Aware of Emerging Sense Communications
- Panda Bear Energy Helps Humans Resolve Conflicts
- ET Scientist Seeks Out Unusual Life
- Time-Traveling Orion ET Visits Future Jupiter

THROUGH ROBERT SHAPIRO

TOTALITY AND BEYOND

The Search for the Origin of Life — and Beyond

Book 20

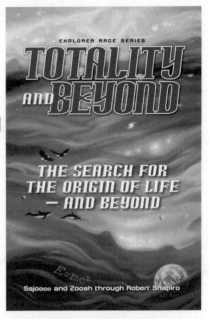

"The book you are about to read attempts to explain and, to a degree, put an order to existence. You might reasonably ask, 'What is the purpose?' The purpose is very simply this: In order for you now to be able to function in a world of responsibilities well beyond your own physical life, you need to be able to understand the functionality of creation and the confidence you need to have in simply emerging from seemingly nothing. 'Nothing' is not really zero. Nothing is a matrix available to create something. It will always be that, and it has always been that.

"This book will explain, with some wide variety of points of view at times, those points, and over the next few hundred years, you can consider them as you blend with your total being, creating and re-creating what is now in order to bring it to a more benevolent state of being."

—Ssjoooo, September 18, 2015

$24.95 • Softcover • 416 PP.
978-1-891824-75-3

CHAPTERS INCLUDE

- The Thirteen Envision the Worlds within Worlds
- The Loop of Time
- An Unending Parade of Existence
- Disentanglement
- Disentangling Cords of Discomfort
- All Creation Responds to Need
- Every Action Has a Reaction: It's Mother Nature's Plan
- Love and Care for Others to Embrace the Totality
- Feel Heat to Learn Oneness
- You Planned Your Journey
- The Reservoir of Being

BOOKS THROUGH ROBERT SHAPIRO

Are You a Walk-In?
Book 19

From the walk-in's perspective, the benefit of this new form of birth is coming into an adult body and being able to bring one's gifts to humanity without having to take the time to go through the usual birth process. The other side of this is that the walk-in has to resolve the physical, emotional, and spiritual issues that the walk-out left behind in order to completely express its own personality.

"This book is intended to be practical advice for day-to-day living for people who know they are walk-ins, for people who believe they might be walk-ins, or for the family and friends and business associates of people who are believed to be walk-ins. In short, this book is intended to serve the community to understand the walk-in phenomenon and for those who are experiencing it personally to be able to apply it in such a way as they are able to live easier, more comfortable, more useful, and more fulfilling lives."

— Reveals the Mysteries

$19.95 • Softcover • 304 pp. • ISBN 978-1-891824-40-1

ARE YOU A WALK-IN?

A NEW FORM OF BENEVOLENT BIRTH IS NOW AVAILABLE ON EARTH

Zoosh, Isis, Reveals the Mysteries, and More
through **Robert Shapiro**

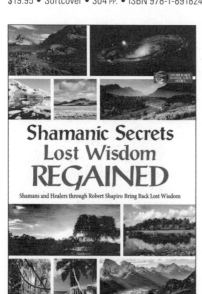

Shamanic Secrets Lost Wisdom REGAINED

Shamans and Healers through Robert Shapiro Bring Back Lost Wisdom

Shamanic Secrets: Lost Wisdom Regained
Book D

Due to wars, natural disasters, a shaman not being able to train a successor, and many other reasons, Isis (through Robert) says that 95 percent of the accumulated shamanic wisdom has been lost. Now it is important to regain this wisdom as young people who are able to learn and use these processes are being born now.

Beings who lived as shamans and healers on Earth at various times now speak through Robert Shapiro and bring these lost teachings and techniques to a humanity waking up and discovering it has the talents and abilities to use this wisdom for the benefit of all.

$16.95 • Softcover • 352 pp. • ISBN 978-1-62233-049-2

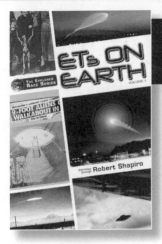

ETs ON EARTH
VOLUME 1 · BOOK 18

Chapters Include

- Blue Spiral Light over Norway
- Humans Are Going through Rapid Changes on Earth
- You Traverse to Your Home Planet in Deep Sleep
- Will There Be a Phony ET Invasion on Earth?
- Beware of a Staged ET Invasion
- You Moved Earth Out of Phase to Test Your Creator Abilities
- ETs Land in Soviet Union September 1989
- Brave ETs Stayed Behind so the Rest of Their People Could Go Home
- ETs Visit with Russian Politician in Moscow
- ET Contact with the President of the Russian Republic of Kalmykia
- Crop Circles and Benevolent Magic for Oil Spill
- Your New Stage of Transformation Is Causing Others Discomfort

$16⁹⁵

Plus Shipping
ISBN 978-1-891824-91-3
Softcover · 352 pp.

ETs ON EARTH 2
VOLUME
BOOK 21

Chapters Include

- Dolphins: Creators of Time Bridges
- Physical Feelings Are the Language of Physicality
- ET Sightings Will Increase as Earth Becomes More Benevolent
- Pleiadians Request ETs' Help in Project to Help Humans Awaken
- The Mountain Energies Are a Gift to Amplify Your Consciousness
- ETs Disarmed Nuclear Missiles
- ET Colonizers of Chinese See Promising Signs
- Fake ET Invasion — Why?
- On 1–11–11, a New Stable Pathway to the Next Dimension Was Created

$16⁹⁵

Plus Shipping
ISBN 978-1-62233-003-4
Softcover · 416 pp.

BOOKS THROUGH ROBERT SHAPIRO

Book 14

$29⁹⁵

Plus Shipping
ISBN 978-1-891824-81-4
Softcover • 704 pp.
6 x 9 Perfect Bound

ASTROLOGY

Planet Personalities and Signs Speak

12 Planets, 12 Signs
Plus: The Thirteenth Sign and a Planet to Balance Mother Earth

The planets and signs of astrology speak to us through superchannel
Robert Shapiro — sharing not only LONG-LOST INFORMATION but also
NEW WAYS OF BEING for an awakening humanity.

As the planets and signs speak through Robert, their personality
traits and interests, many of which have been unknown since
ancient times, can be clearly heard and felt. In addition, you —
humanity — have made such progress that other new energies
and traits of the planets and signs are expressed through their
words. These energies, traits, and characteristics were only
potential in earlier times but now are becoming available to you
to become aware of and to express within your life on Earth as
you awaken to your natural self.

TIME AND THE TRANSITION TO NATURAL TIME

THE EXPLORER RACE

TIME
Transition to Natural Time

Book 17

$16.⁹⁵

ISBN 978-1-891824-85-2
Softcover, 352 pp.
6 x 9 Perfect Bound

"The purpose of this book is to provide a context for your lives in the sequence
you find yourselves in now. This explanation of time — and, to a degree, its variables — is being provided for you so that you will understand more about your
true, natural, native personalities and so that you will be reminded that you are, as
you know, in a school and that this school is purely temporary.

You don't come here very often to this place of linear time; like in your own human lives, you are in school for only so long, and then you live your lives. When
you exist beyond this school, you will find all those lives infinitely easier, and even
as the Creator, your lives will be easier than they are in the single, linear lives that
you're living now, because you will have all your components."
— Founder of Time

Chapters Include
- Time Is Now Available for Your Personal Flexibility
- Your Blinders Are Coming Off
- You Live in a Stream Hosted by Planet Earth
- Time Is an Application for Expansion
- You Are Moving toward Complete Safety and Benevolence
- You Can Transition to the Future in Warmth and Safety
- The Gift of Time
- Your Future Selves Are Linking to You

THROUGH ROBERT SHAPIRO

ET Visitors Speak
Volume 2 • Book 15

For those of you who've always wanted to meet somebody completely different, here's your opportunity. This book contains the continuing adventures of visitors to planet Earth. In a strange sense, you might include yourself as one of those, as the human race does not really claim the title of full-time and permanent Earth citizen.

So when you're reading this book, think about it as if you were visiting another planet. What would you say in reaction to the local population, their habits, and so on? Put yourself in the picture so this isn't just a meaningless travel log from various beings that you don't know and may never meet.

Make it personal this time because the time is coming, maybe even in some of your lifetimes, when you might just be one of those extraterrestrials on another planet. So you might as well practice now and get your lines down right.

THE EXPLORER RACE

ET Visitors Speak Vol. 2

THROUGH ROBERT SHAPIRO

$19.95 • Softcover • 512 PP.
978-1-891824-78-4

- Odin, the Norse God: How the Myth Began

- Sirian Researches Earth Life Forms and Their Harmonious Interactions

- An ET Visitor from the Twelfth Planet Looks for His Planet in the Future

- Individual-Specific Communion Among Human Beings

- Predictions for the Past-Anchored Timeline and the Future-Anchored Timeline

- The Key to Life

- Orion's Visitors Remain on Earth

CHAPTERS INCLUDE
- ET Greeters to Future Mars Earth Colony
- Harmony Is a Way of Life on Future Earth
- ETs Create an Alternate Path to Earth
- A Being from Planet Odin Visits the Iroquois Nation in the Thirteenth Century

♣ *Light Technology* PUBLISHING *Presents*

TO ORDER PRINT BOOKS
Visit LightTechnology.com, Call 928-526-1345 or 1-800-450-0985,
or Check Amazon.com or Your Favorite Bookstore

THE EXPLORER RACE SERIES

ZOOSH AND HIS FRIENDS THROUGH ROBERT SHAPIRO

The series: Humans — creators in training — have a purpose and destiny so heartwarmingly, profoundly glorious that it is almost unbelievable from our present dimensional perspective. Humans are great lightbeings from beyond this creation gaining experience in dense physicality. This truth about the great human genetic experiment of the Explorer Race and the mechanics of creation is being revealed for the first time by Zoosh and his friends through superchannel Robert Shapiro. These books read like adventure stories as we follow the clues from this creation that we live in out to the Council of Creators and beyond.

❶ THE EXPLORER RACE
You are truly a result of the genetic experiment on Earth. You are beings who uphold the principles of the Explorer Race. The key to empowerment in these days is not to know everything about your past but to know what will help you now. You are constantly being given responsibilities by the Creator that would normally be things that Creator would do. The responsibility and the destiny of the Explorer Race is not only to explore but to create.
ISBN 978-0-929385-38-9 • Softcover • 608 PP. • $25.00

❷ ETs and the EXPLORER RACE
In this book, Robert channels Joopah, a Zeta Reticulan now in the ninth dimension who continues the story of the great experiment — the Explorer Race — from the perspective of his civilization. The Zetas would have been humanity's future selves had humanity not re-created the past and changed the future.
ISBN 978-0-929385-79-2 • Softcover • 240 PP. • $14.95

❸ EXPLORER RACE: ORIGINS and the NEXT 50 YEARS
This volume has so much information about who we are and where we came from — the source of male and female beings, the war of the sexes, the beginning of the linear mind, feelings, the origin of souls — it is a treasure trove. In addition, there is a section that relates to our near future — how the rise of global corporations and politics affects our future, how to use benevolent magic as a force of creation, and how we will go out to the stars and affect other civilizations. It is full of astounding information.
ISBN 978-0-929385-95-2 • Softcover • 384 PP. • $14.95

❹ EXPLORER RACE: CREATORS and FRIENDS, the MECHANICS of CREATION
Now that you have a greater understanding of who you are in the larger sense, it is necessary to remind you of where you came from, the true magnificence of your being. You must understand that you are creators in training, and you were once a portion of Creator. This book will allow you to understand the vaster qualities and help you remember the nature of the desires that drive any creator, the responsibilities to which a creator must answer, the reaction a creator must have to consequences, and the ultimate reward for any creator. ISBN 978-1-891824-01-2 • Softcover • 480 PP. • $19.95

❺ EXPLORER RACE: PARTICLE PERSONALITIES
All around you in every moment, you are surrounded by the most magical and mystical beings. They are too small for you to see individually, but in groups, you know them as the physical matter of your daily life. These particles might be considered either atoms or portions of atoms who consciously view the vast spectrum of reality yet also have a sense of personal memory like your own linear memory. Some of the particles we hear from are Gold, Mountain Lion, Liquid Light, Uranium, the Great Pyramid's Capstone, This Orb's Boundary, Ice, and Ninth-Dimensional Fire.
ISBN 978-0-929385-97-6 • Softcover • 256 PP. • $14.95

❻ EXPLORER RACE and BEYOND
With a better idea of how creation works, we go back to the Creator's advisors and receive deeper and more profound explanations of the roots of the Explorer Race. The Liquid Domain and the Double Diamond Portal share lessons given to the roots on their way to meet the Creator of this universe, and the roots speak of their origins and their incomprehensibly long journey here.
ISBN 978-1-891824-06-7 • Softcover • 384 PP. • $14.95

⚜ *Light Technology* PUBLISHING *Presents*

THE EXPLORER RACE SERIES

ZOOSH AND HIS FRIENDS THROUGH ROBERT SHAPIRO

7 EXPLORER RACE: COUNCIL of CREATORS

The thirteen core members of the Council of Creators discuss their adventures in coming to awareness of themselves and their journeys on the way to the council on this level. They discuss the advice and oversight they offer to all creators, including the Creator of this local universe. These beings are wise, witty, and joyous, and their stories of love's creation create an expansion of our concepts as we realize that we live in an expanded, multiple-level reality.
ISBN 978-1-891824-13-5 • Softcover • 288 PP. • $14.95

8 EXPLORER RACE and ISIS

This is an amazing book! It has priestess training, shamanic training, Isis's adventures with Explorer Race beings — before Earth and on Earth — and an incredibly expanded explanation of the dynamics of the Explorer Race. Isis is the prototypal loving, nurturing, guiding feminine being, the focus of feminine energy. She has the ability to expand limited thinking without making people with limited beliefs feel uncomfortable. She is a fantastic storyteller, and all of her stories are teaching stories. If you care about who you are, why you are here, where you are going, and what life is all about, pick up this book. You won't put it down until you are through, and then you will want more.
ISBN 978-1-891824-11-1 • Softcover • 352 PP. • $14.95

9 EXPLORER RACE and JESUS

The core personality of that being known on Earth as Jesus, along with his students and friends, describes with clarity and love his life and teaching 2,000 years ago. He states that his teaching is for all people of all races in all countries. Jesus announces here for the first time that he and two others, Buddha and Mohammed, will return to Earth from their place of being in the near future, and a fourth being, a child already born now on Earth, will become a teacher and prepare humanity for their return. This text is so heartwarming and interesting, you won't want to put it down.
ISBN 978-1-891824-14-2 • Softcover • 352 PP. • $16.95

10 EXPLORER RACE: EARTH HISTORY and LOST CIVILIZATIONS

Speaks of Many Truths and Zoosh, through Robert Shapiro, explain that planet Earth, the only water planet in this solar system, is on loan from Sirius as a home and school for humanity, the Explorer Race. Earth's recorded history goes back only a few thousand years, its archaeological history a few thousand more. This book opens up as if a light is on in the darkness, and we see the incredible panorama of brave souls coming from other planets to settle on different parts of Earth. We watch the origins of tribal groups and the rise and fall of civilizations, and we can begin to understand the source of the wondrous diversity of plants, animals, and humans that we enjoy here on beautiful Mother Earth.
ISBN 978-1-891824-20-3 • Softcover • 320 PP. • $14.95

11 EXPLORER RACE: ET VISITORS SPEAK

Even as you are searching the sky for extraterrestrials and their spaceships, ETs are here on planet Earth. They are stranded, visiting, exploring, studying the culture, healing Earth of trauma brought on by irresponsible mining, or researching the history of Christianity over the past 2,000 years. Some are in human guise, and some are in spirit form. Some look like what we call animals as they come from the species' home planet and interact with their fellow beings — those beings who we have labeled cats or cows or elephants. Some are brilliant cosmic mathematicians with a sense of humor who are presently living here as penguins. Some are fledgling diplomats training for future postings on Earth when we have ET embassies here. In this book, these fascinating beings share their thoughts, origins, and purposes for being here.
ISBN 978-1-891824-28-9 • Softcover • 352 PP. • $14.95

12 EXPLORER RACE: TECHNIQUES for GENERATING SAFETY

Wouldn't you like to generate safety so you could go wherever you need to go and do whatever you need to do in a benevolent, safe, and loving way for yourself? Learn safety as a radiated environment that will allow you to gently take the step into the new timeline, into a benevolent future, and away from a negative past.
ISBN 978-1-891824-26-5 • Softcover • 208 PP. • $9.95

ᕬ *Light Technology* PUBLISHING *Presents*

BOOKS THROUGH ROBERT SHAPIRO

SHIRT POCKET SERIES
Carry the Wisdom with You

Benevolent Magic & Living Prayer
This first book in the Feminine Science series provides an easy-to-read, introduction to benevolent magic and living prayer.
$9.95 • 3.75 x 5 • Softcover • 96 PP.
978-1-891824-49-4

Feeling Sedona's ET Energies
Intended to support Earth and its people, this book uses the energies in Sedona to motivate and stimulate potential actions.
$9.95 • 3.75 x 5 • Softcover • 96 PP.
978-1-891824-46-3

Touching Sedona
Speaks of Many Truths teaches how to communicate with the natural, powerful elements and wonders of Sedona in this title.
$9.95 • 3.75 x 5 • Softcover • 96 PP.
978-1-891824-47-0

BOOKS THROUGH DRUNVALO MELCHIZEDEK

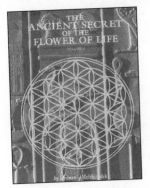

THE ANCIENT SECRET OF THE FLOWER OF LIFE
VOLUME 1

Once, all life in the universe knew the Flower of Life as the creation pattern, the geometrical design leading us into and out of physical existence. Then from a very high state of consciousness, we fell into darkness, and the secret was hidden for thousands of years, encoded in the cells of all life.

$25.⁰⁰ • 240 PP. SOFTCOVER • ISBN 978-1-891824-17-3

THE ANCIENT SECRET OF THE FLOWER OF LIFE
VOLUME 2

Finally, for the first time in print, Drunvalo shares the instructions for the Mer-Ka-Ba meditation, step-by-step techniques for the re-creation of the energy field of the evolved human, which is the key to ascension and the next dimensional world. If done from love, this ancient process of breathing prana opens up for us a world of tantalizing possibility in this dimension, from protective powers to the healing of oneself, others, and even the planet.

$25.⁰⁰ • 272 PP. SOFTCOVER • ISBN 978-1-891824-21-0

LIVING IN THE HEART
Includes Heart Meditation CD

"Long ago we humans used a form of communication and sensing that did not involve the brain in any way; rather, it came from a sacred place within our hearts. What good would it do to find this place again in a world where the greatest religion is science and the logic of the mind? Don't I know this world where emotions and feelings are second-class citizens? Yes, I do. But my teachers have asked me to remind you who you really are. You are more than a human being, much more. Within your heart is a place, a sacred place, where the world can literally be remade through conscious cocreation. If you give me permission, I will show you what has been shown to me."

— Drunvalo Melchizedek

$25.⁰⁰ • 144 PP. SOFTCOVER • ISBN 978-1-891824-43-2

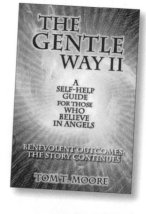

☥ *Light Technology* PUBLISHING *Presents*

299

TO ORDER PRINT BOOKS
Visit LightTechnology.com, Call 928-526-1345 or 1-800-450-0985,
or Check Amazon.com or Your Favorite Bookstore

BOOKS THROUGH TINA LOUISE SPALDING

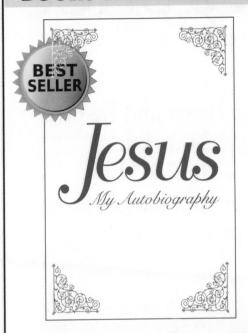

BEST SELLER

Jesus: My Autobiography

This insightful book is designed to free you from the limitations of your conditioned mind and to give you a better understanding of Jesus's life and teachings so that you can begin to transform your mind, your heart, and the world. Through Tina Louise Spalding, Jesus tells his story in his own words, clearing up misconceptions and untruths and describing his physical and nonphysical journeys that led to enlightenment.

$16.95
Softcover • 304 pp.
978-1-62233-030-0

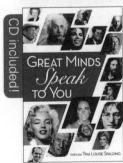

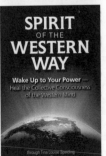

Love and a Map to the Unaltered Soul
$16.95
Softcover, 240 pp.
ISBN 978-1-62233-047-8

**Making Love to God:
The Path to Divine Sex**
$19.95
Softcover • 416 pp.
978-1-62233-009-6

Great Minds Speak to You
$19.95
Softcover • 192 pp. • CD
978-1-62233-010-2

**Spirit of the Western Way: Wake Up
to Your Power — Heal the Collective
Consciousness of the Western Mind**
$16.95
Softcover • 176 pp.
978-1-62233-051-5